Mennonites And Baptists

A Continuing Conversation

Perspectives on Mennonite Life and Thought is a series jointly published between Kindred Press, the Historical Commission of the General Conference of Mennonite Brethren Churches and the Center for Mennonite Brethren Studies of Winnipeg, Manitoba, Fresno, California and Hillsboro, Kansas.*

1. Paul Toews, ed., *Pilgrims and Strangers: Essays in Mennonite Brethren History* (1977)
2. Abraham Friesen ed., *P.M. Friesen and His History: Understanding Mennonite Brethren Beginnings* (1979)
3. David Ewert, ed., *Called to Teach* (1979)
4. Heinrich Wölk and Gerhard Wölk, *Die Mennoniten Bruedergemeinde in Russland, 1925-1980; Ein Beitrag zur Geschichte* (1981)
5. John B. Toews, *Perilous Journey: The Mennonite Brethren in Russia 1860-1910* (1988)
6. Aaron A. Toews, *Mennonite Martyrs: People Who Suffered for Their Faith 1920-1940*, translated by John B. Toews (1990)
7. Paul Toews, ed., *Mennonites and Baptists: A Continuing Conversation* (1993)

*Volumes 1-4 were published by the Center for Mennonite Brethren Studies (Fresno)

Mennonites And Baptists

A Continuing Conversation

PAUL TOEWS, EDITOR

WINNIPEG, MB CANADA  HILLSBORO, KS USA

Kindred Press

MENNONITES AND BAPTISTS
A Continuing Conversation

Copyright © 1993 by the Centers for Mennonite Brethren Studies, Fresno, CA; Winnipeg, MB and Hillsboro, KS.

All rights reserved. With the exception of brief excerpts for reviews, no part of this book may be reproduced without written permission of the publisher.

Canadian Cataloguing in Publication Data
  Toews, Paul
  Mennonites and Baptists
  (Perspectives on Mennonite life and thought ; 7)
  ISBN 0-921788-16-9

  1. Mennonites - Relations - Baptists. 2. Baptists - Relations - Mennonites. I. Toews, Paul. II. Series.

  BX8115.M45 1993   289.7   C93-098088-3

Published simultaneously by Kindred Press, Winnipeg, MB R2L 2E5 and Kindred Press, Hillsboro, KS 67063

Cover design by Gerry Unrau McKay Goettler, Saskatoon, Saskatchewan

Book design by Fred Koop, Winnipeg, MB

Printed in Canada by Christian Press, Winnipeg, MB

International Standard Book Number: 0-921788-16-9

Table of Contents

Acknowledgments		ii
Introduction *Paul Toews*		iii
I	Sixteenth-Century Anabaptism and the Puritan Connection: Reflections upon Baptist Origins *William R. Estep*	1
II	Baptist Interpretations of Anabaptist History *Abraham Friesen*	39
III	Baptists and Mennonites in Poland and Prussia *Peter J. Klassen*	73
IV	Baptists and Mennonite Brethren in Russia (1790-1930) *John B. Toews*	81
V	Mennonite Brethren and German Baptists in Russia: Affinities and Dissimilarities *Albert W. Wardin, Jr.*	97
VI	Russian Mennonites and Baptists (1930-1990) *Walter Sawatsky*	113
VII	The Russian Mennonite Brethren and American Baptist Tandem in India (1890-1940) *Peter Penner*	133
VIII	Mennonite Brethren-Baptist Relations in the United States *Clarence Hiebert*	147
IX	Baptists and Mennonite Brethren in Canada *Abe J. Dueck*	177
X	Augustus H. Strong: Baptist Theologian for the Mennonite Brethren *Howard J. Loewen*	193
XI	The Baptist and Mennonite Vision *James Wm. McClendon, Jr.*	211
Endnotes		225
List of Contributors		261

Acknowledgments

Most books are collaborative efforts. This book is so in several ways. It began as a possible project for the Historical Commission of the General Conference of Mennonite Brethren churches. The Commission on several occasions offered counsel regarding its conceptual development. The essays are the collaborative work of 11 different authors.

Several successive Mennonite Brethren Biblical Seminary student assistants in the Center for Mennonite Brethren Studies, Fresno worked at systematizing both text and endnotes. Special thanks to Wayne Siemens, Jon Isaak and Joanne Klassen. Kevin Enns-Rempel, Archivist of the Center provided invaluable judgement on many details. Joan Ashley Becker did much of the copy editing. Marilyn Hudson at Kindred Press steered it through the entire publication process.

Paul Toews,
Editor

PAUL TOEWS

Introduction

In the early years of the seventeenth century Mennonites and Baptists conversed together in Amsterdam. That meeting was between English and Dutch religious dissenters, both small, marginal and still somewhat harried from their precarious position in Dutch and English society. In 1992, again in Amsterdam, Mennonites and Baptists met to discuss issues of mutual interest. This time the participants were members of the Mennonite World Conference and the Baptist World Alliance, global fraternities who now speak for thousands and even millions. The nearly four hundred years between these meetings contain a history of Mennonite-Baptist conversation. The essays in this book seek to reconstruct and understand part of that dialogue.

These essays center on Baptist-Mennonite relationships in the Northern European Anabaptist-Mennonite stream (Dutch, Prussian and Russian contexts) that gave birth to the Mennonite Brethren. They also focus on the continuing contacts between Mennonite Brethren and Baptists. Those contacts into the early years of the twentieth century were primarily with German Baptists and their allies in Russia and North America. The importance of the relationship, at least for Mennonite Brethren, is suggested by Clarence Hiebert's observation that when meeting people unfamiliar with Mennonites, Mennonite Brethren frequently comment that "we are almost like the Baptists." For those who continue to use Baptist identifications to explain Mennonitism this book will offer both support and critique. The story that unfolds in these essays points to both similarities and differences.

The origins of Anabaptist and Baptist contact, like many things, remain shrouded in uncertainty. It is clear that Continental Anabaptists were in England during the reign of Henry VIII, which concluded in 1547. Anabaptists were part of a larger migration of Dutch refugees who migrated for reasons of political and religious persecution from the hands of their Spanish overlords. If some Anabaptists sought refuge in England, some English dissenters also

iii

sought refuge in the Netherlands. Beginning in 1593 English Separatists sought out Amsterdam as a haven. The initial English Separatists, known as the Ancient Church, were not the ones who entered into a sustained dialogue with Mennonites. Rather, it was a group that migrated in 1608 under the leadership of John Smyth.[1]

John Smyth and his congregation from Gainsborough, England were not drawn to Amsterdam by the Mennonite presence. They came because the United Provinces of the Netherlands were entering the Golden Age of Dutch history. During the previous century the Dutch gained their independence from Spain and began an economic and cultural development that was to make Amsterdam a tolerant, wealthy and urbanized city. The English dissenters, like other minorities—Mennonites, Jews, free-thinkers, Remonstrants (Arminian dissidents from the Dutch Reformed Church), Arminians, and Roman Catholics—were tolerated if not welcomed.[2]

William Estep revisits these early discussions between the Mennonites and Baptists. John Smyth is the critical figure. Estep notes that in Amsterdam Smyth was identified in the Singel Canal Mennonite Church as one of the English-speaking elders of a congregation that joined the Waterland Mennonites shortly following his death in 1612. In a different part of the city the John Smyth Memorial Baptist Church gives testimony to his role in Baptist history. For Estep the symbolism appropriately reflects the importance of the sixteenth-century connection between these two dissenting groups.

Though Amsterdam churches recognize the symbiotic relationship between the two groups, historians have a long history of contentious discussion as to exactly what kinds of interactions and influences extended from this initial contact. Abraham Friesen recounts some of that discussion in his essay on "Baptist Interpretations of Anabaptist History." What Friesen and others have established is that the interpretation of these contacts is both restrained and polemical. Vigorous defense of perceived theological and historical legitimacy is common to many historiographical traditions. In the case of these Baptist-Anabaptist connections the task has been complicated by the problem of establishing historical influence. There was contact between the two. But the impact of those meetings, whether and to what degree the sixteenth-century contacts became carriers of ideas, is another kind of question. Friesen makes it clear that Baptist historians have not always agreed.

Mennonite historians have also disagreed in their thinking

about the impact of the Baptists on the Mennonites. The essays by Peter Klassen, Albert Wardin and John B. Toews offer an abundance of evidence about Mennonite-Baptist contact in nineteenth-century Prussia and Russia. Ministers moved back and forth between the two groups and ideas traversed the boundaries just as easily. No one doubts that Baptists nourished the beginnings of the fledgling Mennonite Brethren group in Russia. What is debatable is the role and influence of those connections. Toews, Wardin and Klassen offer overlapping but also differing assessments of the impact. In doing so they also stand in a long Mennonite Brethren historiographical tradition. In 1896 an unidentified author asked a question in the *Mennonitische Blätter*: "Who are the Members of the Mennonite Brethren Church?" The answer pointed to the commonality shared by Baptists and Mennonites who participated in the mid-century Russian revivals. Elder John F. Harms of the United States replied in the *Zionsbote*, the North American paper of the Mennonite Brethren, that while there were commonalities they were in fact two quite different movements.[3]

Sixty-four years later, Frank C. Peters, a Mennonite Brethren historian, asked the same question. "The Early Mennonite Brethren Church: Baptist or Anabaptist?" published in 1959 reasserted the Harms conclusion. But asking the question in almost identical form revealed the persistent confusion regarding the nature of the 1860 movement in Russia.[4]

By now historians recognize that posing the question in an either/or form hardly recognizes the complexity of forces at work among the emerging Mennonite Brethren and Baptist communities in nineteenth-century Russia. Differing religious currents were blowing through Russia. The Mennonite Brethren certainly were born of pluralistic and even contradictory currents. British evangelicalism, European Pietism, German Baptists and historic Anabaptism were all present at the 1860 creation of the Mennonite Brethren. In addition, Lutherans and Moravians mediated reforming ideas and dispositions.[5] These essays also suggest that the Baptists were not immune from the religious pluralism of the Russian environment.

The story of the Mennonite Brethren and German Baptist dialogue is not only the story of people seeking each other because of similar theological interests. In both Russia and North America they were strangers in a foreign land. In both places they were German speaking islands within the larger Russian and American culture.

v

Finding each other was a means of reinforcing old values in a bewildering and sometimes even hostile world. Preserving "Germanness," at least for a time, was a common hedge against varying forms of theological and cultural transformation. Clarence Hiebert's essay notes that the extensive North American connections of the first Russian MB immigrant arrivals in the late nineteenth century had as much to do with culture as with theology. Walter Sawatsky's essay on the shared trauma of Mennonites and Baptists in the Soviet Union also illumines the tendency of kindred spirits finding each other in dislocated times and spaces.

For Mennonite Brethren, particularly during the first fifty years of the story, German Baptists offered more advanced institutional programs than they had developed. The German Baptists had well established theological training centers in Hamburg, Germany and Rochester, New York. Mennonite Brethren who were interested in theological or missiological training easily gravitated to these centers. The first Mennonite Brethren missionaries to foreign lands, of both Russia and North America, went under Baptist auspices. Peter Penner's research in hitherto unused Baptist archival sources reclaims the story of the Russian Mennonite Brethren-Baptist missions program in India.

Mennonite Brethren started attending these Baptist seminaries in the late nineteenth century. Due to the opening only in 1955 of the Mennonite Brethren denominational seminary, attendance at Baptist seminaries was common into the middle of the twentieth century. Thus it was also not surprising that Baptist theologians continued to inform Mennonite Brethren theology. Howard Loewen analyzes the impact of one such important Baptist figure: Augustus H. Strong. Through a case study of Strong's influence on selected Mennonite Brethren theologians we gain a sense of both the expanse and limits of such theological borrowing.

This book was commissioned by the Historical Commission of the General Conference of Mennonite Brethren Churches. It reflects the Commission's recognition that the Baptist-Mennonite Brethren connection is an important part of our past. With the exception of the essay by James McClendon, which is an adaptation of an earlier work, the essays are all published here for the first time. They collectively probe what is shared and what is distinctive in both traditions. While the essays reflect on Mennonite influences on Baptists the emphasis is much more in discerning the Baptist impact on the evolution of the Mennonite Brethren.

In publishing these essays, the Commission also recognizes the importance of ecumenical dialogue. In the diversity of the Baptist and Mennonite worlds there are some denominational groups that share more in common than others. Overriding the specific historical, cultural, theological and even political differences is a common vision that James McClendon articulates. In a world growing ever more secular it is imperative that Christian communities recognize those elements that permit them to ally together with others who seek to build the "kingdom of God." The "Anabaptist vision," a phrase Mennonites commonly utilize to point to the center of their tradition, or the "baptist vision" as identified by McClendon, contain elements that can reinvigorate not only these two Christian communities but also the larger Christian fraternity.

WILLIAM R. ESTEP

Sixteenth-Century Anabaptism and the Puritan Connection:
REFLECTIONS UPON BAPTIST ORIGINS

The question of Baptist origins is both intriguing and complex. One of the central questions is why the first identifiable Baptists felt it imperative to separate themselves from both the English Separatists and the Dutch Mennonites. The answers may lead the present generation of Baptists to a correct understanding of their unique heritage.

In an attempt to trace, accurately, Baptist origins, the historian must discard any preconceived assumptions about Baptist succession. Similarly, we cannot depend upon a Congregational historiography to explain Baptist origins.

What we must depend on, however, is what happened in the light of the available evidence, both historically and theologically. A crucial question, for instance, is not whether John Smyth was influenced to adopt believers' baptism due to direct Mennonite influence, but to what extent did Thomas Helwys and his congregation carry back to England a faith and order that was neither Mennonite nor Separatist but incorporated elements of each? Both a textual analysis of the documents involved as well as a careful examination of the historical context will provide the distinctions we need to answer our inquiries.

This chapter explores one possible tributary in the rise of the English Baptist stream. While the earlier impact of Anabaptist teaching and influence in England still needs further study, the research of Champlin Burrage, Irvin Horst, Keith Sprunger, and Michael Watts indicates that Anabaptism in England in the sixteenth century was more than a mirage. In fact, as early as 1531, William Barlow, a re-

1

pentant Roman Catholic priest and later bishop, published *A Dialoge Describing the Original Ground of these Lutheren Faccions and Many of their Abuses* in which he revealed his former fascination with the Reformation on the Continent and his subsequent disillusionment. Although his glowing report of the Anabaptists' devotion to Christ, to Scripture, baptism, pacifism, and conduct under severe persecution was tempered by their perceived divisions and alleged crimes, Barlow gave the English of the sixteenth century a fairly accurate picture of Anabaptism. Of the *Thirty-nine Articles* of 1563, at least seventeen and perhaps eighteen criticized the supposed errors of the Anabaptists.

Thus, it seems more than plausible that there was considerable Anabaptist influence in England in the sixteenth century. The known presence and execution of those accused of Anabaptism persisted from the time of Henry VIII to James I. Doubtless, these public executions had a profound effect upon the audiences. Surely, their doubts about a state-church increased with every fresh demonstration of its intolerance toward the courageous faith of the martyrs.

We can readily see that Anabaptism comprised a fairly well-defined element in the English religious milieu of the times. It, along with other forms of the Reformation from the Continent, created a potpourri of religious fare. Evidence is not lacking to prove that English Separatism owed some of its characteristics to this amalgam of religious fare. Burrage's contention that Anabaptism in England was of little, if any, consequence, since it was a foreign import of limited influence, seems unsubstantiated by the evidence available.

Tradition and Spirit in Sixteenth-Century Anabaptism

Surely Baptists are indebted to the Anabaptists for some basic characteristics of their faith but there were other sources as well. By attempting to understand these we may better understand what Baptists and Mennonites hold in common and what differences distinguish Baptists from Mennonites within the Free Church movement. We will succesively examine the Anabaptists on the Continent, the English Puritan-Separatist John Smyth, and finally Thomas Helwys, who died in Newgate prison for his faith. A helpful way of unraveling these complex developments is to begin with an examination of Anabaptist and Baptist beginnings in light of both "Tradition" and "Spirit."

In this discussion, Tradition refers to the traditional dogmas and practices of medieval Catholicism. Although evangelicals tend to use the term in a pejorative sense, it has value in this study. Without tradition in some form, both the continuity and meaning of the Christian faith can be lost from one generation to the next. Yet accumulated traditions can form a straight jacket that immobilizes the church and quenches the Spirit.

The term Spirit also means different things to different people. The *Spiritualisten* of the sixteenth century were quite sure that they had a direct line to the Holy Spirit independent of Scripture through visions, dreams, and trances. For them ultimate authority resided in neither Scripture nor Tradition but in revelations of the Spirit. The Zwickau Prophets, Thomas Müntzer, Caspar Schwenckfeld, and the Münsterites fall into this category with a good many, such as Hans Denck, Melchoir Hofmann, and Sebastian Franck. Tradition meant nothing to the Spiritualists, the would-be prophets of the Spirit. They are best described as "free spirits"—free from the restraints of church, state, and Scripture. They represented a radical critique of the politico-religious establishments of the age. The Anabaptists shared this critique while rejecting the more extravagant claims and eschatological programs of the revolutionary Spiritualists.

SWISS ANABAPTISM

The Anabaptists, often confused with the Spiritualists by the Reformers, rejected both the *corpus christianum* (state church) of medieval Catholicism and the *solo Spiritus* (by the Spirit alone) of the Spiritualists while retaining elements of both. The *fidei regla* (standard of faith) by which the Anabaptists discerned the spirits and discarded or retained elements of traditional Catholicism was the New Testament. However, the tension or imbalance between Tradition and Spirit remained when either became dominant. The struggle to keep the balance by applying New Testament principles to a given situation is one way to take a fresh look at both Anabaptist and Baptist beginnings.

There are four central documents concerning the emergence of Swiss Anabaptism that reveal the inner struggle between the competing attractions of Tradition and Spirit. In chronological order they are: "The Eighteen Articles" (April 1524); The Letters to Thomas

Müntzer (September 1524); "Concerning Heretics and Those Who Burn Them" (September 1524); and "The Schleitheim Confession" (February 1527).

The Eighteen Articles

The Reformation of the sixteenth century challenged medieval Catholicism at several points. Luther first raised the issues that precipitated the break with the Roman Church. Later his insights, which soon found expression in print, stimulated a plethora of reformatory efforts that met with mixed responses. Among these was the Anabaptist movement that first arose within the context of the Swiss Reformation. Although recently there has been a revival of older theories of Anabaptist origins which attribute the movement to Thomas Müntzer or the Zwickau Prophets, this polygenesis concept is more plausible when limited to Zürich and Waldshut. Balthasar Hubmaier, of Switzerland and South Germany, was moving in the direction of Anabaptism in 1524 and was apparently in contact with the Grebel and Mantz faction in Zürich by the October Disputation of 1523.

The clearest demonstration of Hubmaier's thinking at this stage of his development is found in *The Eighteen Articles* of April 1524.[1] He had attended the Second Disputation held in Zürich on October 26-28, 1523. There he had an opportunity to compare notes with both Zwingli and Grebel. Even at this early date, Hubmaier discussed baptism with Zwingli and later cited the exact time and place where this conversation took place. After returning to Waldshut, he attempted to enlist the other priests in his chapter by drawing up in Zwinglian fashion eighteen articles for their consideration. These articles reveal both the influence of Luther and Zwingli and yet there is something more, which we now recognize as incipient Anabaptism.

Perhaps Hubmaier was the furthest removed from the *Spiritualisten* and the closest to the magisterial Reformers of any of the Swiss Brethren. His break with traditional Roman Catholicism and its scholasticism appears decisive and his own independent course is evident. The first three articles deal with faith. Instead of declaring with Luther that faith "justifies," Hubmaier wrote that faith makes us "holy" before God. He defined faith as something living and dynamic, not *assensus* (intellectual assent) or a mere historical faith. The most significant aspect of his concept of faith, however, is its ethical dimension as written in the third article: "Such faith can not remain passive but must break out (*müss aussbrechen*) to God in thanksgiving and to mankind in all kinds of works of brotherly love. Hence all vain religious acts, such as, candles, palm branches, and holy water will be rejected."

Although Luther broke with tradition when he affirmed his doctrine of justification by faith, Hubmaier went further when he clearly implied that God changes a person's heart from within. He later refered to this experience as the "*Wiedergeburt*" (second birth). This meant that out of the heart or spirit of the new creation, there springs an irrepressible expression of gratitude to God and a desire to serve others motivated by the love of Christ. An article that characterized good works as only those which God had commanded followed these first three articles. The next four reflect the consensus of those present at the Second Zürich Disputation regarding images and the mass. In addition, there was an appeal for the preaching of the gospel in the language of the people when the Lord's supper is observed. The eighth article affirmed the priesthood of believers with an indirect reference to believers' baptism, which suggests that in Hubmaier's mind this was already an assumed truth. The ninth article taught the centrality of Christ as redeemer, intercessor, and mediator. Articles ten through twelve rejected all traditional rites of the medieval church not supported by Scripture along with Aristotle, while affirming *sola scriptura* (scripture alone).

Many of these articles were enunciated with a Zwinglian accent. For example, articles fourteen through eighteen could have been lifted out of The Sixty-seven Articles of Zwingli. They condemned the dogma of purgatory, the practice of celibacy, unchastity, and idleness, while, by implication, justifying marriage for priests. Much of what Hubmaier wrote in *The Eighteen Articles* has a familiar ring. It reflects both Lutheran and Zwinglian influence—but there is more. The perception of faith here is not a faith in faith concept, but faith in Christ, which is a faith that evokes a profound change in the redeemed. Personal responsibility that expressed itself in a confession of faith, baptism, and participation in the Lord's Supper according to the scriptural model was set forth. Congregational support of pastors was advocated perhaps for the first time, in reformatory literature. In these three points, it is possible to detect an advance beyond both Luther and Zwingli.

With every positive statement of faith and order in these articles, there is a corresponding rejection of traditional dogmas and practices of the medieval church. By the term "Word of God," Hubmaier apparently meant, in this context, the Bible. He ended this brief summary of Reformation principles with the motto: *Die Warheit ist Untödlich* (The Truth is Immortal). Truth for Hubmaier had now replaced a blind adherence to Tradition.

Letters to Thomas Müntzer

The letters to Thomas Müntzer, dated September 5, 1524, represent a further development of an incipient Anabaptist theology. Although not meant for publication at the time, they give the modern reader several insights into the thinking of the Grebel-led group at this juncture in their development. Here that which was only implicit or cautiously advanced in Hubmaier is boldly stated. Acting upon fragmentary information derived from Müntzer's earlier tracts and hearsay reports, these former disciples of Zwingli, alienated and increasingly isolated, wrote in hopes of gaining an ally. They knew of his bold pronouncements against the perceived shortcomings of the Lutheran reform. Still, they wished Müntzer to know exactly where they stood on certain issues.

Before outlining for him their program for reform, they wrote: "We therefore entreat and admonish you as a brother, . . . to esteem as right and good only what is found in crystal-clear Scripture, to reject, hate, and curse all proposals, words, rites, and opinions of all men, even your own."[2] The writers then took Müntzer to task for a number of innovations that they considered unsupported by Scripture, such as singing during worship, preserving the mass (though in German, "since it is still only the mass"), engraving the ten commandments upon stone and placing it in front of the congregation, and using the sword. Rumors that Müntzer was advocating the use of the sword on behalf of the peasants against the princes disturbed them greatly.

These letters expressed several new ideas, which were implemented by the Swiss Brethren within a few months. While their view of the Lord's Supper was basically Zwinglian, in the light of their understanding of the New Testament, the Lord's Supper was more than a simple symbol. "Although it is simply bread, yet if faith and brotherly love precede it, it is to be received with joy, since when it is used in the church, it is to show us that we are truly one bread and one body, and that we are and wish to be true brethren with one another."³ In addition to the admonition that the Lord's Supper should be observed with the elements and in accordance with the relevant passages of Scripture, which were cited, the young men reminded Müntzer, "But one must eat and drink in the Spirit and love." These two words "Spirit" and "love" add a new dimension to their understanding of the nature of the Lord's Supper which was lacking in all previous formulations of the mass by both Luther and Zwingli. Hence for them the Lord's Supper was a communion (*koinonia*). The association of discipline with the Lord's Supper, however, was not a new idea but in accord with the traditional practice of the Roman Church. But the way in which it was to be practiced in the fellowship of believing disciples was different. Again, the attempt to adhere to the New Testament in all things made a significant difference.

The exposition of the writers' understanding of the teaching of the New Testament on baptism demonstrates that a great deal of thought had gone into the nature, purpose, and meaning of baptism. This is easily the most important point of the letters and reveals that on this issue the brethren had reached a consensus that they held with conviction. The harsh denunciation of infant baptism as "the senseless, blasphemous form of baptism," attributed to Luther, Leo Jud, Osiander, and the men at Strassburg, was due, in part, to the depth of conviction on the subject that characterized these sincere young men. It can also be attributed to youthful enthusiasm over the discovery of truth that had lain hidden beneath an accumulation of the debris of traditional misconception and practice for more than a thousand years.

Sensing that this last attempt to make their position on biblical authority absolutely clear might be a little much, they concluded this last admonition with an accolade for the preacher from Alstedt.

> We entreat you not to use nor to accept the old
> customs of the Antichrist, such as sacrament, Mass,

signs, etc. Hold to and rule by the Word alone, as should all ambassadors and especially you and Carlstadt, and you do more than all the preachers of all nations.[4]

From this earliest known systematic presentation of their views, it is evident that the New Testament was the rule of faith by which the Swiss Brethren had been working through both the heritage of the medieval church and the reshaping of that heritage by Luther and Zwingli. While it reflects an advance over Hubmaier's *Eighteen Articles* and some fundamental differences between their understanding of a biblical faith and that of the magisterial Reformers, it is also clear they had not rejected all traditional practices of the Roman Church nor all the teachings of Zwingli.

Concerning Heretics and Those Who Burn Them

In the same month in which the young men from Zürich were writing their letters to Müntzer, Hubmaier published his treatise on religious liberty. Due to the threat of an Austrian invasion of Waldshut, Hubmaier sought refuge in the Benedictine cloister in Schaffhausen. Although doubtless stimulated by his confinement and the plight of Waldshut, *Von Ketzern* is an abstract of tenets calling for religious freedom, the cessation of persecution of heretics, real or imaginary, and the separation of church and state. It was meant for universal application.

As early as the Second Zürich Disputation, Harold Bender detected the first emergence of the ideas that Hubmaier articulated in this treatise in the unwillingness of Grebel to accept the judgment of the city council regarding the implementation of the Lord's Supper in place of the mass. John Howard Yoder saw the break coming around December 19, 1523 when Zwingli bowed to the judgment of the city council and ceased to press for the change that did not come until Easter, 1525. Whatever the exact date of the break between Zwingli and his disciples, it appears that the question of church-state relations was involved. It was Hubmaier who first clearly expressed principles that were implicit from the beginning of the Anabaptist movement and basic to an Anabaptist understanding of the nature of Christian faith, the gospel, and the church. At each of these points, Hubmaier challenged the medieval tradition as taught by Rome and the magisterial Reformers alike.[5] Upon the basis of Scripture, Hubmaier redefined heresy and rejected the persecution or the coercion of heretics. Many reasons derived from his understanding of Scripture were given for his position: God alone was the judge and humankind's ultimate fate was in his hands, faith could not be coerced but was the result of the convicting power of the gospel and the Holy Spirit, the state had no jurisdiction in matters pertaining to one's relationship to God; therefore, even the atheist must not be punished for his unbelief or deprived of his civil rights as long as he obeyed civil law. To put a heretic to death appeared to be a pious act but in reality it was a *denial of the incarnation*. Finally, Hubmaier stressed that truth cannot be destroyed even though you burn those who proclaim it for "*Die warheit ist untödlich*" (The Truth is Immortal). Throughout the work there were references that indicate Hubmaier held that both church and state were ordained of God. However, for the state to punish heretics upon the orders of the church was unwarranted by Scripture, the nature of the Christian faith, the church and the state.[6]

Although *Von Ketzern* charted a new course for church-state relations beyond both Marsilius of Padua and Erasmus, it was hardly a well-written treatise. It was doubtless written in haste and like many of Hubmaier's works meant to be suggestive rather than exhaustive. Nevertheless, writing under the assumption that God works among humankind through the Word and the Spirit, Hubmaier rejected the traditional concepts of heresy, persecution of heretics, the gospel, church, and the state while offering creative alternatives, best described as the use of spiritual means to obtain spiritual ends. In the final analysis, it was Scripture interpreted by the Holy Spirit that God had ordained to bring his saving gospel into the arena of human affairs, and not a coerced faith, which, according to Hubmaier, was no faith at all.

The Schleitheim Confession

By February 1527, when the Schleitheim Confession was adopted, the Anabaptist movement had generated a number of documents as booklets, tracts, letters, and court records. Archduke Ferdinand was in the process of moving against the Anabaptists in

Moravia. On January 5, 1527, Felix Mantz, executed by drowning upon orders of the Zürich City Council, became the first martyr to die at the hands of Protestants. A few months before, Eberli Bolt had been burned to death at Schwyz, a Catholic dominated city. Both Catholic and Protestant authorities apparently felt threatened by the movement that had received so much popular support in several Swiss and German centers. Under the circumstances, it was not surprising that some Anabaptists had apparently begun to talk of arming themselves for matters of defense. Possibly some had cited Hubmaier's position, although his treatise *On the Sword* was not yet published. Hubmaier argued that a Christian could be a magistrate. Apparently other Anabaptists or possibly some of the same group had embraced antinomian beliefs and were acting accordingly. Clearly the Anabaptist movement was facing a crisis from without and within. The seven articles of Schleitheim were directed to the perceived crisis within, which, if left unchecked, could have led to the disintegration of the movement.

These articles were diametrically opposed to the position advocated by the antinomians. Although not a complete or balanced confession, the Schleitheim Articles became the first group confession adopted by any Anabaptist assembly. As such it provides us with another basic document that indicates how Tradition and Spirit were understood and co-joined in what became Anabaptism. As William Lumpkin points out, the Schleitheim Confession is of "supreme importance as a source document for the study of the views of the Swiss Brethren. Indeed, most later confessions and doctrinal summaries of the Anabaptists are based upon it."[7]

Like virtually all Anabaptist writings until those of Menno, there was a noticeable lack of attention to the doctrine of God. The few direct and indirect references to deity show that the Anabaptists had no quarrel with the traditional idea of the trinity. The opening sentence of the introduction to the Schleitheim Confession included an implied acceptance of the triune God of Nicene orthodoxy. From other sources, we know that these early Anabaptists refused to deify the Virgin Mary. In these articles, as in the previous articles examined, an implied Christology was paramount. It was both the teaching and example of Christ that were appealed to as the ultimate authority on the two crucial articles: "Separation from the Abomination" and "The Sword." These two articles receive the bulk of attention. Little notice was given to baptism, the Lord's Supper, and pastors, since the articles on "The Ban" and "The Oath," both of which are very closely related to those on separation and the sword, get the most attention.

Obviously, the Schleitheim Articles were based upon certain assumptions from both traditional Catholicism and Reformation sources. For example, even though the article on "The Breaking of Bread" was basically in accord with Swiss Brethren understanding and practice, the article on "Pastors in the Church" implied that the bread was still elevated just as the host was elevated in the Roman Catholic celebration of the mass. Again, at the close of the salutary section the traditional Catholic greeting was invoked: "Grace and peace of heart be with you all. Amen."

A careful examination of the Schleitheim Confession confirms the impression gleaned from other documents written in the first decade of Anabaptist gestation and birth. While the attempt was made to make a radical break with Tradition, by using Scripture under the guidance of the Holy Spirit, it was neither complete nor accomplished without a struggle. Remnants of the medieval church's Tradition appeared in Anabaptist writings throughout the sixteenth century. On the other hand, the temptation to abandon the clear teachings of the New Testament for immediate revelations of the Spirit was often difficult to resist. What helped these earnest disciples to discern the spirits and unravel the traditions was their attempt to adhere strictly to Scripture. On the surface this appeared nothing more than that which Luther, Zwingli, and later, Calvin were attempting to do. But there was a difference. Apparently it was the difference between Law and Gospel, but there was also more. The revelation of God in Christ to which the New Testament bears witness became the touchstone of truth and the criterion by which all else was measured in the Christian life. That witness for them was not only credible but authoritative. In the final analysis, it was the Lordship of Christ as revealed in the New Testament that became the final criterion for determining the nature of discipleship, the church, its ordinances, and its purpose and function in the world.

In the reshaping of Dutch Anabaptism after Münster, Menno rejected the charge of Faber "that we have brought the ministers (of the state church) into disrepute." Instead, Menno wrote, it was "because we reprove them in unfeigned love, and point them by doctrine and life to Christ's example, spirit, and Word," although some were more fit to be "swineherders than shepherds of the sheep of Christ."[8] It was clear from this and many other statements that Menno's supreme authority was the revelation of God in Christ. In his *Reply to Gellius Faber* he added the example of Christ to the authority of the Word and the Spirit. It was also evident that the ethical dimension in soteriology and the finality of the revelation of God in Jesus Christ became increasingly determinative in sixteenth-century Anabaptism as Menno and his followers attempted to discern the spirits in breaking with Tradition under the leadership of the Holy Spirit.

JOHN SMYTH: PURITAN, BAPTIST, MENNONITE

On a wall in the foyer of the Singel Canal Mennonite Church in Amsterdam is an old chart with a list of elders of the church from its inception to the present. John Smyth's name stands at the head of the list of English-speaking elders of the English congregation that did not become an integral part of the Waterlander Church until two years after his death in 1612. In a newer section of the city there is another church, the John Smyth Memorial Baptist Church, which bears his name. The English Baptist movement has revered Smyth as its founder for the better part of four centuries. Similarly, the Waterlander Mennonite Church has honored him as an elder of their church. "How can this be?" is a question that naturally arises. The answer lies in attempting to understand the remarkable changes that took place in Smyth's life during a ten year period, from 1602 to 1612. In order to understand those years, we need to catch a glimpse of Smyth's life and ministry within the religious context of the closing years of Elizabeth's reign and the first years of that of James I.

John Smyth: Puritan, 1586-1606

Little is known about Smyth's early life. Apparently a gifted student, but without funds, he matriculated at Christ's College, Cambridge University in March 1586. He paid his way as a *sizar*, which meant he acted as a valet to other students and professors. Francis

Johnson, later pastor of the Ancient Church of English Separatists at Amsterdam, and one of the leading Puritan professors at Cambridge, was his tutor. Smyth graduated with a B.A. degree in 1590. In the same year, the university expelled Johnson for advocating the Presbyterian system of church government as more scriptural than the Episcopal. Since the danger of the Spanish Armada had passed, Elizabeth turned her attention to enforcing the religious settlement of 1559 upon all her subjects. Puritans such as Johnson were suppressed and the Separatist leaders Greenwood, Barrowe, and Penry were executed. Doubtless, the significance of these events did not escape the attention of young Smyth.

Smyth stayed on at Cambridge and in 1593 completed a master's degree. During this period he took advantage of the opportunity to study medicine on his own in addition to taking the required courses. He became a fellow of Christ's College at the Michaelmas term in 1594. This required him to take an oath of allegiance to church and crown. Within a year Smyth was ordained to the priesthood of the Church of England by Bishop Wickham of Lincoln. For four years, he taught at Christ's College. His teaching career ended when he married. The next two years Smyth apparently supported himself in various capacities in or around Cambridge. In 1600 he became the city lecturer of Lincoln, a position he held for little more than two years.

While at Lincoln, Smyth was a staunch supporter of the Anglican establishment, although he still considered himself basically a Puritan. His sympathies with the Puritan party were made public as early as 1592. An attempt to reconcile the Calvinistic philosophy of the four-fold ministry with that of the Church of England marked his Lincoln years. In his *A Patterne of True Prayer* (1605), he listed "officers of the Kingdom" as Doctor (teaching), Pastor, Elder (ruling) and Deacon. He displayed an unwillingness to debate differences between various parties in the Reformed tradition regarding the actual function of those officers. However, he went on to pay homage to the authority of the king and bishops.

> We acknowledge euery King in his Kingdome, the supreme Gouernor in all causes, and ouer all persons, aswell ecclesiasticall, as ciuill, next and im-

mediately vnder Christ: which Prince hath authoritie to substitute ecclesiastical Magistrates according to the word, for the polity of the Church, in the exercising of iurisdiction, visitation of Churches, and ordination of Ministers; which persons in England are called Bishops.[9]

In spite of, and perhaps because of, the Hampton Court Conference (1604) in which King James had rejected the Puritan program of reform, Smyth was clearly on record in support of the episcopal establishment.

John Smyth: Separatist, 1606-1608

Although the whereabouts of Smyth from 1603 and 1606 are difficult to determine, he must have lived in Gainsborough north of Lincoln. However, he did not secure a license to serve a parish church. Occasionally, he led worship in the local parish church in the absence of the parish priest. An episcopal visitation uncovered this irregularity and Smyth was severely reprimanded. Although documentation is lacking regarding the frequency with which Smyth led divine services, the following that he soon developed seems to suggest it was not just a one time experience. By 1606, after nine months of deliberation and prayer with both ministers and lay members, Smyth made the fateful decision to break with the Church of England. He then led in the formation of a Separatist church.

This step was the first of many that led the former Cambridge fellow from the Church of England into Anabaptism and such a move did not come easily. As late as 1605, in *A Patterne of True Prayer*, Smyth wrote: "When there is a Toleration of many Religions, . . . the kingdom of God is shouldered out a doores by the diuels kingdome."[10] Smyth went on to insist that magistrates should be Christians and careful to enforce the laws against heretics. "Wherefore the Magistrates should cause all men to worship the true God, or else punish them with imprisonment, confiscation of goods, or death as the qualitie of the cause requireth."[11] This position was to come under careful scrutiny once Smyth and his congregation had arrived in the Netherlands.

According to William Bradford (Governor of Plymouth colony),

Smyth drew up a brief covenant patterned after that of the Old Testament saints that read:

> They shooke of this yoake of antichristian bondage, and as ye Lords free people, joyned them selves (by a covenant of the Lord) into a church estate, in ye fellowship of ye gospell, to walke in all his wayes, made known, or to be made known unto them, according to their best endeavours, whatsoever it should cost them, the Lord assisting them.[12]

Separatist churches had been formed in England for some time in similar fashion. The covenant of Francis Johnson's church in Amsterdam was the most recent example. However, a comparison of the two covenants reveals a remarkable difference. In the Gainsborough covenant, beyond the expressed desire to walk in all the "wayes of the Lord," there is both a tacit admission that those signing the covenant do not possess ultimate truth and a willingness to remain open to the Spirit's leadership. The Gainsborough covenanters, therefore, were breaking with Tradition as it had found expression in the Anglican Church, which now appeared beyond the hope of reform. They were also taking a giant step of faith into an unknown future with the sole assurance that the Lord would, in time, make known more fully his ways.

Separatism in England was not new. There were Separatist conventicles as early as the Elizabethan Settlement, if not earlier. The nature of these early conventicles is not entirely clear. As Irvin Horst has shown, there is no question that Anabaptists were in England by 1534. Although their numbers may never have been large, their influence and fear of their influence made their impact upon the English religious scene something other than a negligible factor. Some of the English, such as Joan Bocher, Henry Hart, Robert Cooche, and Humphrey Middleton embraced certain Anabaptist teachings.[13] Even though there may have been Anabaptist conventicles in England and probably were, the later Separatist congregations were characterized by Calvinism, imported from Geneva, through the returning Marian exiles and via the Genevan Bible.

15

It is quite evident that by the time the Smyth-led Puritans became Separatists, Separatism in England was Calvinistic and not Anabaptist. Like Smyth, Separatists were Puritans who refused to accept the new canons that resulted from the Hampton Court Conference. They considered the Church of England beyond the hope of reform and, therefore, a false church (Babylon), from which they must separate. When Smyth exited from the Church of England and its ministry, he embarked upon a spiritual pilgrimage that would not end until his death in August 1612, in Amsterdam.

These Separatists counted among their number several ordained Anglican clergymen, and a few gentry. Most were commoners but unusually well educated.[14] Ninety-eight percent could read and write, which was considerably above both English and Dutch literacy rates. Coupled with the fact that these were people of deep convictions and considerable influence, it is not surprising that the authorities determined to crush this fresh outcropping of Separatism with a new wave of persecution.

Since it was reported that toleration was possible in the Netherlands, even for English Separatists, the entire church, which by 1607 may have numbered 150 or more, decided to leave England for Amsterdam. William Bradford wrote of the decision:

> Yet seeing them selves thus molested, and that ther was no hope of their continuance ther, by joynt consente they resolved to goe into the Low Countries, wher they heard was freedome of Religion for all men; as also how sundrie from London, & other parts of the land, had been exiled and persecuted for the same cause, & were gone thither, and lived at Amsterdam, & in other places of the land.[15]

About a year after the formation of the Smyth Separatist church, the members began to leave England. Families were divided. Some of those who remained were imprisoned. A furious storm in the North Sea threatened to sink one of the boats. By the spring of 1608, the entire congregation had succeeded in getting to Amsterdam. Their faith had been sorely tried and their understanding of the covenant severely tested. Smyth and a large part of the church were in Amsterdam as early as the summer or fall of 1607. John Robinson was among the last to arrive in 1608. By that time he discovered that Smyth was raising serious questions about the order of ministry in the Ancient Church and the use of books in the act of worship. Within a few months Robinson and William Brewster made plans to move on to Leyden where they settled within the year. (This church became the mother church of the Pilgrim Fathers). Smyth and the remaining Separatists from the Gainsborough area found themselves increasingly isolated from their fellow citizens.

Smyth and Anabaptism

The open-ended covenant subscribed to by Smyth and his fellow Separatists apparently precluded the possibility of adopting Anabaptist concepts. In fact Smyth was well aware of the dangers the removal of his church to Amsterdam faced in this regard. Upon arriving in the Netherlands, Smyth reportedly said: "Truely wee being Now Come into a place of libertie are in Great danger if we look not well to our wayes, for wee are like men sett upon the Iyce and therefore may esely slyde and fall."[16] Doubtless Smyth was aware that some English Separatists who had come from London with the Ancient Church before it settled in Amsterdam had done exactly this. Some had returned to England before the turn of the century with news of their remarkable experiences during their sojourn at Kampen and Naarden in 1597. Nevertheless, Smyth was a man of integrity and courage. He remained open to the truth as he understood it, despite the consequences. Once the New Testament had become his *regla fidei* (rule of faith), his rejection of tradition became even more radical and his spiritualism more refined.

Like the early Anabaptists, Smyth and his little company were faced with achieving a scriptural balance between Tradition and Spirit. Like them, his radical rejection of Tradition subjected him to misunderstanding and ridicule. On two points he questioned both the Anglicans and the Separatists. These involved the nature of the ministry of each particular church and its worship.

Smyth's *Principles and Inferences Concerning the Visible Church* (1607) was probably printed in Amsterdam. It clearly indicates that he had already made a basic shift in his biblical hermeneutics. An appeal to the New Testament, which, he argued, alone provides the guidelines for "administering the covenant since the death of Christ" replaced the Puritan and Calvinistic orientation with its heavy emphasis upon the Old Testament. He continued: "In this little treatise the ordinances of Christ for the dispensing of the covenant since his death are described."[17] Clearly, for Smyth, the New Testament alone had begun to provide the criteria for determining the nature of the church. In a sense this work constituted a personal confession of faith and an apologetic for separating from the Church of England. (It abounds in Scripture references from the New Testament with a scattering of Old Testament references.) It also provided the basis for his critique of contemporary churches. As such, it was the first of three works, which, examined together, point the direction in which Smyth's thought was rapidly moving.

Smyth's *Principles and Inferences* was soon followed by *The Differences of the Churches of the Separation*. In the introduction Smyth indicated that this work was based upon the standards set forth in the previous work. This treatise demonstrated an intimate knowledge of the "Ancient Church" in Amsterdam and was a thorough critique of its ministry and worship, and, by inference, that of the Reformed Church and the Church of England, as well. The concern of Smyth at this point was the nature of true spiritual worship.

> Wee hould that the worship of the new testament properly so called is spirituall proceeding originally from the hart: & that reading out of a booke (though a lawful ecclesiastical action) is no part of spirituall worship, but rather the invention of the man of synne it beeing substituted for a part of spirituall worship.[18]

Up to this point, Smyth's position represented the most radical critique of his fellow Separatists yet launched. In a sense it was a reaction to worship in the Anglican Church, which all Separatists considered book-bound and lifeless. His major objection seems to have been based upon the nature of all translations of the Bible, which he held were in reality commentaries and when used in worship fell into the category of read prayers or the singing of Psalms. He apparently believed in serious and thorough Bible study done in the biblical languages, if possible. He did not object to reading the Scriptures before preaching or engaging in worship but drew the line between true spiritual worship that comes from the heart and liturgical reading. Smyth cited many passages of Scripture and numerous examples from both the Old and New Testaments to support his position, that in worship the Holy Spirit must have full sway. Above all, he appealed to the example of Christ.

His opposition to the use of the English Bible may also have solidified because of the Genevan version in use in the Ancient Church and the English Reformed Church in Amsterdam. The Geneva Bible contained notes advocating Calvinistic theology and ecclesiology which Smyth was no longer willing to accept uncritically. While wishing to free the Spirit's work, Smyth did not mean to leave the reading of the Bible out of the activities of the church, even on a Sunday set aside for worship.[19]

Smyth's second major concern in *The Differences of the Churches of the Separation* was the ministry of the Ancient Church. For Smyth the elders of the church were to be chosen by the will of the people. Even when thus chosen, they did not possess alone the privilege of preaching, teaching, praying, and singing that belonged to all the brethren.

By 1609, Smyth and his followers had come to the conclusion that their church, founded upon a covenant, must be disbanded and reorganized upon the basis of individual confessions of faith and believers' baptism. *The Character of the Beast or The False Constitution of the Church* (1609) gave the reasons for this action and answered the criticisms of Richard Clifton. Clifton, a former member of Smyth's church, left the congregation for the Ancient Church. Therefore Smyth considered Clifton the spokesman for the Amsterdam English Separatists and the one among them he knew best. Unfortunately Smyth's manner of inaugurating believers' baptism by first baptizing himself became so magnified in the controversy, that many Separatists seemed to have lost sight of the significance of the event.

Nine years later Robinson called attention to Smyth's self-baptism:

> Mr. Smith, Mr. Helw:[ys] & the rest haveing vtterly dissolved, & disclaymed their former Ch:[urch] state, & ministry, came together to erect a new

> Ch:[urch] by baptism: unto which they also ascribed so great virtue, as that they would not so much as pray together, before they had it. and after some streyning of courtesy, who should begin, . . . Mr. Smith baptizd first himself, & next Mr. Helwis, & so the rest, making their particular confessions.[20]

The question immediately arose, "Why did Smyth baptize himself?" It was obvious that he either saw no need for seeking baptism at the hands of the Mennonites or from some of the English who had previously received believers' baptism in the Netherlands. Smyth knew well, as apparently his English critics did not, that there was historical precedent for self-baptism. *The Character of the Beast* suggests Anabaptist influence at several points. However, Smyth indicated that though he was almost persuaded, he was not yet fully convinced the Mennonite position on the magistracy was biblical. He also clearly rejected the Hofmanite Christology in favor of traditional Chalcedonian orthodoxy.[21]

In spite of the two reservations, Smyth made it clear that he considered Mennonite churches true churches and all churches that practiced infant baptism false churches. It is equally evident that he wrote with deep conviction supported by his own careful study of the relevant New Testament passages. By all appearances Smyth had become an Anabaptist, despite his previous warnings concerning the dangers of Anabaptism. The sequence of events with their accompanying changes had been rapid: he was a staunch Puritan and Anglican in 1602; became a Separatist after considerable thought, consultation, and prayer in 1606; upon arriving in Amsterdam in 1607, he registered his dissatisfaction with the Separatist worship and ministry. Less than a year later, he reorganized his church upon the basis of personal confessions of faith and believers' baptism. This almost certainly occurred in the fall or winter of 1608. The weather would have been no deterrent to Smyth's baptism since it was by affusion.

The rapid shifts in his position subjected Smyth to merciless criticism from his compatriots. The defense of his actions is a classic apologetic for changing one's religious opinions, once they are recognized as erroneous. With evident conviction Smyth wrote:

> The true constitution of the Chu. is of a new creature baptized into the Father, the Sonne, & the holy Ghost: The false constitution is of infants baptized: we professe therfor that all those Churches that baptise infants are of the same false constitution: & al those Chu. that baptize the new creature, thos that are made Disciples by teaching, men confessing their faith & their sinnes, are of one true constitution.[22]

Baptist or Mennonite?

Isolated and terminally ill with tuberculosis, Smyth increasingly turned to the Mennonites for fellowship. There seems little doubt that Mennonite influence played a role in his rethinking the biblical teachings on baptism and the church. *The Character of the Beast* reveals a mind in transition. Once he saw his way clear to accept Hofmanite Christology, it was but a short step to seek union with the Waterlander Mennonites.

Jan Munter, the owner of a bakehouse which Smyth and his congregation used for worship services on Sundays was a possible initial contact between Smyth and the Mennonites. Besides the Waterlanders, there were both High German and Flemish Mennonite churches in the city. In possibly a year or less after the inauguration of believers' baptism, Smyth petitioned the Mennonites for union with them as a true church of Christ. The letter contained the signatures of fifteen men and seventeen women. A brief confession of faith containing twenty articles accompanied the letter. The petition read:

> The names of the English who acknowledge this their error and repent of it, viz., that they took in hand to baptize themselves contrary to the order established by Christ, and who now wish to come to the true church of Christ as quickly as possible.[23]

Hans de Ries, a well educated and leading Waterlander Mennonite elder from Alkmaar was anxious to accommodate the English. There was very little in the twenty articles with which the Mennonites could find fault. It declared that *Corde credimus, et ore confite-*

mur (we believe with our heart and we confess with our mouth) all the basic Mennonite beliefs on the nature of the church, its ministry, and its ordinances. It was also clear that the Smyth-led Separatists had abandoned their former Calvinistic soteriology. However, since the confession was incomplete at several points and not explicit on others, Hans de Ries and Lubbert Gerritsz drew up a confession of thirty-eight articles which became the basis for negotiations that never reached a satisfactory conclusion during Smyth's lifetime. The exchange of confessions, however, stimulated both Smyth and Helwys to draw up and submit for Mennonite scrutiny new and much more carefully composed confessions on behalf of their respective congregations. Smyth's confession, apparently published shortly after his death in 1612, numbered 100 articles in English and 102 in the Dutch version. This confession reveals that Smyth was one with the Mennonites even in the points that still presented problems for him when he published *The Character of the Beast*.

Smyth and his congregation had begun to seek union with the Mennonites in February 1610. By this time, Helwys, his leading layman and chief supporter, along with nine or ten others had broken with Smyth and the majority. In 1611 they presented their own confession of faith of which Lumpkin writes: "The confession shows considerable independence of thought and is rightly judged the First English Baptist Confession of Faith."[24] The articles on the magistracy show the major point of difference between the Smyth and Helwys confessions. Smyth's confession of 1612 became the first confession of faith in English to set forth the principles of complete religious liberty and the separation of church and state. Although it is questionable whether it should be called a Baptist or a Mennonite confession, in a sense, it was both. From this time down to the present, virtually every major Baptist confession has incorporated certain distinctive features reminiscent of this confession.

For example, articles eighty-four and eighty-five from the English edition are most significant for the Baptist development of the principle of religious liberty.

> 84. That the magistrate is not by virtue of his office
> to meddle with religion, or matters of conscience,
> to force or compel men to this or that form of reli-

gion, or doctrine: but to leave Christian religion free, to every man's conscience, and to handle only civil transgressions (Rom. XIII), injuries and wrongs of man against man, in murder, adultery, theft, etc., for Christ only is the king, and lawgiver of the church and conscience (James IV. 12).

85. That if the magistrate will follow Christ, and be His disciple, he must deny himself, take up his cross, and follow Christ; he must love his enemies and not kill them, he must pray for them, and not punish them, . . . he must suffer persecution and affliction with Christ, and be slandered, reviled, blasphemed, scourged, buffeted, spit upon, imprisoned and killed with Christ; and that by the authority of magistrates, which things he cannot possibly do, and retain the revenge of the sword.[25]

In article eighty-four, Smyth stated clearly for the first time in English the principle of religious liberty and the separation of Church and State. Baptists have claimed this principle as their own, often under the mistaken notion that it originated with them. Article eighty-five stated the position that a magistrate cannot be a Christian without giving up his magistracy. Implied is the principle of nonresistance. Some early English Baptists also held this position, but at this point Helwys drew the line. Subsequently, most Baptists followed Helwys rather than Smyth.

Smyth left the Baptists a significant legacy. Fittingly enough, that legacy comprises a spiritual heritage. Few in the history of the church have so single-mindedly rejected Tradition at the prompting of the Spirit. Smyth recognized, as few have, that "God is a Spirit and those that worship Him must worship Him in Spirit and in truth."

THOMAS HELWYS AND THE
CONTINUING BAPTIST-MENNONITE DIALOGUE

By May 23, 1610, John Smyth and most of his followers had decided to unite with the Waterlander Mennonite Church in Amsterdam. Forty-two Englishmen, including Smyth, signed the short confession drawn up by Hans de Ries and Lubbert Gerritsz. Smyth's correspondence reveals that he considered himself one of Menno's followers. Concurrently, the strained relationships that characterized Thomas Helwys and nine or ten others had reached the breaking point. Helwys, while indicating an indebtedness to the Mennonites for that which they had taught them, nevertheless considered the Mennonites and Smyth in error. The four points he considered erroneous were: 1) on the incarnation; 2) on Sabbath day observance; 3) ministerial succession; and 4) the magistracy. Although Helwys may not have realized it then, the division between him and his mentor was perhaps essential to the rise of the English Baptists as a separate movement distinct from that of the Mennonites. To place this whole development in its historical context, we turn now to the role of Thomas Helwys of Gray's Inn.

Helwys at Gray's Inn

Thomas Helwys, son of Edmund Helwys of Broxtowe Hall in Nottinghamshire, entered Gray's Inn in London in 1593. Gray's Inn was the most famous law school in England. Its reputation was enhanced in part by the fact that Thomas Cromwell and Francis Bacon were once numbered among its students. Students received a general education with special attention given to the reading of English Common Law. That was a notable year.

While Helwys entered Gray's Inn, Queen Elizabeth, threatened by the rising tide of dissent and intent on maintaining the religious settlement of 1559, ordered the execution of John Greenwood and Henry Barrowe. They had been in prison seven years for "publishing and distributing seditious books." Six months later a Welshman, John Penry, suffered a similar fate for his Separatist convictions. A fresh visitation of the ever-recurring plague underlined the turbulence of the times.

The fact that Helwys chose Gray's Inn instead of Cambridge is significant. Certainly, Cambridge was closer to Basford than Gray's Inn. His Uncle Geoffrey, who was a wealthy London merchant and later Sheriff (1607), may have influenced him in that direction. Whether this was so or not, Gray's Inn was the logical choice for a gentleman's son who had little interest in pursuing a career in the church. Although a student would escape the ecclesiastical environment of an Oxford or Cambridge at Gray's, he could not escape the effects of the Conventicle Act that Parliament passed the same year, 1593.

Smyth and Helwys

In 1595 Helwys returned to Nottinghamshire to claim his bride, Joan Ashmore, of the Bilborough Parish. They set up housekeeping at Helwys' ancestral home in Broxtowe Hall. It was here that John Smyth became closely associated with Thomas Helwys and his growing family. The first of seven children came along the next year. Subsequently, the Helwys household became a congenial gathering place for like-minded friends and "a home away from home" for Smyth suffering from a bout of tuberculosis. In 1606 while visiting Broxtowe Hall, Smyth preached at the local parish church at Basford. Three days later the vicar and church wardens were cited before the archdeacon's court and admonished.[26] Clearly the death of Elizabeth had brought no friend of the Puritans or Separatists to the English throne.[27] Evidently Smyth had already broken with the Church of England and established a Separatist conventicle in Gainsborough. This much is certain, Smyth was a marked man and Helwys was numbered among his staunch supporters.

The Gainsborough Separatists formed their church by drawing up a covenant after the pattern of "the Old Testament saints."[28] Ironically, the Scrooby Manor House, belonging to the Archbishop of York, became an additional meeting place for the Gainsborough Separatists. This was due to the rapid growth of the Separatists in the area.[29] It appears that while Smyth was the pastor, Richard Clifton and John Robinson were his assistants. Although they made every attempt to keep the clandestine meetings as quiet as possible, such defiance of the Conventicle Act could hardly be tolerated, nor was it. In July 1608 Joan Helwys, the wife of the leading lay member of the Gainsborough Separatists, was arrested and imprisoned in York Castle. Apparently Thomas escaped a similar fate only by his absence. He was probably already in Amsterdam with the Gainsborough congregation. By 1608 the Scrooby congregation had also resettled in the Netherlands.

The Smyth-led Separatists seem never to have worshiped with the Ancient Church led by Francis Johnson. However, this does not seem to have been the case with the Scrooby congregation that had developed its own separate identity under the leadership of John Robinson. From the beginning it appears that Smyth and his congregation continued their own separate existence.[30] From 1610 the Smyth congregation was evidently worshipping in a bakehouse owned by Jan Munter, a Mennonite elder. Members of the congregation also rented living quarters from him around a quadrangle on the Amstel River adjoining the bakehouse. The Scrooby congregation soon moved on to Leyden where it sought to avoid continuing contact with and the influence of both Smyth's church and the Ancient Church.

The shattering of whatever harmony may have existed among these three exiled English Separatist congregations was exacerbated by a quarrel between Francis and his brother, George, over Mrs. Johnson's lifestyle and stylish apparel and the adoption of believers' baptism by John Smyth and his new-formed church. That Smyth had no intention of taking his followers into the church led by his former Cambridge don is evident from a work published in 1608 in which he delineated the differences between his own church and that of Francis Johnson. Smyth took issue with the Amsterdam Separatists on the use of the Bible in worship and the nature of the ministry of the church.

We may assume that Smyth's, *The Character of the Beast* (1609), represented Helwys as well. In this work, Smyth set forth the conviction that only "new creatures" were suitable subjects for baptism and that churches which practice infant baptism were built on a false foundation. His criticism included all the Separatist churches as well as the Church of England. Smyth wrote, "al[l] those Chu[rches] that baptize the new creature, those that are made Disciples by teaching, men confessing their faith & their sinnes, are of one true constitution."[31] He insisted that a proper subject for baptism "must bee one that confesseth his Fayth and his sinnes, one that is regenerate and borne againe: The forme must bee a voluntary delivering up of the party baptized into the Name of the Father, Sonne, and Holy Spirit, by washing with water."[32] Against the charge of denying the Old Testament, Smyth answered: "the ordinances" of the Old Testament are abolished which were the "Types & shadowes of Gods things to come, but the body is in Christ. Col. 2. 14-17.20."[33]

Instead of denying the Lord's day, as charged by fellow Separatists, he insisted that his church observed the Lord's day by assembling for worship on the first day of the week. Also, instead of denying the magistracy, Smyth affirmed "that they [the magistrates] are the ministers of God to take vengeance on them that do evil."[34] Although Smyth affirmed the legitimacy, even the necessity of the state and magistrates, he confessed that those who are "admitted into the Chu[rch] by baptisme, ther may many questions be made, which to answer neither wil we if we could, neither can we if we would."[35]

Smyth brought this interesting work to a close when questioning the whole process which identified certain people as heretics by various factions, including Roman Catholics, Anglicans, and Separatists. He said it was not the affirmation of a label without evidence that made a man a heretic but "wilful obstinacy in error."[36] By inference Smyth was saying that those who continue to practice infant baptism and defend it are true heretics and not those who reject it. *The Character of the Beast*, therefore, documents fundamental changes in Smyth's thinking from his former Puritan and Separatist positions.[37]

The Parting of the Ways

The Character of the Beast represents Smyth's thought in transition. If he had already reached the position that once a magistrate had become a Christian and a member of the church he must give up his magistracy, he refused to say so due, perhaps, to the opposition of Helwys and others. By 1610, if not before, Smyth and Helwys had come, however, to a parting of the ways.[38] According to Burgess, a few had previously separated from the Smyth congregation over a difference in Christology.[39] While Helwys accused Smyth of holding to a Hofmanite Christology, which was characteristic of most of the Dutch Mennonites, on this point Smyth seems to have vacillated. There is no doubt that he was unwilling to make the controversial teaching a point of fellowship.

Since Smyth's self-baptism had evoked such a sharp reaction among the English Separatists, he decided, after considerable soul-searching, that he had acted precipitously. For the sake of order, he decided to retrace his steps. Therefore, he renounced his baptism and expressed the "desire to come hence to the true Church of Christ as speedily as it can be done."[40] This decision by Smyth and the majority of the church led Helwys and about ten others to withdraw and excommunicate the majority, insisting that they, and, they alone, constituted the original church. A flurry of confessional statements followed. All parties involved—Waterlander Mennonites, Smyth, Helwys, and their respective congregations—prepared statements. From these confessions and the correspondence of Helwys with the Mennonites, it is possible to detect the emergence of a distinctive Baptist faith.

Issues that Divide

An attempted reconstruction of the historical scenario that led to dissension within Smyth's congregation includes factors hardly subject to documentation. Among these is the impression that Helwys had never intended the Amsterdam exile to become a permanent arrangement, though he had apparently been the chief agitator in seeking a refuge in the Netherlands.[41] However, the Dutch sojourn brought many new insights, convictions, and changes. With the recent turn of events, Helwys doubtless began to see that if the new overtures of Smyth received a favorable response, the arrangement might become permanent. The English could lose their identity as well as the urge to return home to share the gospel with their new understanding. He concluded that the flight from England to escape persecution was a mistake.

Therefore, Helwys and his followers determined to clarify their position for the Waterlanders hoping to forestall the union of Smyth and his congregation with the Amsterdam church. For this purpose, as Burrage suggested, Helwys sent a letter in Latin, probably written in 1610, addressed to "Charissimi fratres fidei vinculo" (Dearest brothers by the bond of faith) discouraging the Mennonites from accepting one whom they (Helwys' congregation) had excluded.[42]

Shortly afterwards (February or March 1610), Helwys drew up a confession of faith entitled *Synopsis fidei, verae Christianae Ecclesiae Anglicanae, Amsterodamiae* (A Synopsis of Faith of the true English Christian Church [in] Amsterdam). The confession had nineteen articles that reflected basic agreement with the Latin confession that Smyth probably presented to the Mennonites a month or so before. There was apparently a studied attempt on Helwys' part to avoid duplicating the phraseology of Smyth. In most cases Helwys' Latin was simpler and his statements shorter than those found in Smyth's confession. However, the underlying theological concepts on God, original sin, the general atonement, justification by faith alone, baptism of believers only, and the Lord's Supper were virtually identical with those of Smyth.

The two major points at which Helwys took issue with Smyth were evident in Articles six and nine. In Article six, Helwys made clear his acceptance of traditional Christology.[43] He declared that Christ was the seed of Abraham, Isaac, Jacob, and David according to the flesh. As a true man, he wrote, he was circumcised, baptized, crucified, died, was buried, resurrected, and ascended into heaven. He closed the article by asserting, "Et vna persona, verus Deus et verus homo" (and in one person a true God and true man).[44] The full import of Helwys' formulation can only be seen in contrast with that of Smyth who stated in Article seven, "Iesum Christum, quod ad carnem attinet, per spiritum sanctum in vtero Virginis Mariae conceptum fuisse, postea-natum, . . . fuisse." (That Jesus Christ, because he pertains to the flesh, was conceived through the Holy Spirit in the womb of the Virgin Mary . . . [and] was afterwards born.)[45] The phrase "per spiritum sanctum in vtero Virginis Mariae conceptum, fuisse" was identical with the Christological formula of Menno Simons and the Waterlanders. Helwys viewed Smyth's position as completely unacceptable.

The second major point at issue between Smyth and Helwys was the authority of a particular church to administer the ordinances. Article nine was the second longest article in the "Synopsis of Faith." In this article Helwys defined a "church as an assembly [*Coetus*] of believers baptized in the name of the Father, Son, and Spirit who have confessed their faith [repented of] their sins [and] who have the authority of Christ to preach the Word, baptize and administer the Lord's Supper, even in the absence of ministers according to the rule of Christ."[46] Two cryptic references that hinted at Helwys' mature thought on shunning and the autonomy and freedom of the local church appeared in Articles sixteen and seventeen, which read:

> 16. Quod Excommunicati respectu civilis societatis non sint fugiendi. (That with respect to excommu-

nication they should not avoid the private citizens of the society.)

17. Quod adiaphora non fuit ecclesiae, aut alicui membro ecclesiae imponenda: sed Christiana libertas . . . restituenda est. (That it was not a matter of indifference to the church or must be imposed on some member of the church; but Christian freedom must be restored.)[47]

In a closing paragraph Helwys expressed his heartfelt gratitude for the instruction and kindness that they had received from the Mennonites.[48] The paragraph ended with a petition asking the Lord Jesus Christ to guide by his Spirit both Mennonites and the Helwys Church into all truth.[49]

Apparently the correspondence and "Synopsis of Faith" led to a conference about which, upon reflection, Helwys had some misgivings. This led to another letter written in English. Helwys blamed his inability to use other languages for the lack of clarity in expressing his true position. This March 12, 1610 letter was signed, in addition to Helwys, by William Pigott, Thomas Seamer, and John Murton.[50] The burden of the letter was the matter of succession that affected the validity of Smyth's self-baptism and, consequently, the baptism of those baptized by Smyth. As yet the Mennonites had not arrived at a solution to the problem. They were kindly disposed toward Smyth but extremely cautious about accepting him and his followers without careful study and further instruction. This situation led Helwys and his little flock to set forth their position even more fully and forcefully in the hopes that they would at least be heard, if not heeded. Helwys sounded very much like Conrad Grebel in his letter on behalf of the Swiss Brethren when he argued against succession.

And now for the other question, that Elders must ordeyne Elders, if this be a true perpetuall rule, then from whence is your Eldership come, and if one Church might once ordeyne, then whie not all churches alwaies. Oh that wee migh be though[t] worthie to be aunswered in these thinges, or that the poore aduise of so few, so simple, and so

> weake might prevaile with you to cause you to looke circumspectlie to your waies in these thinges. The lord that knoweth all harts knoweth ours towards you herein, that wee do desire that there may be found no way of error in you, but that you and wee might walke vprightlie in the waiers of God: casting vtterlie away all the traditions of men, and this wee are perswaded is your vnfained desire also; now fulfill our perswasion herein, and trie your standing in these pointes, and respect not how manie hold these thinges with you, but respect from what ground of truth you hold them.[51]

He may have hoped to persuade Smyth and his company to desist in their efforts to unite with the Waterlanders by persuading the Mennonites that the New Testament did not support their position on succession. Helwys closes the English letter as he had his previous letter and Synopsis of Faith with a fervent admonition and expressions of gratitude and hope.

> Thus beseeching the lord to perswade your hart, that your hand may not be against his truth and against vs ye lords vnworthie witnesses, wee take leaue, commending you to ye gracious protection of ye almightie, and to the blessed direction of his word and spirit, beseeching ye lord to do by you according to the great loue and kindnes that you haue shewed vnto vs./ Grace and peace be with you. Amen.[52]

Although the appeal had been to the Word and the Spirit repeatedly against the traditions of humanity, a favorable response was evidently not forthcoming. Positions hardened and Helwys felt all the more alienated not only from the English Separatist congregations of Amsterdam and Leyden but also from Smyth and the Waterlanders.

After Smyth and his congregation had drawn up a confession of faith to present to the Mennonites, Helwys, with the help of his brethren, drew up a new confession that was much more extensive than the "Synopsis of Faith." Entitled *A Declaration of Faith of English People Remaining at Amsterdam in Holland*, it was printed in 1611. Burgess referred to it as "the earliest printed Baptist Confession of Faith."[53] Before Helwys' English confession could be formulated and printed, he sent a letter to the Mennonite church unburdening his heart. It revealed both a high regard for his "brethren in Christ" while at the same time, it took issue with their insistence upon an orderly succession in the ministry. He argued that succession "is Iewish and Ceremoniall, an ordinance of the old testament, but not of ye new."[54] This point must have been very keenly felt for it appealed to the same hermeneutical principle the Anabaptists had been using for almost a century. Helwys was also clearly agitated about the validity of Smyth's baptism.

> And this is our warrant by ye Word of truth. First, for our baptisme./ Iohn Baptist being vnbaptized preached the baptisme of repentance and they that beleeued and confessed their sinnes, he baptized. And whosoeuer shall now be stirred vp by the same spiritt, to preach the same word, and men thereby being converted, may according to Iohn his example, wash them with water and who can forbid./ And wee pray that wee may speake freelie herein, how dare anie man or men chalenge to themselues a pre-heminence herein, as though ye spiritt of God were onelie in their harts, and the word of God were only to be fetched at their mouethes, and the ordinances of God onelie to be had from their hands, except they were Appostles, hath ye Lord thus restrained his spirit, his word, and ordinances as to make particular men lords over them, or ye keepers of them, God forbid.[55]

The question of the validity of orders was inevitably involved in holding to the necessity of succession of elders to ordain elders. "If this be a true perpetuall rule, then from whence is your Eldership come," he asked.[56] The letter ended with a reference to "the great loue and kindnes that you haue shewed vnto vs./ Grace and peace be with you. Amen./ Your brethren in the faith/ Thomas Helwys, William Pigott, Thomas Seamer, Iohn Murton."[57] Helwys' arguments against succession did not convince Smyth or the Mennonites. Instead, Smyth countered by claiming that such a position would lead to innumerable baptisms by unqualified persons and much confusion.

Undaunted, Helwys and his small congregation continued to hold to the conviction that each church, however small, had the authority of Christ to baptize and observe the Lord's Supper. This much became clear in the eleventh article of the confession of 1611.

> That though in respect off CHRIST, the Church bee one, Ephes. 4.4. yet it consisteth off divers particuler congregacions, even so manie as there shallbee in the World, every off which congregacion, though they be but two or three, have CHRIST given them, with all the meanes off their salvacion. Mat. 18.20. Roman. 8.32. I Corin. 3.22. Are the Bodie off CHRIST. I Cor. 12.27. and a whole Church. I Cor. 14.23. And therefore may, and ought, when they are come together, to Pray, Prophecie, breake bread, and administer in all the holy ordinances, although as yet they have no Officers, or that their Officers should bee in Prison, sick, or by anie other meanes hindered from the Church I:Pet. 4.10 & 2.5.[58]

Helwys' deep feeling regarding this matter can be explained by the fact that he felt the validity of his baptism and the viability of his church were at stake.

Both the dependence of Helwys upon Smyth for his basic insights regarding the nature of the church and its relation to the state were revealed. His own creative reinterpretation was evident in Article twenty-four on the magistracy, the first part of which was taken verbatim from *The Character of the Beast*. Helwys added that magistrates "may bee members off the 'Church off CHRIST' retaining their Magistracie, for no Holie Ordinance off God debarreth anie from being a member of CHRISTS Church." The articles continued, "They beare the sword off GOD, which sword in all Lawful administrations is to be defended and supported by the servants off GOD that are under their Government, with their lyves and al that they have according as in the first Institution off that Holie Ordinance."[59] This article was exceedingly important. It articulated a far more positive attitude toward the state than either Smyth or the Mennonites had expressed. Once Baptists were distinguished from Anabaptists, this position, alone, would give their movement not only a chance of survival but also the possibility of influencing society through an active participation in government that the Mennonites never enjoyed. It further separated Helwys' little group from the Mennonites and Smyth. Indeed, it became the single most important doctrinal difference as subsequent correspondence was to demonstrate.

Freedom and Responsibility

Helwys' position on the magistracy now called for further clarification of his views on religious freedom. The last confession drawn up by Smyth before his death in August 1612, was available to Helwys and pointed the way out of the dilemma created by his views on a Christian magistracy, i.e., "How then is religious freedom assured if the magistracy is ordained of God to wield the sword when the magistrate is a member of the church?" *Helwys solved the problem by limiting the magistrate's authority to the secular affairs of state.* Before leaving the Netherlands he wrote, and probably had printed, a little book (212 pages) entitled *The Mistery of Iniquity*.

There is evidence that as early as 1610, Helwys had come to the conclusion that his exodus from England was ill-conceived. Article sixteen in its cryptic phraseology exhibited as much. Probably the death of Smyth triggered Helwys' return home. The last year in Amsterdam had been a difficult one. In the spring, news from England told of two who were put to death for heresy; Bartholemew Legate, a cloth merchant who had been in contact with certain Mennonites in the Netherlands, was executed by burning at St. Paul's Cathedral, London, in March 1612. The following month Edward Wightman was burned to death at Lichfield. Helwys' sense of guilt must have increased with every fresh account of these barbarous acts. With the death of Smyth, he sensed the end of a chapter and the need for another beginning. There was nothing more to be gained by further delay. Perhaps he envisioned that his almost certain imprisonment and possible death would firmly plant the Baptist faith in England. Upon his return to England with about ten others, Helwys established a Baptist church on English soil for the first time. It was hardly the same church in faith or practice that John Smyth had led to Amsterdam in 1608. Nor was it identical with that of the Mennonites with whom they shared so much common ground. The little group that gathered to worship at Spitalfield (Spittlefields) represented something new under the English sun.

These returning exiles, like the Marian exiles half a century before, immediately made their presence felt. A copy of Helwys' book was promptly inscribed and sent to the king, James I. This bold witness cost Helwys his life. Apparently he had anticipated this, for in the inscription Helwys reminded the king that, although he was a king, he was but a mortal man. As a mortal man he had no authority whatever over the consciences of his subjects. To use the words of Helwys, it was not the king's prerogative, "to set up spiritual lords and to make laws and ordinances for them."

In short, religion for Helwys was a personal matter. However, he also informed the king that they, "his poor subjects," intended to be obedient citizens, even to death.[60] If King James ever read the book, he must have found it as curious as it was objectionable. In its pages, Helwys lambasted the Roman Catholic Church as the first beast of Revelation, the Anglicans as the second beast, the Puritans as the third, and the Separatists as the fourth. Their "false teachings" condemned them all. Yet the remarkable thing about the little book was not its polemics, typical of the religious climate of the times, or its unpolished style, but its concept of religious freedom.

> We still pray for our Lord the King that wee be free from suspect. For haeving anie thoughts of provoking evil against them of the Romish religion in regard of their profession, if they be true & faithful subjects to the king for wee do freely professe, that our lord the King hath no more power over their consciences then over ours, and that is none at all: for our lord the King is but an earthly King, and he hath no authority as a King but in earthly causes,

35

> and if the Kings people be obedient and true subjects, obeying all humane lawes made by the King, our lord the King can require no more: for mens religion to God is betwixt God and themselves; the King shall not answere for it, neither may the King be jugd betweene God and man. Let them be heretikes, Turcks, Jewes or whatsoever, it apperteynes not to the earthly power to punish them in the least measure.[61]

Such a bold declaration of the principle of religious freedom and the limitation of the king's authority could hardly have evoked from James' mentality anything other than total rejection. Consequently, the author was arrested and imprisoned, possibly in the early months of 1613. A letter, attributed to Helwys by Burrage, bore the mark of Helwys' mature thought. It was addressed to Parliament and pointed out that Roman Catholics who took the oath of allegiance to the king were freed from prison but indicated that it was not so with the author and many of his fellow prisoners:

> But when wee fall vnder the handes of the Bishops wee can have no benifitt by the said oath, for they say it belongeth onely to Popish recuzantes, & not to others; but kept have wee bene by them many yeres in lingering imprisonmentes, devided from wives, children, servantes & callinges, not for any other cause but onely for conscience towardes God, to the vtter vndoeing of vs, our wives & children.[62]

It appears the letter was of no avail. A notation on the letter read: "rejected by the committee."[63]

The Continuing Dialogue

The early General Baptists reflected an indebtedness to the Mennonites in spite of their differences. Both John Murton and Mark Leonard Busher were numbered among them. Murton succeeded Helwys after his imprisonment in 1613. At least three and possibly four books came from his pen, all of which reveal the dependence of the emerging Baptist movement upon Mennonite teachings. After Murton's death in Newgate prison, his widow returned to Amsterdam and joined the Waterlander Church without undergoing another baptism. In fact, apparently none of the English baptized by Smyth were rebaptized when union was finally achieved in 1615.

Mark Leonard Busher seems to have been in Amsterdam, and the pastor of another English Anabaptist congregation, when Smyth and Helwys were there. As early as 1614, he published a book in English, designed to influence Parliament to consider the advantages of religious freedom, entitled *Religion's Peace: A Plea for Liberty of Conscience*. This work has long been considered a product of an English Baptist author. Although Busher was apparently born in London and well-acquainted with Helwys, Murton, and other English Baptists, he identified with the Flemish Mennonites in 1642.

In 1626, five small English Baptist churches wrote to the Mennonites seeking to compare notes leading to mutual recognition and fellowship. The English Baptist historian, A.C. Underwood writes in his, *A History of English Baptists* of this episode:

> In 1626, Murton's church, associated with churches at Lincoln, Coventry, Salisbury, and Tiverton made an approach to the Dutch. In that year these five churches sent two messengers with a letter to the Waterlander church intending to strengthen friendly relations. Again, the same difficulties arose. The two delegates insisted that unordained members of the church might "preach, convert, baptize, and perform other public actions with the consent of the church, when bishops are not present." They also defended the right of a Christian to accept the office of magistrate and to bear arms. In the end the Mennonites, who throughout the negotiations had displayed a brotherly spirit, declined to enter into organic union, though they were prepared to maintain friendly relations.[64]

The Amsterdam Mennonites considered English Baptists the English counterpart to their fellowship. In 1630, the English-speaking branch of the Waterlander Church sent John Drew, originally from Lincoln, to England. He brought letters from the church that admonished the Baptists "not to be too hasty in disciplining any member" and to restore as soon as possible any who had been disciplined. Apparently some English Baptists had written the English-speaking Mennonites for assistance in one or more cases of discipline.

Individual English Baptists from 1615 through 1650 continued to join the Mennonites in Amsterdam from time to time. Keith Sprunger indicates that possibly as many as eighty-five English joined the Waterlander Church exclusive of those belonging to the Smyth-led congregation. Among these, several were admitted without baptism with the notation that they had been baptized in England.[65] The Baptists, who became known as Particular Baptists, sent one of their number, a Richard Blunt, to Holland in 1641 to secure baptism from the Collegiates at Rynsburg.

After 1650, contacts between the English Baptists and Dutch Mennonites seemed to have ceased except for a couple of isolated incidents. Later, the General Baptists sent Christian Ludwig to Amsterdam in 1696 to explain to the Waterlander Mennonites the Standard Confession of 1660.

Since the end of the seventeenth century, Baptists and Mennonites have, for the most part, gone their separate ways. Yet, as subsequent essays in this book indicate, there is a continuing story of contact and dialogue. In the last one hundred years, Baptist historians, beginning with A.H. Newman, have attempted to help present day Baptists understand that we are kindred people, both historically and theologically. Since 1967 there have been a number of Believers' Church Conferences that have heightened an awareness of the unique heritage that Baptists, Mennonites, and other free church people share. This is a step in the right direction. Is it too much to hope that, as the twenty-first century dawns, Baptists and Mennonites might rediscover each other and walk more closely together as "the Lord's free people?"

ABRAHAM FRIESEN

Baptist Interpretations of Anabaptist History

On December 30, 1909, Henry Elias Dosker, then professor of Church history at the Presbyterian Theological Seminary in Louisville, Kentucky, read a paper on the Dutch Anabaptists at the annual meeting of the American Society of Church History.[1] Rather than open with a statement on the central theme of his subject, Dosker chose to castigate Baptist historians for their reliance on the writings of Ludwig Keller, observing:

> Since 1885 when Ludwig Keller published his *Reformation und die lteren Reformparteien. In ihrem Zusammenhange dargestellt* (Leipzig), the question of the true origin of the Anabaptists has been a matter of debate. With considerable ingenuity and show of reason, Keller argues for the historical genesis of the sect from the well-known medieval movements of the Petrobrusians, the Apostolic Brothers, the Arnoldists, the Moravian Brethren, and the German Mystics. [Theodor] Kolde and Carl Müller have shown the untenability of this theory, and yet it is appealed to again and again by that class of Baptist historians who endeavor to set up for their theological views a quasi apostolic succession[2]

Dosker did not divulge what he might call such Baptist historians, but he did argue that "sober historians," among whom he appears to have numbered himself, saw "'a fanatical ultra reformatory movement'" in Anabaptism "which revealed itself first in Germany in the so-called 'Wittenberg fanaticism' of 1521-1522 . . . [and] later associated itself with the atrocious Peasant War."[3]

Dosker's condemnation of a Baptist appropriation of an apparently discredited Keller thesis notwithstanding,[4] E.H. Broadbent pro-

39

claimed in his The Pilgrim Church, first published in 1931 and repeatedly thereafter:

> Perhaps the largest use has been made of the works of Dr. Ludwig Keller, especially for the history and teaching of the Waldenses.[5] His position as Keeper of the State Archives, giving access as it does to most important documents, has been used by him to investigate the histories of those known as "heretics", and his publications are an invaluable contribution to the understanding of these much misunderstood people. Dr. Keller's book, "Die Reformation und die lteren Reformparteien" [sic] is a mine of information and all who can do so should read it. Use has also been made of his book "Ein Apostel der Wiedert ufer" [sic] and of a number of others written or issued by him.[6]

Like many other Baptist historians who adopted Keller's reversal of the established churches' claim to sole legitimacy, Broadbent asserted that the apostolic faith had been passed down through the centuries, not by the dominant Roman Catholic Church or even its reformed Reformation counterparts, but by the persecuted, dissenting minority groups of Christians who had rejected the Constantinian compromise from late Antiquity to the Reformation and beyond.[7] Such a thesis had of necessity not only to be challenged but also condemned by the apologists of the established churches. That minorities, non-conformists, dissenters, "outsiders" all, should be considered the transmitters of the authentic "deposit of apostolic faith and practice" posed a threat to these churches not even a Dosker could ignore.[8] How could erstwhile heretics suddenly become orthodox disciples? How could such a dramatic reversal of established ecclesiastical norms even be contemplated? And yet, this was unambiguously Keller's and Broadbent's intent. Thus Broadbent wrote in the concluding paragraph of his introduction:

> The tragedy and the glory of "The Pilgrim Church" can only be faintly indicated as yet, nor can they

be fully known until the time comes when the Word of the Lord is fulfilled: "there is nothing covered, that shall not be revealed; and hid, that shall not be known" (Matt. 10. 26). At present, albeit through mists of our ignorance and misunderstanding, we see her warring against the powers of darkness, witnessing for her Lord in the world, suffering as she follows in His footsteps. Her people are ever pilgrims, establishing no earthly institution, because having in view the heavenly city. In their likeness to their Master they might be called Stones which the Builders Rejected (Luke 20. 17), and they are sustained in the confident hope that, when His kingdom is revealed, they will be sharers in it with Him.[9]

Broadbent's version of the Keller thesis is held in some Baptist circles to this day. Jack Hoad, in *The Baptist* (1986), cites an extensive Baptist bibliography to confirm such a position. He observes that "many American Baptists claim John, the Forerunner of Jesus Christ, as the first 'baptist' and trace their beginnings from him."[10] In so doing, Hoad continues, "they advance a continuity which claims to trace their churches' history through various separatist movements, such as the Montanists, Novationists, Donatists, Cathari, Paulicians, Petrobrusians, Waldenses and Anabaptists, down to the baptist churches of today."[11]

Hoad does not appear altogether persuaded, observing that this thesis "smacks of the classical catholic doctrine of 'apostolic succession'";[12] nevertheless, he does lend some credence to it, quoting the great evangelist, Charles Haddon Spurgeon, who asserted: "We have an unbroken line to the apostles themselves. We have always existed from the days of Christ, and our principles, sometimes veiled and forgotten, like a river which travels underground for a season, have always had honest and holy adherents." Long before Protestants had been heard from, Spurgeon boasted, "anabaptists were protesting for the 'One Lord, one faith, one baptism.'"[13] More intriguingly, Hoad also quotes from two eminent sixteenth-century Catholics. The one, Cardinal Stanislaus Hosius, later president of the Council of

Trent, wrote in 1524: "'Were it not that the baptists had been grievously tormented and cut off with the knife during the past 1200 years, they would swarm in greater numbers today than all the reformers.'"[14] The second comes from a memorandum of the council of the Archbishop of Cologne to Charles V which told the latter to "'suppress the "anabaptists" because they seek to introduce the community of goods . . . etc., even as has been the nature of the anabaptists throughout the ages, as the old Imperial law over a thousand years testifies.'"[15] And so even Hoad, as late as 1986, can introduce his history with the following somewhat modified version of the discredited Keller thesis:

> The baptist heritage is an immensely rich record of the grace of God in preserving a biblical church witness throughout the centuries of a christian era. In repeated upsurges of a revived testimony to the rugged simplicity of the New Testament principles, the Lord of the churches has proclaimed the heretical departure of those claiming to be main-line christianity.[16]

Nothing could be more obvious: those who formerly considered themselves the carriers of orthodoxy are here proclaimed heretics.

Dosker, however, was mistaken in his charge: Keller was not the first to formulate the theory, nor did the Baptists borrow it from him. It can be found in the writings of Baptist historians well before Keller's time. As early as 1846, J. Newton Brown, in *The Life and Times of Menno, the Celebrated Dutch Reformer*,[17] spoke of "Waldensian Baptists" finding refuge in Frisia four centuries before Menno's birth,[18] though Menno had not been aware of their existence until the rebaptism of Sicke Snyder in 1531.[19] With this established, Brown could assert that the Münsterites "had nothing in common with the Baptists, except the denial of infant baptism—for they held to a worldly, not a spiritual kingdom."[20] Quoting Cardinal Hosius and Seisellius, Archbishop of Turin, with reference to heresy in the Church prior to the Reformation, Brown proclaimed: "Such are the concessions of illustrious Romanists to the long, unbroken line of our martyr witnesses."[21]

An excellent example of the similar, but broader, theory, can be found in J.M. Cramp's *Baptist History from the Foundation of the Christian Church to the Close of the Eighteenth Century*, first published without date by the American Baptist Publication Society of Philadelphia. A second edition appeared in 1865, and a third in 1868. An English edition was produced in London in 1868 and another in 1871. Even a German translation was published by the J.G. Oncken Verlag in 1870.[22] Obviously, the book travelled well in Baptist circles. Cramp, a professor of church history at Acadia College in Nova Scotia, voiced his Baptist orientation early in the study:

> Unquestionably the progress of religion in the community, which was emphatically designated "The Church," was altogether downward during the "Transition Period" [from Constantine to the close of the "Dark Ages"]. It is an interesting inquiry, how far the spirit of the gospel was preserved, and its essential truths maintained, by those whom ecclesiastical historians have denominated "heretics" and "schismatics." I shall pursue this inquiry in succeeding chapters. In order to find the true church, we must look out of the "Church" commonly so called.[23]

Cramp traced this "decline" of the Church, especially in regard to baptism, from its inception to the rise of Scholasticism. It was in the wake of the latter movement that groups of dissenters, who sowed the seed of the later Baptist harvest, had arisen. Not yet the authentic product, they "had [nevertheless] imbibed the right principle." Cramp observed, "One cannot help thinking that they must have been Baptists, so entirely does the position they maintained harmonize with our own."[24] Having all but declared these "heretics" Baptists, Cramp proceeded to trace the fate of men like Henry of Lausanne, Arnold of Brescia, Berenger, Wycliffe, the Bohemians. From this context he then asserted:

> When Luther blew the trumpet of religious freedom, the sound was heard far and wide, and the

Baptists came out of their hiding-places, to share in the general gladness and to take part in the conflict. For years they had lived in concealment, worshipped God by stealth, and practiced the social duties of Christianity in the best manner they could, under the most unfavourable circumstances, and fondly expected to enjoy the co-operation of the reformers in carrying into effect those changes which they knew were required in order to restore Christian churches to primitive purity. They were doomed to bitter disappointment. The Reformers had no sympathy for Baptist principles, but strove to suppress them.[25]

When it came to Anabaptism proper, Cramp seems to have relied on one major publication as his source: an abridgement of Van Braght's *Martyr's Mirror* published as the *A Martyrology of the Churches of Christ, Commonly Called Baptists, During the Era of the Reformation* published for the English Baptists Hanserd Knollys Society.[26] Whether Van Braght provided Cramp with his larger "Baptist" context, or merely confirmed it, Cramp's narration of Reformation "Baptist" history consisted primarily of vignettes of Anabaptist martyrs found in the *Martyr's Mirror*. For describing Menno Simons, he not only drew, as had J. Newton Brown before him from the Martyrology, but also from Menno's "Narration of his Secession from Popery," published in the *London Baptist Magazine* by the Rev. William Rowe.[27] Clearly, Cramp provided an "insider's" account of sixteenth-century Anabaptism from materials published largely by the English Baptists themselves.

Even before Keller, Edward Bean Underhill of Oxford, England, general editor of the Hanserd Knollys Society, produced another Baptist interpretation of continental Anabaptism. In 1846 he published a series of tracts on religious liberty also under the auspices of the Society. In the preface, Underhill presented a general survey of "Baptist" history during the Reformation. Unlike Cramp, who appears to have written later,[28] Underhill did not indulge in a lengthy pre-history of ancient and medieval "Baptists," but stated simply: "The Reformation had scarcely boasted an existence of five years, when, from the midst of its adherents, men arose who declared it to be insufficient."[29] Quoting Mosheim, on whom Underhill relied heavily for information on the Anabaptists, he argued that the basic principle of the movement had been to establish "The kingdom of Christ, or the visible church . . . on earth." This desire not only brought the Anabaptists into conflict with the reformers, but also with the magistrates who were quick to persecute them, "not for sedition, treason or crime, but for matters of opinion and faith."[30] Their crime was that "they rejected secular interference in the church of God; it was the boast of the reformers everywhere to employ it: the natural fruit of the one was persecution, of the other liberty."[31] As it had at Münster, on occasion this persecution led to revolution. Not that one should condone such an uprising, Underhill remarked, but one could understand it, for it derived from that oppression "which makes [even] a wise man mad" at times.[32]

Underhill, too, had Van Braght's *Martyr's Mirror* at his disposal, but cited it only occasionally, relying instead on Pierre Bayle's interpretation of Anabaptism[33] to make the case of religious liberty. Underhill saw the continental Anabaptists standing in the vanguard of this struggle. "The baptists were and ever have been opposed" to surrendering their understanding and conscience, he observed, "inasmuch as they conceive that the marks of infallibility have never yet been discovered, engraven by divine skill, either on the 'holy Roman church,' or on that constituted by legislative enactments of king Edward and his successors on the British throne."[34]

This Baptist interpretation of Church history may well have found its justification, though not its source, in the writings of Ludwig Keller. Baptist Church historians, like their Mennonite counterparts, turned to Keller for confirmation of views and interpretations already well established. As an impartial outsider—Keller belonged to the German Reformed Church—he provided them with an obviously "unbiased" scholarly foundation for their theories.

The common source of all these interpretations, however, seems to have been the Protestant martyrologies in general,[35] and Van Braght's *Martyr's Mirror* in particular. John Foxe, for example in the opening lines of Acts and Monuments, cited Christ's promise, made in his response to Peter's confession in Matthew 16:16, about building his church "on this rock . . . and the gates of hell will not prevail against it," implying the unbroken existence of Christ's true church here on earth. It was the same passage that served the Roman Catholic church for its doctrine of apostolic succession.[36] In chapter IV, however, Foxe arrived at what he called "papal persecutions." Here it was that he indicated he no longer considered the papal church to be the true church:

> Popery having brought various innovations into the Church, and overspread the Christian world with darkness and superstition, some few, who plainly perceived the pernicious tendency of such errors, determined to show the light of the Gospel in its real purity, and to disperse those clouds which artful priests had raised about it, in order to blind people, and obscure its real brightness.[37]

These few who had perceived the Church's "pernicious tendency of . . . errors," men like Berenger, Peter of Bruges, Henry of Toulouse, Peter Waldo, the Albigenses, Wycliffe and the Lollards, became in Foxe's hands the forerunners of the reformers and the carriers of the true church which would be fully restored in the Reformation.

A similar argument came from the pen of Van Braght; only in his account the Anabaptists represented the line of the true church from Antiquity to the Reformation:

> Some will not admit that the Anabaptists, or those who maintain such a confession as they do, have existed through every century, from the days of Christ up to the present time.[38]

Later he observed:

> Now the question arises, whether our church of the present day, called the Anabaptists, has truly descended, and derived her succession, from the aforementioned church of God which has existed from the beginning and kept the commandments of God in purity.[39]

In Van Braght's apostolic succession the Waldenses, with whom Foxe had initiated his true church under the false papal church, became the crucial link to the sixteenth-century Anabaptists.[40] No wonder Mosheim could write in his *Ecclesiastical History*:

> The modern Mennonites not only consider themselves as the descendants of the Waldenses, who were so grievously oppressed and persecuted by the despotic heads of the Roman church, but pretend, moreover, to be the purest offspring of these respectable sufferers, being equally averse to all principles of rebellion, on the one hand, and all suggestions of fanaticism on the other.[41]

In the view of these martyrologists, the pope became the Antichrist and the Roman Catholic Church the Babylonian whore. It was a view that had its source in Martin Luther and was given great currency in England by no less a person than Sir Isaac Newton in 1733[42] and Richard Hurd, Bishop of Worcester, in 1772.[43] It would appear, therefore, that the interpretation promulgated in Protestant martyrologies, based on an impulse received from Luther himself is the probable source for the Baptists position, especially since both Cramp and Brown relied heavily on Van Braght's *Martyr's Mirror*.

The dissenting voice of Walter Rauschenbusch, son of August Rauschenbusch, father of the Social Gospel and himself a Baptist, should nonetheless be heard. Writing in the partial autobiography of his father, he observed:

> Given the paucity of historical evidence [concerning Baptist as well as Anabaptist beginnings], many Baptists, especially those from the Southern States, had pieced a kind of ideal history together for themselves. One knew that churches, at the time of the apostles, had consisted of believers who had been baptized by immersion on their confession of faith. One knew that in the second quarter of the seventeenth century Baptist congregations had arisen in England from which the present-day Bap-

47

> tists had descended. But what about the long period of time between these two points? Should the true baptism and the true church have disappeared from the face of the earth for such a long time? No, for already one hundred years earlier, among Germany's Anabaptists, and Holland's Mennonites, apostolic baptism had been practiced. Furthermore, one had some knowledge of the Bohemian Brethren, the Waldensians and Albigensians of France and Italy, the Petrobrusians and Paulicians who had all protested the Roman apostacy and had sought to reestablish apostolic Christianity. Therefore they must also have been opposed to infant baptism. Upon pillars such as these one sought to build a bridge backwards to the time of the apostles. There must, therefore, always have been secret authentic Christian churches that stood in historical connection to one another and that passed the true baptism from one to the other so that at all times those truly and correctly baptized passed this baptism on to others so that apostolic baptism had been handed down to us by an unbroken chain of succession. Everyone knew, of course, that there was no certain proof of this, but they believed that the missing historical links would yet be found. In the meantime, the theory had to substitute for the missing evidence. Since this was the way it must have been, this was the way it was.[44]

The activating assumption behind this theory, Rauschenbusch continued, was the doctrine of apostolic succession promulgated by the Roman Catholic Church and adopted by the Anglican Church, a church from which the Baptists had separated in the seventeenth century. This theory, Rauschenbusch asserted, "continued, as a dogmatic inheritance from the Anglican Church, to work among the Baptists, only in a transformed fashion."[45] Like his father, August, before him, Walter rejected the theory, arguing instead with Irenaeus: *Ubi ecclesia, ibi Spiritus Sanctus* (Wherever the Church, there is the

Holy Spirit). It was not the external continuity that mattered to Walter Rauschenbusch, but faith in Christ.

In this larger portrayal of Baptist Church history, Anabaptism appeared merely as one of the links, albeit a major one, between the primitive church and the inception of the Baptists. Even as such, however, Baptist scholars early turned their attention to its study, even before they encountered the writings of Ludwig Keller. That is not to say, however, that Keller did not play an important role in the early stages of the Baptist interpretation of Anabaptist history. On the contrary. The first work of any substance to appear was J. Newton Brown's biography of Menno Simons. Based essentially on Menno's description of his departure from the Catholic Church, Brown compared him with the other reformers in the following manner:

> In this sketch, we aim to present our readers with the portrait of a man worthy to be held in everlasting remembrance; but of whom little is generally known. Among the great reformers of the sixteenth century, he certainly was one of the first order—in some respects, we do not hesitate to say, the very first. Luther, Melanchthon, Zwingli, Calvin, Know, Cranmer, were men who displayed high talents and virtues—men whose consecrated learning and genius shed lustre on the cause of Truth, and gave both form and impulse to their age after ages. The world will never forget them. Their names are dear to the bosom of the Church. Their influence as reformers will never die. But there stood one among them whom they knew not; who was greater than they—more truly eminent in the likeness of their common Lord.[46]

Brown concluded his brief account of Menno by asserting:

> Indeed, of all the illustrious names recorded in church history, for the last six hundred years, we know of none superior to his. Others may think differently. But for ourselves, taking all circum-

> stances of his times into account, we know of none whose place in heaven we should prefer, to that which his faithful Lord has marked out for Menno Simons.[47]

Brown, however, worked essentially from one document: Menno's very personal descriptive justification of his departure from the Catholic Church.

After August Rauschenbusch took up his duties in the German Department at Rochester Theological Seminary in the mid-nineteenth century it soon became the most influential center for Anabaptist studies within the Baptist community.[48] Howard Osgood, librarian at Rochester, began to develop what became the finest collection of *Anabaptistica* in North America during the latter half of the century. He assisted Henry S. Burrage with his studies of Swiss Anabaptism,[49] inspired Henry C. Vedder to write Balthasar Hubmaier's biography,[50] and may also have furthered the work of Albert Henry Newman who taught at the seminary from 1877 to 1881. In this work Osgood was assisted by August Rauschenbusch. From the outset the two appear to have focused their attention on Hubmaier, yet the first substantive Baptist history of the Anabaptists dealt with the Swiss movement and was written by Henry S. Burrage, a Baptist minister from Portland, Maine, and a prolific local historian.[51]

Baptist historians were, from the outset, determined that the Anabaptists would be accorded a fair treatment. After all, had they not, in Underhill's words, been the defenders of religious liberty? Burrage reflected this determination in the preface to his book:

> No one among us would be satisfied with a history of the Reformation in Germany, prepared by Dr. Eck or any of Luther's opponents; but works concerning the Anabaptists, written by their bitterest enemies, are received by writers of almost every name as trustworthy history. Books of this character are cited as authorities in Anabaptist history.[52]

After enumerating a representative sampling of such works, Burrage proceeded to cite a particularly glaring example from J.P. Thompson's *Church and State*, where the author had asserted that "The Anabaptists in Germany in the sixteenth century had most of the characteristic features of Mormonism." But Thompson had, as Burrage noted with satisfaction, immediately been challenged by Osgood.⁵³ Burrage, focusing on the Swiss movement, was clearly adopting a point of departure different from those of Dosker and Thompson, whose ideal types were the Zwickau Prophets and the Münster revolutionaries respectively.

Burrage knew the secondary literature on his subject; he was also conversant with the primary sources. In his treatment he was more historian than theologian, taking political, economic and other non-theological matters into account. Tracing the radical tendencies in Ulrich Zwingli's followers to the reformer himself, Burrage depicted a movement that had early on developed the concept and reality of the believers' church.⁵⁴ From this vantage point the Anabaptists had begun to doubt the validity of infant baptism, believing, as Burrage said, along with Luther and Zwingli, that "faith was indispensable to baptism."⁵⁵ Earlier, Zwingli had himself "entertained the view that it would be better not to baptize children until they were somewhat advanced in years," but because of "his opposition to the radicals he was led to abandon it."⁵⁶ Quoting from Dorner's *Geschichte der Protestantischen Theologie*, Burrage noted that for Zwingli setting aside infant baptism was tantamount to abandoning the national church.⁵⁷ Burrage proceeded to trace the development of Anabaptism in Switzerland from the initial refusal to baptize infants, to the first believer's baptism, the establishment of the new church in Zollikon and the resulting persecution by Zwingli and the Zurich authorities. Burrage also had some wise things to say about Conrad Grebel's famous letter to Thomas Müntzer, so often interpreted from prejudicial points of view. Nor did Burrage give Bullinger's account much credence:

> Here, Bullinger says, Müntzer was invited by Grebel, Mantz and others, but no record of the conference has been preserved. Nor do we find that the leaders of the Swiss radicals had any subsequent dealings with him. As Grebel's letter shows, he and his associates were not in agree-

51

ment with Müntzer in reference to baptism. They did not believe in the use of the sword as he did. Doubtless, they now found that in purpose they and the Saxon Reformer differed widely. Müntzer's aims were social and political chiefly. . . . But Grebel and his friends, who were also in sympathy with the oppressed peasants, would bring about a better state of things, not by revolution, but by restoring primitive Christianity: and so believing in different methods of accomplishing the great end they had in view, they seem to have separated without forming a closer alliance, and took the different paths they had already marked out. (Italics mine.)[58]

The other striking aspect of Burrage's history—and of other Baptist histories as well—was empathy with and sympathy for the peasants during the critical years of social upheaval. In contrast to Dosker and the generally received theological assessment—Dosker called it "the atrocious Peasant War"—Burrage spoke of a "movement for political reform," of "the grievances of the common people." And of the relationship between Anabaptism and Peasant War, Burrage remarked:

They [the Anabaptists] would not aid the endeavor to right them [the peasant grievances] by the sword. Their view of the independence of the churches, however, and of the limits of the power of the magistrates, as well as the general distress of the people under the tyranny of their oppressors, prepared the way in many hearts for the words of those who preached a gospel of hope for the children of toil and want.[59]

Burrage, though devoting considerable time and space to Hubmaier as one of the important early leaders of Swiss-South German Anabaptism, was not yet party to that Baptist predilection for Hubmaier because of his position on the sword. Nor did Burrage glorify him. Willing to rest his case on the evidence—in Hubmaier's case he even received the original German confession from the Zurich archives—Burrage candidly conceded that Hubmaier had offered to recant his Anabaptist views there in 1526.[60] When it came to baptism by immersion, another special point of Baptist interest, Burrage quoted Osgood (who had himself been to St. Gall in 1867) that Grebel, in the Sitter River in late March or early April 1525, had manifestly moved from sprinkling to immersion as the preferred mode of baptism.[61]

Quoting Emil Egli, whose *Aktensammlung* he had used to good advantage, that the principles from which the Anabaptists proceeded "unquestionably . . . manifest a powerful grasp of original Christian ideas,"[62] Burrage concluded his study with the following observation:

> All of these principles are accepted by the Baptist churches of today. But they have obtained a wider recognition. In churches whose creeds still solemnly inculcate infant baptism, we find this fruitful source of evil from the third century is almost wholly ignored. At the present time, also, other than Baptist churches insist upon a regenerated church membership, the independence of the churches, religious liberty, and the separation of Church and State. Insofar, succeeding ages have justified the principles of the Swiss Anabaptists, and it can hardly be doubted that the ages that shall follow will justify yet others. Certainly, not in vain did the Anabaptists of Switzerland adopt these principles, and sacrifice so much in maintaining them.[63]

It can only have been Burrage's familiarity with the most recent European studies on Anabaptism by Cornelius, Egli, Füsslin and others that had drawn his attention to the Swiss Anabaptists. Even before his book appeared (1882), he obtained and read Keller's history of the Münster revolution.[64] On July 6, 1882, he wrote Keller to tell him:

> In reading this book I have not been able to detect a party bias. I have found nothing that shows

53

whether you are a Catholic or a Protestant. This is as it should be. Men too long have been accustomed to read history through their prejudices. What we want are the facts, and these, as it seems to me, you have honestly endeavored to give.

While he had "no sympathy with the Münster fanatics," Burrage concluded, "their history too should be given in accordance with the facts," since their "record was dark enough when truthfully presented."[65]

On December 28, 1882, after receiving Keller's second book, *Ein Apostel der Wiedert ufer*, Burrage wrote observing that had he possessed it for his own study, it "would have aided me greatly."[66] On April 5, 1883 he sent another letter responding to Keller's request for help in circulating his works in America. Burrage informed Keller that he had recently translated Keller's essay, "Ein Apostel der Wiedert ufer" which appeared in the September 1883 issue of the *Preussische Jahrbücher*. Moreover Burrage had read it "before a historical society in Boston." Burrage hoped to publish the translation in *Bibliotheca Sacra*, but it was published instead in the *Baptist Quarterly Review* in 1885.[67]

In the meantime, Keller must have written Burrage to thank him for translating his essay and to enquire whether Burrage was planning to write a Hubmaier biography. Apparently, Dr. Underhill of Oxford had so informed Keller.[68] Burrage denied the report, suggesting, in a letter of April 14, 1885, that Keller undertake the project together with an edition of Hubmaier's writings. At the same time, he remarked that he had just "recently received a copy of your new work 'Die Reformation, etc.'" Whereas he had just begun to read it, the part he had completed "has greatly interested me, and you have done a good work in making prominent the facts in reference to the earlier reform parties. There can be no question," Burrage concluded, "but that these parties prepared the soil for the seed sown at the time of the Reformation."[69] There was no indication, however, that he saw the implications of Keller's thesis for a Baptist interpretation of the larger outlines of church history.

Early in 1884 Keller, seeking American contacts, must have written to Gustav Schwab, a New York businessman and son of the

Swabian poet.[70] Schwab, in a letter of March 12, 1884, gave him the name of August Rauschenbusch.[71] Nearly a year later, on March 7, 1885, Keller wrote Rauschenbusch. By this time August Rauschenbusch had already been interested in Anabaptist studies for some thirty years. He began such study shortly after his 1850 rebaptism from Lutheranism to the Baptists. In June 1851, he conducted evangelistic services in Ontario, Canada, where contact with local Mennonite congregations had prepared great numbers of people for the Gospel and believers' baptism. By November he had returned home to Elberfeld, Germany, only to find himself accused of being an Anabaptist of the Münsterite ilk.[72] In 1868, when he next returned to Germany, he searched in southern Germany for his Anabaptist "roots," to which his Elberfeld experiences and the study of Church history were directing him. As his son, Walter, observed:

> He planned to write a history of the Anabaptists, and gathered materials for it on this trip. In Landshut, the former locale of Hubmaier's activity, in Zurich, Basel, Freiburg and other university cities, he sought the remains of Waldensian and Anabaptist writings in the libraries, had copies made of rare manuscripts and purchased an impressive number of important original documents. He also visited different scholars who had occupied themselves in a special way with this portion of history, e.g., Dr. Schreiber in Freiburg, the librarian of the city library of Zurich, a learned Catholic priest in Waldshut, three professors in Ulm and, in particular, the Catholic Professor Cornelius in Munich, whose study on the Münster revolt he held in especial high esteem.[73]

August Rauschenbusch, as a result of his Anabaptist studies, arrived at the conviction that of all the medieval heretics only Peter of Bruges demanded believers' baptism and that it "had only been reinstituted in 1525 by the Swiss Anabaptists." But even these had not practiced immersion. With respect to John Smyth, he argued that Smyth had probably baptized himself, with baptism by immersion first coming to England in 1641.⁷⁴

In the summer of 1870, August Rauschenbusch presented two lectures on his Anabaptist research at a summer school for preachers at the University of Chicago. Over two hundred Baptist ministers and many seminary professors were in attendance. In these lectures, Rauschenbusch challenged the inherited Baptist position on baptism and its apostolic succession, creating consternation in many Baptist circles. The reverberations still were felt years later. Thus, by the time Keller began to correspond with Rauschenbusch, the latter was already firmly entrenched on the opposite side of the Keller thesis.

Rauschenbusch, in his response to Keller of May 29, 1885, made no mention of the latter's thesis. He did, however, respond to Keller's suggestion that Rauschenbusch publish the writings of Hans Denck, observing that an edition of Denck's writings would not find much support among American Baptists.

> Permit me to tell you quite frankly that Denck would not find much sympathy among Baptists because he is, even more so than other Anabaptists, *a semipelagian*; the Baptists, in contrast, are Augustinian."⁷⁵

In a letter of August 4, 1885, which referred to Keller's interpretation of the Waldensians in his *Die Reformation*, Rauschenbush laid out why Baptists had an interest in the medieval sectaries at all: "For in the eyes of the Baptist," Rauschenbusch observed, "whether or not the Waldensians are to be considered forerunners of the Anabaptists depends entirely upon their teaching and mode of baptism," not on any historical connectedness or Baptist version of apostolic succession. In the same letter Rauschenbusch referred to a notice of Keller's book in the July 1885 issue of the *Baptist Quarterly Review* by Albert Henry Newman, then of Toronto. "He speaks of it with praise and respect," he reported, "but it served him only as excuse to discuss Dieckhoff's and other newer works on the Waldensians."⁷⁶

By the time Newman wrote to Keller on September 15, 1886, he had already staked out his own position in an 1884 essay on "The Reformation from a Baptist Point of View" in the *Baptist Quarterly Review.*

Christ did not convert men by nation, neither did Paul. Mohammed and Charlemagne did. Hubmaier did not make Protestants by nations. Luther did. Christ made individual, earnest Christians. Charlemagne made hypocrites and cringing slaves to external forms. Hubmaier made, with divine help, self-sacrificing Christians. Luther made self-indulgent Protestants![77]

Luther, Newman continued, "could be Biblical when it suited his purpose";[78] when pressed by those who adhered to the "Biblical principle," he said it was sufficient "if prevalent practices were not *distinctly forbidden* by Scripture."[79] Being destructive rather than constructive in his writings, Luther failed "to develop an apostolical [sic] in the place of a monkish piety in his followers."[80] And the "most vicious point in Luther's system was the maintenance of the union of Church and state."[81] Luther could be forgiven had his generation been without witnesses to the truth, but this had not been the case. There was Hubmaier, whose motto had been: "The truth is immortal."[82] The choice, then, was between "Hubmaier or Luther." Newman chose Hubmaier: "The man that, at the very beginning of his career, could write the ablest plea of the age for liberty of conscience, who showed forth an apostolic faith and suffered an apostolic martyrdom."[83] In contrast, Newman characterized Luther as

> the man who put himself at the head of the politico-religious movement, who drove to despair and to death such as refused to yield to his *ipse dixit*, whose controversial language was more becoming to a fish-woman than to a theologian, who did not blush to hold the most unworthy inducements to those whose alliance he would gain, whose arrogance was equalled only by his exceeding bitterness of spirit.[84]

About a year later an essay by Newman on "The Early Waldenses" appeared in the same journal. By this time he had read Keller's *Die Reformation*, and he said of it:

> It is Dr. Ludwig Keller's great merit to have traced the history of the old evangelical party through the dark ages of persecution, and to have exhibited, in a masterly manner, the relations of this party to the great religious, social, industrial, and scientific movements of the later Middle Ages, and so to the Protestant revolution of the sixteenth century. . . . These results are in the highest degree gratifying to evangelical Christians in general, and especially to Baptists. Keller insists throughout that the old evangelical party was fundamentally Baptist, and that its failure to carry out its fundamental principles with logical consistency, and so to attain fully the Baptist position, was due to the unfavorableness of the circumstances. He shows, moreover, that just in proportion as this party had freedom to develop itself the Baptist position was reached.[85]

Already during the last two hundred years, Newman concluded triumphantly, "The great Baptist movement . . . had revolutionized the religious thinking of the world . . . and [would] sooner or later sweep away the last vestiges of Popery from the doctrines and practices of the great evangelical denominations."[86] Then the revolution begun by the "old evangelical parties" of the Middle Ages would have reached completion.

On September 15, 1886, Newman wrote Keller:

> I have read with great pleasure and profit your various works bearing upon the Reformation and Baptist history, and I have also read a number of critiques to which you refer in your latest book. Allow me to say that Kode's strictures in the "Zeitschrift f. d. Kirchengeschichte" impressed me when I read them as utterly unscrupulous and partisan,[87] and that I regard your self-vindication as complete. From being deeply interested in your writings I have come to feel considerable personal interest in yourself and it has occurred to me to

> publish in a leading New York Review a sketch of your life and works, if I can acquire the necessary materials. If you would kindly furnish me with a sketch of your life, and with whatever other information with reference to your position and plans for future literary work, I would endeavor to make such use of them as would tend to bring your work more into notice and to increase your influence for good.[88]

One year later Newman published his *A History of Anti-Pedobaptism from the Rise of Pedobaptism to A.D. 1609*.[89]

There can be little doubt that Keller's *Die Reformation und die älteren Reformparteien* served as a model for Newman's study, for, though narrower in scope, it concentrated on the theme of baptism. The opening paragraph clearly falls into the pattern of Keller's "discredited" thesis and the Baptist view of Church history.

> The claim of Baptists that in doctrine and in polity they are in substantial accord with the precept and the example of Christ and his apostles would seem to make it incumbent upon them to account for the early departure of the great mass of Christians from the apostolic norm.[90]

Newman saw the "departure . . . from this apostolic norm" coming "early in the second century, possibly during the last decade of the first," when "the idea came into vogue that while instruction in Christian truth and morals, repentance, faith, fasting, and prayer must precede baptism, the remission of sins takes place in connection with the baptismal act."[91] Therefore, Newman argued, the postapostolic church had "already begun to yield to the all-pervasive pagan idea of the magical efficacy of water baptism."[92] From this beginning, Justin Martyr, but especially Tertullian and later Church Fathers, developed their theology of baptismal regeneration.

Newman, in the second chapter, confronted the Baptist theory of "apostolic succession" in the Church to the tenth century. In effect he rejected it and argued that "the best example of the persistence of a somewhat primitive type of Christianity is probably that of the ancient British church."[93] But even here he did not find enough evidence to demonstrate "that the Iro-Scottish church rejected baptismal regeneration of infant baptism."[94] Not until the twelfth century, Newman argued, "do we encounter Christian doctrine that we can with confidence recognize as measurably conformable to the apostolic standard."[95] He regarded Peter of Bruges, Henry of Lausanne and Arnold of Brescia as the first exemplars, followed by the Waldensians. But Newman rejected the argument of "many Mennonites and some Baptists," that Waldo had simply attained to the leadership of an ancient evangelical party going back to apostolic times and not founded a new group.[96] Nevertheless, with Waldo the succession had begun:

> It is probable [Newman declared] that Waldo and his immediate followers held to a set of views that soon became characteristic of the Waldenses, and were communicated by them to the Bohemian Brethren, and by both these parties to the Anabaptists of the sixteenth century.[97]

Having made this assertion, Newman turned his attention to the Reformation. Here he reiterated the charges against Luther he had levelled in his essay, "The Reformation from a Baptist Point of View." Caught between the forces of reaction and what Dosker had called an "ultra-reformatory" movement, Luther had been unwilling to apply the same biblical norms to the Left he had applied to the Right. On the Left were Thomas Müntzer and the Zwickau Prophets. Influenced in his assessment of the latter by Wilhelm Zimmermann and other Liberal-Radical historians,[98] Newman, like Burrage before him, adopted a very positive attitude toward the peasants:

> We must distinguish between the aspirations and strivings of the peasants in Swabia and Alsace, and the fanatical procedures of Müntzer and [Heinrich] Pfeiffer. The cause of the peasants was a righteous cause. If ever an oppressed class was justified in rebelling against constituted authority, the peasants of

Germany were surely justified in organizing themselves as they did and in venturing their lives for civil and religious liberty. The oppression under which they groaned had become intolerable, and the enthusiastic utterances of Luther and others had given them a clear consciousness of the rights of man and of the unjustifiableness of tyranny. . . . The twelve articles in which they set their demands, as has been justly said, are worthy of a Solon. There is not a trace of fanaticism in the document. It is in the spirit of the best medieval evangelical thought. It is in accord with the best that was contained in Luther's earlier utterances. *It is in accord with Baptist views of civil and religious liberty.* It is in accord with modern democratic principles. There is no demand for community of goods. There is no suggestion of theocratic government. The people claim the right to appoint and remove pastors and to insist upon the preaching of the gospel in its purity and simplicity. They demand the abolition of oppressive laws as regards wages, rents, tithes, the "heriot" or death gift, hunting, fishing, the use of forests for fuel and timber, etc. The demands are all most reasonable and Christian. Moreover the authors of the demands express a willingness to abandon any one of them that shall be shown to be out of accord with Scripture. *So thoroughly sound are these articles that they have by some been attributed to Hubmaier, who probably came nearer to the modern Baptist position than any man in the sixteenth century.* There is nothing in them that he might not have written, and he was certainly in thorough sympathy with the just demands of the peasantry, it is not improbable that he had at least something to do with the drafting of the document. (Italics mine.)[99]

Having rejected Müntzer and affirmed Hubmaier and the justifiable use of the sword, Newman turned to the Swiss movement. In this portrayal, Grebel, Felix Mantz and the others fade behind the prominence of Hubmaier. The latter, it was argued, "found little satisfaction in Denck's mystical views."[100] Hubmaier was described as the "greatest leader" of the Moravian Anti-Pedobaptists, the "ablest and soundest advocate" of the cause of radical evangelical reform. "In point of ability and character," Newman asserted, "Hubmaier deserves a high place among the evangelical leaders of the church universal."[101]

Newman was one of only a few Baptists who dealt with the entire movement, covering Roll and Rothmann, Hoffmann and Münster, as well as Menno Simons and the Anabaptists in England. He placed the responsibility for the revolution in Münster primarily on the "oppressors of the working classes, or rather on the institutions that made such oppression possible,"[102] even though he had little sympathy for the "prophetico-mystical chiliasm of Nicholas Storch and Thomas Müntzer [that] was perpetuated by Hans Hut, Melchior Rinck, and Melchior Hoffmann."[103] Menno Simons, however, "was to gather out of the wreck . . . the sound evangelical elements and to carry forward along *old evangelical lines* [Keller's term] the work of restoring primitive Christianity."[104]

Newman posited the same origin for the Lollard movement in England that Keller had used to explain the beginnings of Anabaptism: they, too, were a part of the "old evangelical" church even though "diligent research" had as yet "failed to discover any case of Anti-pedobaptism" before it had arrived from the continent after 1530.[105] The English General Baptists, advocates of the freedom of the will, had in fact, he argued, been "greatly influenced . . . [by the] Polish anti-trinitarian Anti-pedobaptist movement" and maintained close ties to them. It was from their leader, Fausto Socinus, that baptism by immersion had been adopted.[106]

Newman's selection of Hubmaier as the "ablest and soundest advocate" of the Anabaptists had its source in the fact that Hubmaier "probably came nearer to the modern Baptist position than any man in the sixteenth century."[107] In the concluding chapter, Newman described the "narrowness and . . . erroneous views" of the Anabaptists as due in large part to the persecution. The last vestiges of the "narrowness"—its anti-Augustinian doctrine of free will—had been overcome by the English "Particular" Baptists who had seceded from

the "General" Baptists in 1633.[108]
   In 1899 Newman published his very influential *A Manual of Church History*. Repeatedly reprinted because of its widespread use in theological seminaries, the *Manual* contained a section on "The Anti-Pedobaptist Reformation" where, long before George Hunston Williams,[109] Newman attempted a typology of Anabaptism. He divided the parties into "Chiliastic Anabaptist," "Soundly Biblical Anabaptist," "Mystical Anabaptist," "Pantheistic Anabaptist" and "Anti-Trinitarian Anabaptist." In the first category he included Thomas Müntzer, though he argued Müntzer "was never really an Anabaptist";[110] Hans Hut, of whom he said: "The corrupting influence of Hut on the Anabaptist movement can hardly be overestimated";[111] Melchior Hoffmann; Jan Matthys and the Münster kingdom. Under the "Soundly Biblical" Anabaptists Newman put the main Swiss-South German movements and the Mennonites. The "Mystical" Anabaptists were Hans Denck, Ludwig Hätzer and others like Jakob Kautz and Caspar Schwenckfeldt. David Joris and Heinrich Nicläs came under "Pantheistic" Anabaptists. Johannes Campanus, Michael Servetus and the Italian and Polish Anabaptists he captioned Anti-Trinitarian Anabaptists. What is especially intriguing about Newman's description in this section of his *Manual* is 1) his quite open acknowledgement of Hubmaier's meeting with Müntzer in Waldshut;[112] 2) his implied criticism of pacifism; 3) his rejection of oaths and political office of the group he called the "soundly biblical" Anabaptists;[113] 4) his consequent elevation of Hubmaier because no one in his age had "more ably expounded the distinctive principles of the Baptists";[114] and, 5) his rejection of the "objectionable" teachings of Hans Denck.[115] Newman not only knew the literature on the Anabaptists well; he judged the movement from his Baptist vantage point.
   In 1890, the Assembly of the Baptist Union [Calvinist],[116] meeting in Cardiff, Wales, adopted a resolution designed to stimulate interest in Baptist history by providing a "chapter of the more general history of the denomination," as George P. Gould, the General Editor put it. The first volume in the series to appear (for lack of reader interest only three appeared, two of which were biographies) was on Continental Anabaptism by Richard Heath.[117] Heath was a close friend and collaborator of Walter Rauschenbusch and both were influenced by English Fabian Socialism.[118] That influence certainly in-

formed their understanding of Anabaptism and brought both men close to E. Belfort Bax's interpretation as contained in his 1903 study, *The Rise and Fall of the Anabaptists*.[119] Heath, writing for a wider audience, took his material from secondary, largely German sources. Though published in 1895, Heath appears not to have consulted Keller's *Die Reformation*, for he still saw Anabaptism as originating in Zwickau—as had Dosker as late as 1909—and ending in Münster. Nevertheless, Heath had read Keller's biography of Hans Denck and his history of the Münster rebellion. Of Keller Heath wrote:

> Keller's book, *Ein Apostel der Wiedertäufer*—the biography of Hans Denck—contains summaries of the writings of the most original thinker among the early Anabaptists. This book and Dr. Keller's *Geschichte der Wiedertäufer* have been much consulted. The difference in tone of these two works with regard to Anabaptism is striking testimony to its intrinsic worth, and encourages the belief that the more its history is carefully and critically studied, the more it will emerge from the fog of prejudice in which it has been enveloped.[120]

Heath had also read the works of the Dutch Mennonite Steven Blaupot ten Cate as well as J.P. Müller's *Die Mennoniten in Ostfriesland* and Anna Brons' *Ursprung und Schicksale der Taufgesinnten oder Mennoniten*. Indeed, Müller, pastor at the Mennonite church in Emden, Germany, had apparently provided Heath with a great deal of material.

More than any previous Baptist historian, Heath—as one influenced by Fabian Socialism—was an advocate of the common people. He referred to Anabaptism as the faith of the poor and argued that it could not "be limited to its strict meaning of second or adult baptism, for it represents historically a movement having for its aim social and political as well as religious reform."[121] The Peasant War, he argued, "was in fact an effort of the People to make the Reformation thorough."[122] And though "Luther's own sympathies were not democratic,"[123] the translation of the Bible he unleashed "proved wholly and entirely on the People's side."[124] There God revealed himself "as suffering with man and bent on his deliverance."[125] Sympathizing with the downtrodden

> were these reformers:—Dr. Balthasar Hubmaier, of Waldshut; Thomas Müntzer, one of the prophets of Zwickau; Carlstadt, Luther's old colleague; and Carlstadt's brother-in-law, Dr. Gerhard Westerburg. Hubmaier is said to have written the original twelve articles, and Westerburg wrote those for his district. None of them, however, threw themselves into the movement as Müntzer did. He was emphatically the prophet of the insurrection; its spirit of intense animosity against the ruling classes seemed concentrated in him.[126]

Perhaps Heath got his interpretation of these events from Wilhelm Zimmermann's massive 1841-1843 history of the Peasant War, which he cited, or from Bax's study which relied heavily on Zimmermann. But the sentiment must have been there before he took up the subject and speaks volumes for the Baptist—especially the English Baptist—attitude toward social reform, even to the point of justifying revolution. This attitude stands in stark contrast to the Dutch Mennonite paranoia with respect to Menno's possible association with the Münster revolutionaries.[127]

On March 21, 1891, Heath wrote to Keller, citing an article Keller had written on the Anabaptists and their English descendants for the *Contemporary Review*. In doing so, Heath observed, he had "gleaned" in Keller's field, and found Keller's book on Hans Denck "extremely interesting." In contrast to August Rauschenbusch, who had rejected Denck, Heath requested permission to translate the book on Denck.[128] Keller agreed, and Heath received permission from Keller's publisher to do so. On June 6 Heath wrote that the translation was "nearly completed."[129] But he seems not to have been able to find a publisher, for the study never appeared in English. Perhaps "official" Baptist sentiment against Denck prevailed even in England.

As Paul M. Minus, the most recent biographer of Walter

65

Rauschenbusch observed, Heath belonged to a group founded by Rauschenbusch known as the "Brotherhood of the Kingdom" and exerted an "important influence on WR's interpretation of Anabaptism."[130] In the year Heath published his book on Anabaptism, the younger Rauschenbusch made a trip to Münster where he met Ludwig Keller, who taught him that "the Anabaptists contain[ed] more of the future . . . than the Reformers."[131] For Rauschenbusch this future included his proclamation of the Social Gospel, the Gospel of the Kingdom. He observed that whereas Luther "said the gospel was to free the soul and not the body," the Anabaptists said it was to free both.[132] This, indeed, had been Christ's message, and the Anabaptists had sought a return to Christ rather than a return to Augustine and Paul, as had the reformers. Thus, as Minus remarks, the Anabaptist "road to reform, together with their understanding of the church as a disciplined, uncompromising band of believers, won Rauschenbusch's favor and made a lasting impression on his thought."[133]

That the social aspect of Anabaptism was as important for Walter Rauschenbusch as it had been for Richard Heath and some of the other English Baptists can be seen from what one student said at Rauschenbush's funeral:

> Nor could one work with him through Anabaptist history without feeling that the actual course of the social movement which conditioned the religious upheaval known as the Reformation has never been adequately traced and probably never can because the peasant and the commoner were held of so little account; without feeling much more, the passionate interest in the lives of plain people which gave our beloved scholar so great a measure of interpretive insight.[134]

Rauschenbusch, like some of the English Baptists, not only did not shun the "revolutionary" character of Anabaptism, he welcomed it with open arms:

> We were far to the front, on the skirmish line. We were the radicals of the radicals. . . . We were for a

> "reformation without tarrying," even if we had to leave the old church and break it in pieces. We were against clericalism and against all hierarchies. We were for the religious emancipation of the laity. We went as far as the most radical Calvinist in purging religion of superstition, and when he stopped we went on. The others reformed the Lord's Supper, and cleared it of the abuses which had grown up about it, but they feared to attempt the reformation of baptism, for they knew that would shake the foundation of church life. The abolition of infant baptism meant not simply the modification of one church rite, but a revolutionary reconstruction of the very conception of the church.[135]

Rauschenbusch concluded, that the Anabaptists had initiated a revolutionary movement for which they paid with their blood. But God had vindicated them, for "in the long, slow sweep of four centuries, often by devious and pathetic ways, the course of religious development for the Protestant world has been in the direction marked out by the swift rush of radical parties of the Reformation."[136]

In 1903, Edward Carey Pike wrote *The Story of the Anabaptists* as volume two in the series "Eras of Nonconformity," published under the auspices of the National Council of Evangelical Free Churches.[137] Once again, the publications of the Hanserd Knollys Society were cited as important sources, especially the "wonderful *Martyrology* by J.T. van Braght."[138] Richard Heath's book on Anabaptism was also cited, along with "the recent volumes by E. Belfort Bax, on *The Social Side of the Reformation in Germany*, particularly *The Rise and Fall of the Anabaptists.*"[139] Here Anabaptism and the Peasant War were tied closely together with the Anabaptists "fully concurring" in the demands of the common people and Hubmaier lauded as the author of the Twelve Articles.[140] Always democratic in their sympathies, the Anabaptists "were regarded with apprehension, for their doctrines were subversive of the tyranny which in those days passed for government."[141] They were especially so in the histories of Anabaptism by English Baptists, who were strongly influenced by

Fabian Socialism. The theme sounded by Pierre Bayle and recovered for the Baptists by Underhill, had, by the turn of the century, become the dominant theme, with the social significance of the movement all but eliminating the religious aspect. Only in Rauschenbusch, the American Baptist, were the two fully integrated in his Social Gospel.

Only two years later, Henry C. Vedder published his biography of Hubmaier, entitled, *Hubmaier: The Leader of The Anabaptists*.[142] In the preface Vedder praised Carl Adolf Cornelius for first breaking with the ancient disparagement of Anabaptism, Joseph Beck for the "epochal" publication of *Geschichts-Bücher der Wieder-täufer*, and Ludwig Keller for demonstrating "the genetic relation of the Anabaptists of the Reformation to the older reform parties."[143] Time, as Vedder argued, was "bringing about the vindication of these greatly wronged people."[144] But Vedder was not altogether happy with what English Fabians and their Baptist counterparts were doing to the Anabaptists:

> More recently, certain English writers [he cited Richard Heath and E. Belfort Bax], themselves advocates of modern socialistic theories, have represented the whole Anabaptist movement as a splendid but unfortunate attempt to realise a complete socialistic programme, a radical overturning of existing institutions, almost an entire anticipation of the teaching of Lassalle and Marx.
> While the motives of the recent writers are far more laudable than those of the predecessors, the result is almost precisely the same. The contemporary writers wished to load the Anabaptists with obloquy; their English historians wish to crown the Anabaptists with honour, as the first to attempt the application of a theory yet destined to be the salvation of mankind; but in either case the Anabaptists are equally misrepresented, and the opinions of a few are attributed to the whole. The misrepresentation is most serious when the violent measures advocated by Hut and afterwards put in practice at

Münster are represented either as the conviction of the majority or the legitimate consequences of the views of the prevalent body.[145]

To a certain extent Vedder stood at the forefront of a new generation of Baptist scholars of Anabaptist history; to a certain extent he was the heir to the mantle of Henry S. Burrage in his desire to be a critical and impartial historian. There was, he asserted, "no attempt in these pages at idealising Hubmaier."[146] Nonetheless, his very choice of Hubmaier pointed to his Baptist proclivities. His inclusion of Hubmaier's "On the Sword" in the appendix of his book probably also had its "Baptist" reasons.

From Vedder forward Baptist studies on Anabaptism have joined, by and large, the ranks of modern critical scholarship. Aside from the popularizers of some general Baptist church histories, the Keller thesis has, at least outwardly, faded from the scene. A scholar like Kenneth Davis, in *Anabaptism and Asceticism*, picked up a variant of the Keller thesis propounded by Albrecht Ritschl, and sought to connect Anabaptism to the ascetic ideal of holiness in the Franciscan Tertiaries.[147] In *The Anabaptists and the Czech Brethren*, Jarold Knox Zeman of Acadia University (the same institution where Cramp taught in the nineteenth century) tackled the question of the relationship of the Czech Brethren and the Anabaptists.[148] Both Ritschl and Keller, independently of one another, argued for such a connection: the first from the influence of the Franciscan holiness ideal; the second from the ideological parallels and historical links between "the old evangelical brotherhoods."[149] Davis's argument, though based on extensive scholarship, has not proven convincing to Zeman who concluded that the historical evidence in Davis's case was disappointingly limited. Hubmaier, Zeman concluded, knew nothing of the Czech Reformation though he lived in Moravia for over a year:

> The relationship between Hutterites and the Czech Brethren constitutes one of the most ironical, if not tragic, episodes of ecumenical history. The two groups, so much alike in their protest against the established Christendom, lived side by side in one

land for several decades. Yet they ignored each other so completely that the only information which the Hutterite chronicler was able to incorporate in his manuscript was derived from a hundred-year-old book written by the arch-enemy of the Hussites, Aeneas Sylvius. Its contents were mediated by the catalogue of a Dominican inquisitor and the chronicle of a spiritualist.[150]

The most rewarding work from Baptist scholars has been dedicated to studies more central to Swiss Anabaptism. Jan J. Kiwiet and Ekkehard Krajewski have written brief but very useful biographies of Pilgram Marpeck and Felix Mantz respectively. J.A. Moore has done a slender volume on George Blaurock. Above all, however, there is the work of Torsten Bergsten who has written a biography of Hubmaier and edited a critical edition of his writings. Here, in the personality so attractive to Baptists over the last one hundred and fifty years, their best work has been done. Indeed, Bergsten's biography remains the definitive study on Hubmaier.[151] Thus, even in these latest, important studies from Baptist scholars on Anabaptism, the themes sounded early are still the ones that dominate their interest. The scholarship itself, however, has become much less partisan.

Since the volume in which this essay is to appear deals with Mennonite, and more specifically Mennonite Brethren relations with Baptists, a word might be said on the significance this study may have for that larger theme. First, Mennonite Brethren, in particular and Mennonites in general might do well to discard their fear of Müntzer, Münster and social revolution and take a more positive and compassionate look at the oppressed common people of the Reformation. They might also become more aggressive in focusing on the "Social Gospel" aspect of Anabaptist ideas, on the theme of religious liberty, and on the struggle for freedom of expression. In this respect, Mennonite scholars have much to learn from their older—and newer—Baptist colleagues. Furthermore, Mennonites, especially Mennonite Brethren, need to hear the very positive assessment of the Anabaptist movement by Baptist scholars, to the point of lauding it as the prophetic voice for future evangelical Christianity. For, in large part, the Mennonite Brethren are in the process of abandoning that position for a vague "American Evangelicalism." They need to hear J. Newton Brown, Henry S. Burrage and the multitude of other Baptist interpreters of Anabaptism. On the other hand, Baptists would do well not to judge sixteenth-century Anabaptism by the Baptist yardstick. Perhaps Hubmaier *is* to be "corrected" by the nonresistance of a Michael Sattler. Perhaps Christ has indeed called his church to be the reconciling agent in a confrontational world. Erasmus's *Complaint of Peace*, which may well have influenced early Anabaptist pacifist thought, is, after all, a very powerful document.[152] And after Ludwig Keller has been thoroughly studied,[153] we may all forget about theories of apostolic succession—whether Catholic, Anglican, Baptist or Mennonite—and say with August Rauschenbusch: "Wherever the Church, there is the Holy Spirit."

PETER J. KLASSEN

Baptists and Mennonites in Poland and Prussia

For approximately one century before the extinction of Mennonite communities in Eastern Europe during and after World War II, Mennonites and Baptists existed side by side both in Poland and in Prussia. During much of this time, Poland did not exist as an independent political entity, having been divided among its neighbors late in the eighteenth century. Then, with the end of World War I, the state of Poland was reestablished. Throughout this entire period, however, Poles maintained their identity, whether living under Austrian, Prussian, or Russian rule. The vast majority of Poles lived in Russian, or Congress Poland, and so it was not unusual to use the term "Poland" to refer specifically to this area. Baptist congregations began to appear in this region in the late 1850s and drew initial inspiration from German Baptist missionaries.

The birth of the Baptist movement in Poland largely coincided with that of the Mennonite Brethren in South Russia. While historians have given considerable attention to relations between Baptists and Mennonites in South Russia,[1] few have examined the corresponding situation in Poland.

The first Polish Baptist congregation was organized in 1858 under the leadership of Friedrich Alf. Ironically, this pastor and itinerant minister later gave significant assistance to the fledgling Mennonite Brethren movement. Alf, a Lutheran pietist and teacher in the village Mentnow, near Warsaw, combined his instructional responsibilities with efforts to bring a spiritual renewal.[2] He emphasized Bible study, prayer, and the quest for a devout life style. Some local church authorities objected; eventually, they succeeded in removing him from his position. Impoverished and unemployed, he took up residence in his parental home and assisted with farming responsibilities. In the nearby village, Adamov, however, he found spiritual nurture and fellowship with a group of like-minded believers.

At this time, Heinrich Assmann, a businessman from East Prus-

73

sia, came to Adamov and told the group about the Baptist practice of immersing believers. Largely because of the work of Johann G. Oncken, the founder of the German Baptist movement, East Prussia already had several Baptist congregations. Eduard Kupsch, in his *Geschichte der Baptisten in Polen, 1852-1932*, reported that Alf and his fellow believers met repeatedly for prayer and Bible study. After lengthy discussion some participants decided that they would adopt the practice of immersing adult believers; others, however, insisted they would retain infant baptism and work for renewal within the Lutheran Church. Thus, the renewal movement split on the baptism issue.[3]

With this decision to break with the Lutheran practice of baptism, the group attracted considerable attention and opposition. Alf was forced to leave his father's home; he moved to Adamov, some ten miles from Warsaw. Here he was able to acquire a small plot of land, although he remained desperately poor. To provide an orderly transition, Alf and his associates decided to invite a Baptist minister, Weist, from Stolzenberg in East Prussia, to assist them in founding a Baptist church. Accordingly, on November 28, 1858, with the baptism of nine persons, the Baptist Church in Poland came into existence. On the following day, another seventeen were baptized. Adamov thus became the birthplace of the Polish Baptist churches.

This break with established religious procedure in the region elicited vigorous response. Weist and some others were arrested, imprisoned in Pultusk, and brought to trial. An enlightened judge concluded that the defendants had committed no crime and ordered their release. With that, the triumphant, former prisoners returned to Adamov and promptly baptized thirteen more people.[4] Soon the local congregation drew up both a confession of faith and a constitution, based directly on documents received from German Baptists. These served as models for other Baptist churches soon to be established in Poland.[5] Ties with German Baptists remained close. Later in 1859 Alf visited Hamburg to study briefly at Oncken's missionary center there and to gain further insights into Baptist church practices.

When Alf returned to Adamov, he began the first Baptist Sunday School in Poland. Despite vigorous opposition, especially from local Lutheran pastors, the Adamov Baptist congregation grew, and almost immediately erected its own church edifice. In 1860 alone 110 new members were baptized. Meanwhile, because of the missionary efforts of Alf and his associates, several Baptist congregations arose in several nearby villages.

As the movement spread, opposition intensified. Repeatedly, Baptist preachers and converts were abused, imprisoned, and subjected to various indignities.[6] Not until 1879 did Baptists gain official toleration.[7] Most often, local Lutheran clerics led the opposition. In a letter from prison Alf, himself, described some of the physical abuse he suffered.[8]

Meanwhile, the new movement spread, and in some localities, Mennonites decided to become part of this religious awakening. In Wola-Wodzinska, a predominately Mennonite village, a former Mennonite, Johann Penner, played a key role in founding a Baptist church. A resident of Adamov and a member of the Baptist church there, he went to visit his relatives in Wola-Wodzinska. While in the village, he tried to persuade all who would listen to consider the teachings of the Baptists. Immediately, he created a stir, both among local Mennonites and members of other confessions. Local authorities arrested and imprisoned him, then ordered him never to return to Wola-Wodzinska. Nevertheless, in this village and in nearby Kicin, Baptist ideas continued to gain ground and drew significant interest from local Mennonites.

In Kicin the Mennonite, Peter Ewert, provided strong support. When Alf came to this area in 1860, Ewert entertained him. In addition, Ewert allowed Alf to conduct meetings in his home. The number of interested persons grew quickly, so that Ewert's home proved too small; the group moved its services to the hay loft. On August 25, 1860, the first baptisms were conducted in Kicin, and one year later the congregation was formally established.[9] By 1862 the membership had risen to 112. Ewert continued as leader in the congregation and was ordained a Baptist minister in 1865.[10] His efforts brought a number of Mennonites into the Baptist church, and he created a stir when he baptized the 63-year-old wife of a Mennonite minister.[11] Local hoodlums sometimes subjected new converts to mistreatment,[12] but at the dedication of the church building in 1868, government officials came to pay their respects.[13]

As the church in Kicin grew, Baptists of Mennonite background and those with Lutheran roots came into sharp doctrinal controversy. Issues of dispute included views of military service and the practice of footwashing. In addition, Mennonites had for centuries enjoyed special privileges that would be forfeited if they joined another religious body. Johann Penner championed the position that believers should not bear arms, and that footwashing should be observed after the Lord's Supper. Gradually, however, the Baptist position prevailed, and Mennonites who joined the church surrendered their privileges.

As the Baptist movement spread, many of its adherents experienced ridicule, arrest, imprisonment, and physical violence. Leaders such as Alf aroused the wrath of both Lutheran and Catholic church officials, who then brought formal charges before civil authorities. In 1864 Alf moved to Kicin, which now became the Baptist center in Poland. By the end of 1869 the congregation had 771 members.[14]

The Kicin church also served as the focal point for extensive missionary work. It sent one of its members, Peter Ewert, as a preacher to the village of Kurowek. A fruitful ministry followed, so that by 1869 the new congregation numbered eighty-five baptized members.[15] Ewert was also a leader in founding a new Baptist congregation in Zezulin, a village near Lublin.[16] In 1873, the church had 232 members. A few years later some young men in these new congregations began studying in the Baptist seminary in Hamburg, thus strengthening ties between Polish and German Baptists.[17] Ewert continued his activities, and in 1874 baptized several converts in the nearby village of Rabatki.

As the Baptist movement expanded in central and southern regions of Poland, it continued to develop harmonious relations with the newly-established Mennonite Brethren Church in South Russia. The development of the Baptist congregation in the town of Zyrardow, a few miles from Warsaw, demonstrated the mutual respect. The congregation, established in 1868, continued to attract new members, but sometimes experienced a shortage of ministers. From November 1896 until March 1897, Johann Friesen from the Mennonite Brethren Church in South Russia served as minister. Peter Rempel, also from the Mennonite Brethren Church, succeeded him and continued his ministry there until 1899. The members especially appreciated Rempel's ministry, but he emigrated to North America.

Similarly, some Baptist ministers gained the confidence of Mennonites, especially Mennonite Brethren, and served in their churches. As a remarkable expression of confidence in the emerging Baptist Church in Germany, some Mennonite Brethren leaders in South Russia wrote to Hamburg and requested assistance in organizing the new movement.[18] August Liebig arrived in the spring of 1866, chaired a congregational meeting where formal procedures were adopted, and thus helped the Mennonite Brethren end their disarray. He could play this influential role because he had previously served widely as a guest preacher in Mennonite Brethren churches in South Russia. During his stay the authorities accused him of fomenting sectarianism (*Sectiererei*) with his continued preaching. He was arrested, and on June 2, 1866 he wrote to J.G. Oncken from prison: "Mennonites, who also once had to endure prison, delivered me into the hands of the Russian authorities. . . . O that the Lord would . . . take Russia's privileges from them, so that they might again receive God's privilege, to bring sinners to Christ."[19] Local opposition eventually led to his being expelled from Russia, but in 1871 he returned.

For the next several years, Liebig helped to bring greater unity and order to Mennonite Brethren congregations. He simultaneously continued his ministry to Baptist churches in South Russia and in Polish (Congress) Russia. In 1887 Liebig was chosen leader of the Baptist congregation in Lodz. His dynamic church expansion practices and denunciation of what he regarded as evil in church and society aroused considerable opposition, but he continued his ministry. Eventually, since he was not a Russian citizen, authorities used this as a pretext to order him out of the Russian Empire in 1889. He had been a major force in demonstrating that Baptists and Mennonites could enjoy mutual respect and fellowship and also retain their separate identities.

As the Baptist movement continued to expand, contact with Mennonites often increased. In 1876 the Baptist periodical, *Missionsblatt der Gemeine getaufter Christen*, reported that August Penski, minister of the Baptist church in Ksiazki, near Swiecie, had visited sister congregations in South Russia. While there, he also spent time in Mennonite villages, and made the acquaintance of "Mennonite Baptist" ministers such as Abraham Unger and Abraham Schellenberg.[20] He addressed congregations in the "large, beautiful church" in Halbstadt as well as in Rückenau. The dialect he heard there was

77

similar to those spoken in West Russia.[21] In 1877 he became pastor of the Baptist church in Danzig and continued his association with Mennonites.

Throughout the last decades of the nineteenth century, Baptists and Mennonites in Poland and South Russia collaborated in various ways. On May 1, 1884, Baptists organized a Russian Baptist Alliance.[22] Johann Wieler was chosen leader; he had been an active proponent of the Mennonite Brethren. Also, when Baptist congregations arose in Bessarabia and Volhynia, close ties with Mennonites helped to shape the Baptist churches.

Numerous Baptist leaders visited Mennonite communities and often gained new adherents or simply fostered close ties of mutual support. No Baptist, however, had a greater impact on Mennonites in Poland, Prussia, and South Russia, than did Johann Gerhard Oncken, long a prominent preacher, educator, missionary, and church organizer in England, Scotland, Germany, Poland, Russia, the Netherlands, Austria, and the United States.

In 1841 Oncken travelled to Tilsit to "visit the Mennonites," as he noted in his diary.[23] His hope was to preach to them and persuade them to adopt Baptist teaching. He noted that when he went to the place of business of a local Mennonite, he found him operating a distillery, and selling his "poison"[24] to the poor citizenry. Later Oncken met two Mennonite deacons, but concluded that they also knew little of the truth of the Gospel. Undaunted, he requested and received permission to preach to the rural Mennonite congregation. In his diary he recorded his prayer that God might rouse the members from their sleep. Evidently his sermon prompted a response, for Oncken reported that some 200-300 listeners had carefully followed his ninety minute sermon and demonstrated their love for him. Moved to tears, they invited him to return.

Oncken decided to spend some time with several Mennonite communities and went to his "old friends, the Mennonites," in Elbing. There he enjoyed a warm welcome and preached in the Mennonite church in Ellerwald, just a few miles outside the city, as well as in the city church.

Some Elbing Mennonites had earlier made Oncken's acquaintance, and were prepared to do more than give him a friendly hearing. Jakob Braun, who had worked for the local Mennonite minister and been baptized a Mennonite, impressed Oncken so much that the latter invited him to come to Hamburg to assist in the publication work there. Braun soon distinguished himself in this calling.[25] Braun did not restrict his ministry to working with publication of Baptist materials. One of his friends in Elbing, Johann Doerksen, also a Mennonite, joined the Baptist cause. In the summer of 1844, Braun and Doerksen spent four months distributing Baptist literature in Prussia. During this missionary endeavor, more Mennonites, and others, joined the Baptists.[26] In 1844, Baptists established their own church in Elbing.[27]

Oncken continued his ministry to the Mennonites in this area by preaching to congregations in Marcushof, Thiensdorf, and Heubuden. In the latter center, he gained support for a Bible distribution effort. Oncken noted that his host, a Mennonite minister in Heubuden, believed that immersion was the right mode of baptism, but that those baptized by sprinkling need not be rebaptized.[28] In another nearby village, Bröskefeld, Oncken found "pious and zealous" Mennonites who wanted to join in efforts to distribute Bibles. Oncken also visited the Mennonite church in Danzig. The pastor, Jakob Mannhardt, impressed him as devout and intelligent. Oncken was pleased to note that Mannhardt was ready to help in the Bible and tract ministry.

During his missionary tour in Prussia in 1841, Oncken also visited Königsberg. He commented that his efforts there had not been very successful. In his explanations of Baptist teachings on baptism, he needed the "patience of Job" to listen to the "absolute foolishness" of some of his opponents.[29] His reports on Königsberg did not specify any contacts with Mennonites there. However, a few years later, Carl Harder, pastor of the Mennonite church there, expressed his opposition to Baptists, and specifically Oncken, for placing so much emphasis on the mode of baptism. Harder rejected insistence on immersion as a "superstitious veneration" of an external form.[30]

At least on one occasion, Oncken's ties with Mennonites, in an ironic twist, served his interests well. Oncken was attempting to gain approval in Hamburg for a projected expansion of the work of his church. Some city leaders apparently expressed concern about the possible proselyting activities of the local Baptists. A senator of the city then advised authorities that Baptists and Mennonites were very

79

similar, and so one need not worry. As far as any tendency to seek converts might be concerned, Senator Kirchenpauer observed, "no trace could be found" among Hamburg Mennonites.[31] Perhaps this indicates why Oncken felt little inclination to form a close relationship with Mennonites in Hamburg and Altona.[32]

Although Oncken was a tireless itinerant minister, and visited many Baptist and Mennonite churches in Poland and Prussia, he devoted much time and energy to publication and education efforts. His missionary school (later "Prediger Seminar") in Hamburg provided a significant arena for bringing Mennonites and Baptists in contact. Most students came from Germany, but some also regularly came from churches in Prussia and Poland. Then, in 1885, when Heinrich Epp and Abram Friesen from South Russia began their studies there, another aspect of Baptist-Mennonite relations began to develop.[33] In the succeeding years, some Mennonites, mostly but not exclusively from South Russia, studied with Baptists from South Russia, Congress Poland, Prussia and elsewhere. Oncken, who had done much to encourage close ties with Mennonites in Russia, did not live to see them begin sending ministerial candidates to his newly-reorganized seminary. He died in 1884.

It is not surprising that of all Mennonites in Poland or Prussia the Mennonite Brethren developed especially close relationships to the Baptists. The Mennonite Brethren congregation in Deutsch Wymysle, begun as an outpost of a church in South Russia in the 1880s, and made independent in 1895, always maintained close ties to Baptists. There were several Baptist congregations in the area, so that joint church celebrations, music festivals and youth meetings were common.[34] When Poland was reestablished as an independent state, this warm fellowship continued.[35] At least in Deutsch Wymysle, the good relations that existed between Mennonites and Baptists, most of whom were Poles, helped to moderate action taken by military forces in this area during World War II. Both at the beginning and end of the war, Baptists interceded for Mennonites to protect them from actions by the Polish military. Similarly, during the years of war and occupation, Mennonites in Wymysle tried to better the treatment of Poles.[36] It was at least a small tribute to the strength of bonds of faith, which forged in times of peace, were able to temper a virulent nationalism unleashed by war.

JOHN B. TOEWS

Baptists and Mennonite Brethren in Russia (1790-1930)

The Russian Mennonite world which generated the Brethren movement in 1860 had long interacted with strangers. Mennonite forefathers in the sixteenth-century Netherlands or eighteenth-century Prussia, though committed to the ideal of a pure church separated from the world, were subject to varied and ongoing relations with the people and states which encompassed them. Anabaptist carpenters, dike builders, brewers and artists fleeing to cities like Elbing, Königsberg and Danzig, early ensured urbanism as one dimension of the Mennonite experience in Prussia. They, as well as the rural Anabaptist populations engaging in land reclamation in the Vistula Delta, were surrounded by Germans, Poles and Dutch who in turn might be of Catholic, Lutheran or Reformed religious persuasion. As Mennonites plied their crafts and trades or participated in the textile, beer and brandy industries, they not only entered into the world of local and regional market economies but also became subject to the cultural and religious cross currents of their day.

Some of the religious and cultural breadth which the Prussian Mennonite migrants brought to Russia in the late eighteenth and early nineteenth centuries was certainly lost amid the vast steppes of Russia. Here Russian settlement law not only separated Mennonite from Russian, but German Catholic from German Lutheran, and even German Lutheran from Prussian Mennonite. Initially, the priorities of the frontier were related to survival and subsequently to the achievement of a reasonable level of prosperity. Under such circumstances the affairs of mind and soul were easily neglected and religious aspirations were centered on what had been and not on what could be. Faith was routinized and heresy usually meant any challenge to the status quo. School implied the acquisition of essential

81

skills and not the promotion of innovative ideas. Identity and the sense of well-being was related to the yearly cycle of the agricultural calendar, the customs and languages of the village, their affirmation in the school, and their sanctification through traditional liturgies and prayers. Life was a delicate balance easily threatened by changes at any level.

Yet even the vast steppes and the insular village could not prevent the incursion of the outside world. Familial and religious contacts with Prussia meant an ongoing association with Mennonites who were well acculturized and aware of the larger Christian world in Germany. The protracted migration of Mennonites from Prussia to Russia ensured a variety of outlooks and even peoplehoods. Since the immigrants came from different localities in Prussia, variant ecclesiastical practices and even diverse theological viewpoints existed. From the very beginning terms like "Frisian" and "Flemish" reflected the cultural and religious diversity of the incoming population. Several decades often separated migrants arriving from the same area. If their religious or cultural outlooks had been modified by outside pressures in Prussia, the new settlers could easily offend their co-religionists who had preceded them by twenty or thirty years. The Prussian connection assured that the curious and the striving, especially those with visions of cultural and religious renewal, were never completely lost on the remoteness of the steppes. There was still access to the outside world and people could breach traditional restraints in search of new knowledge and new inspiration.

The origins of the Mennonite Brethren were not unrelated to a variety of foreign influences, some of which preceded the movement by almost four decades. Tobias Voth, born in 1791, who arrived in Ohrloff in 1820 to take up his teaching post, had been deeply influenced by the writings of the pietist, Jung-Stilling. In subsequent decades the elder Franz Görz of Rudnerweide promoted missions and small group fellowships while elders Bernhard Fast of Ohrloff and Peter Wedel of Alexanderwohl became active supporters of the British and Foreign Bible Society. The Society's agent, John Melville, travelled throughout South Russia until the 1870s.[1] Some two decades before the arrival of Melville, two Quakers, Stephen Grellet and William Allen, had visited the Mennonite settlements.[2] A gifted family named Lange left the Lutheran church early in the nineteenth century and joined the Prussian Mennonite congregation in Brenkenhofswalde. Forty families from this village settled in Gnadenfeld, Molotschna, in 1835. They were soon known for their Bible Study and mission groups and dominated the religious and cultural life in the Molotschna for the next two decades.

In the 1850s, Mennonites in Russia were looking to Germany as the supplier of both religious books and periodicals. By then Mennonite contacts with the outside world were rather broad-based and yet seemed accidental rather than intentional. Individuals in quest of religious renewal and revitalization were drawn to what was available and accessible. This might involve reading the sermons of the Württemberg pietist, Ludwig Hofacker (1797-1828) or the sermons of the Mennonite minister, Jacob Denner (1659-1746). It might also mean attendance at the Gnadenfeld mission festival or hearing a visiting minister preach. For example, the extended ministry of the Württemberg pietist, Eduard Wüst brought him to various Mennonite pulpits in the Molotschna where his sermons on free grace, missions and discipleship impacted a diverse group of serious Christian pilgrims.[3] In one sense the Brethren-Baptist flirtations after 1860 marked yet another stage of Mennonite contact with the outside world.

Mennonite Brethren beginnings were deeply rooted in the diverse religious cross currents engulfing the Russian Mennonite settlements of the mid-nineteenth century. Fragmentary sources make it difficult to establish the inner character of the pre-1860 revivals. None of them suggest either a direct or indirect Baptist influence. In Chortitza revival began with the quietistic conversion of a young man in Neu-Kronsweide in 1853 and soon spread to other nearby villages. Believers gathering in homes formed loosely structured house churches whose adherents still worshipped in the established church. It was this informal setting which encouraged the emergence of both radical leadership and radical worship styles. A type of self-alienation was initiated by the dissidents' severe criticism of the Old Church on the one hand, while their ecstatic and celebratory meetings incensed the more conservative establishment members on the other.[4] Religious renewal in the Molotschna was characterized by a gradualism involving revival preaching by Eduard Wüst, an interest in missions, and the promotion of fellowship meetings. A minority concern with the pure and separated church and a private celebration of the Lord's Supper resulted in an unexpected explosion of anger at a church meeting. The dissidents withdrew and formed their own group.

In both Chortitza and the Molotschna the process of alienation was rapid. In a world where the affairs of the village and the church were tightly interwoven, dissent immediately became a civil issue. Actual imprisonments and threats of exile soon ended the possibility of reconciliation and further religious dialogue. Some of the destabilization nevertheless came from within. Mennonite teachers often constituted a type of discontented intelligentsia capable of articulating new concerns. Some of these turned out to be radical, frequently self-appointed leaders, incapable of providing a clear sense of direction. Initially, the lack of church polity resulted in chaotic decision-making and disorderly worship. Most of the leaders participated in the exuberance movement (*Fröhliche Richtung*) of the early years and appear to have offered no opposition to the new instruments, the new rhythms which they produced, and the wild jumping and dancing which ensued. They were also guilty of an excessive biblical literalism which at times ignored major hermeneutical principles and focused on inconsequential issues. While it was an exciting period of experimentation, openness and intense searching for a new model of the church, it was also a time of isolation and vulnerability. The early Mennonite Brethren stood outside of the traditional Mennonite world, an orphan in need of parenting. During this period of alienation, the first, almost accidental, contacts with Baptist men and materials occurred.

Meanwhile the baptism of Johann Gerhard Oncken in 1834 marked the beginning of the Baptist movement in Germany.[5] Like the later Mennonite Brethren, Oncken stressed the conversion experience, baptism on faith, and the life of discipleship. Seemingly, no substantial Baptist-Mennonite contacts occurred during the 1850s, though isolated individuals were aware of their published materials. The influences associated with Mennonite Brethren beginnings were diffuse rather than specific and there is no evidence that the German Baptists, while affirming an experiential Christianity, were seminal in the birth of the Brethren. In time, specific theological affinities attracted them to their German friends but this was a later affirming process. Prior to 1860 no one could have predicted the intense and lengthy interaction between Baptists and Mennonite Brethren which would soon follow. Alienation, the need for church polity, a common salvation theology, and sense of spiritual kinship—all these indistinguishably, blended motifs, figured in the relationship.

Few things are as well documented in the early Brethren story in Russia as their continuous involvement with both the German and later the Russian Baptists. The dissenters had barely separated from the Old Church in 1860 when one of their leaders, Johann Claassen, returned to the Molotschna from St. Petersburg with a Baptist pamphlet on baptism. One of the founding fathers of the Mennonite Brethren, Jakob Bekker, noted that at the time of the secession on January 6, 1860, "we did not know any Baptists, nor did we know that there were any Baptists in the world. . . . We were ignorant of and knew nothing about baptism by immersion until the first Sunday of September 1860, when the question concerning baptism arose."[6] Bekker then cites Claassen's tract on baptism, the consensus of some of the Brethren, and his private study of Menno Simons' *Fundamentals* as determinative in his decision to baptize by immersion.[7] For another founding member, Jakob Reimer, the awareness of Baptist practices went back to the 1830s when travel to Prussia as well as a biography of Anne Judson not only raised questions about the meaning but also the mode of baptism.[8] Reimer may have been the exception rather than the rule.

The documents published by P.M. Friesen clearly suggest that like Bekker, the majority of the early Mennonite Brethren initiated their contact with the Baptists after their separation from the Old Church. Their initial concern related to the validity of their baptism in the Old Church, which many felt was a meaningless ritual since it was not based on personal faith. Once convinced of the necessity of rebaptism the Brethren focused on the question of mode. Immersion baptism as set forth in Baptist literature seemed both biblically and symbolically correct.[9] The Molotschna Brethren now began to administer the rite to one another according to the immersion mode. Initially, they baptized forward, later reversing the direction in conformity with Baptist practices. In Chortitza there was some question as to who had the authority to baptize. Abram Unger of Einlage

85

wrote to the German Baptist founder, Johann Oncken in Hamburg requesting a minister to come baptize them. He was dissuaded from this course of action by the Molotschna school teacher, Gerhard Wieler, who subsequently baptized Unger in the Molotschna in 1862. Unger's Baptist affirmation came in 1869 when Oncken ordained him as elder.

German Baptist connections, especially in Chortitza, now intensified. Brethren business meetings, somewhat given to the freedom of the spirit, were modified by Baptists like Carl Benzien and August Liebig, who introduced minute keeping and parliamentary procedure. Liebig mediated the prevailing factionalism generated by the Baptist connection and advocated peaceful co-existence between the two groups. This Baptist missionary was also influential in the formation of the first Mennonite Brethren General Conference in 1872. It was not surprising that the Conference elected several Baptists among the itinerant ministers it appointed. When government pressures demanded a confession of faith from the dissidents, they submitted a slightly revised version of one adopted by the German Baptists at the time of their Union in 1849. Mennonite Brethren additions included references to nonresistance, the oath, and footwashing. The 1873 confession formulation appears to have been intentional and not the action of a minority. All the elders and teachers of the young movement participated in the consultation which adopted it.[10] While it could be argued that the confession was an emergency formulation in response to government pressure, the fact remains that it satisfied a broad spectrum of the leadership at the time. Furthermore, it was only in 1902 that the first, truly independent confession of faith was drafted. By then the Mennonite Brethren were subjected to several new influences.

The first two decades of Baptist-Mennonite Brethren contact were by no means the last. Both the Gnadenfeld mission festivals as well as Wüst's preaching infused the early Brethren with a strong consciousness of missions. This sensitivity was soon strengthened and broadened, thanks to the personal presence of individuals like Benzien and Liebig as well as the availability of Baptist mission materials. Financial support of Baptist foreign missions became more personalized when, in 1885, the Abraham Friesens began training in the Baptist seminary in Hamburg and by 1890 they began their foreign service.[11] All Mennonite Brethren missionaries sent from Russia to India remained under the auspices of the American Baptist Missionary Union until 1914, while their American counterparts were sent by the American Mennonite Brethren Mission.[12]

While Mennonite Brethren foreign missions were "Baptist in all but the name," there were several other areas which also suggested a close affinity between the two groups. One of these related to the question of communion. In part, initial Mennonite Brethren dissent was a protest directed against the undifferentiated communion practiced in the Old Church. Only the true, committed believers were admitted to the celebration. At first rebaptism was not considered an essential precondition to participate, yet the adoption of the Baptist immersion practice brought with it the notion that communion was only for the baptized members of the church.

For some the measure of true spirituality became equated with the baptismal mode. The mode in turn emerged as something of a symbol separating the Mennonite Brethren from the Old Church. All who wished to join the Brethren had to be baptized by immersion. As a result Baptist ministers and congregational members with their clear views on conversion and baptism were welcome at Mennonite Brethren communion services while believing, fellow Mennonites baptized by sprinkling were often not. Little wonder that tsarist authorities frequently identified the Mennonite Brethren as Baptists and that special petitions seeking to clarify the relationship were occasionally submitted to government authorities. All too often Baptist friendship meant alienation from the Old Church.

The formative years of the Mennonite Brethren movement saw another area of intimate interaction with the Baptists: evangelism among both the German colonists and the neighbouring Russians. The terms under which Mennonites settled in Russia granted religious freedom but said little about proselytizing. Nevertheless, the manifestos of Catherine II inviting foreign colonists explicitly prohibited evangelism[13] and in the early decades of settlement most Mennonites observed these restrictions. The Mennonite Brethren of the 1860s did not. Their early missions involved the nearby German Lutheran colonists as well as the Russian population. These efforts helped to lay the basis for an indigenous Baptist movement in the region.[14] Gerhard Wieler and Benjamin Becker baptized German

87

colonists who responded to their preaching in Neu-Danzig as early as 1864. Further baptisms were conducted in Alt-Danzig during the same year.[15] The use of the immersion mode ensured a Baptist orientation. Later when these struggling young congregations turned to Abraham Unger and Aron Lepp in Einlage for help, they directed them to Johann Oncken in Hamburg.[16] Apparently the Mennonite Brethren evangelized and the Baptists organized.

The Baptist-Mennonite Brethren connection not only involved the German colonists but the indigenous population as well. Mennonite Brethren converts among the Russians could not become Mennonites. There were profound cultural and linguistic differences not to mention the prohibitions of tsarist law. Early Mennonite Brethren religious zeal ignored these restrictions. Gerhard Wieler, for example, engaged in personal evangelism, Scripture distribution, preaching and even the baptism of Russian converts. Others shared their new found faith with their hired servants or they invited Russians to their worship services. This kind of activity aided the emergence of an indigenous evangelical movement in South Russia.[17] The new converts soon formed their own churches. The Mennonite Brethren, using the organizational knowledge acquired from the German Baptists, now came to the aid of these scattered communities. In 1882, a special conference of Russian believers convened in the Molotschna village of Rückenau. There were more Mennonite Brethren than Russian Baptists present, yet it was a beginning.

Two years later a broadly representative gathering of Russian believers met in the town of Novo-Vasilevka not far from Berdyansk. Only six of the thirty-three delegates were Mennonite Brethren. The minutes of this founding convention of the Baptist movement in Russia reveal something of the then current Mennonite Brethren-Baptist dynamics.[18] The delegates elected the Mennonite Brethren minister, Johann Wieler[19] as chairman and the Baptist minister, J.G. Kargel,[20] as vice-chairman. The agenda items also reflected this dual heritage. The assembly followed a common Mennonite Brethren practice and elected a number of itinerant ministers for evangelism. They further decided that the Lord's Supper was open to those who had not been baptized by immersion, a move which certainly transcended Mennonite Brethren perimeters. The discussion on the question of footwashing could not be resolved. Wieler felt it to be an essential part of church polity and practice while Kargel believed otherwise. In the end it was left to the discretion of the individual churches. One thing was clear. During the 1880s the Mennonite Brethren bestowed the same gifts of structure and organization upon the evolving Russian Baptists which they had received from the German Baptists in the 1860s.

In the early twentieth century another kind of Mennonite Brethren-Baptist contact emerged from a renewal sparked by the Blankenburg *Allianz* Conference in Germany. As shall be seen, the *Allianz* was a product of the more liberal Darbyite Brethren in Germany and it sponsored special meetings and Bible conferences which generated a new commitment to ministry, a deeper knowledge of the Scripture and an acute consciousness of the larger world. Then, too, periodic revivals in various settlements generated a new awareness of mission. The right of freedom of conscience granted by the October Manifesto of 1905 allowed for a freedom of movement and expression hitherto unknown. For a number of the Old Church and Mennonite Brethren, revival not only meant their own strongly experiential conversions but also a strong sense of calling to Russian evangelism.

The isolated accounts of this activity suggest that it was not centrally organized and characterized by considerable diversity. Cornelius Janz preached in the Samara-Orenburg region, Jacob Wiens was active in the city of Samara while the Old Church member Federau worked in the Crimea. Johann Peters and his associates went to live among the Yakuts of eastern Siberia. Bernhard Klassen went to Siberia while Adolf Reimer became something of an itinerate evangelist preaching in cities like Kharkov and St. Petersburg, in Russian villages, on Russian estates, in factories and prisons, or to new and struggling Russian congregations.[21] During the civil war, Reimer preached to both Red and White army troops, and after an extended ministry in the Kiev area, he succumbed to typhus.

Russian evangelism was also characterized by a sense of the individualistic and spontaneous. People simply responded to the needs of a nearby village or to those of a distant people or city. They worked as carpenters, fishermen or Bible salesmen and, in some cases, adopted local dress and customs. Few seem to have been concerned with a formal calling. Those who were capable travelled and preached while others held house meetings or simply testified to their hired workers or other Russians they encountered. Support for these evangelists often came from individuals or concerned local churches. The general lack of constituency commitment to Russian evangelism usually meant that Mennonite Brethren and Old Church participants formed their own constituencies and support groups. A memoir left by the Old Church adherent, Peter Riediger, succinctly illustrates the dynamic.[22] Jacob Wiens in the city of Samara worked with a Russian officer and a Molokan to organize a church. When the evangelist, Cornelius Janzen, visited the city, he contracted typhus and subsequently died. We learn that he was "surrounded by dear, sympathetic Russian brothers and sisters."[23] The identity of such churches becomes clear in the case of H.P. Sukkau's ministry. He began to preach in Russian in a small Baptist Church and later carried out his ministry under Baptist auspices. When Riediger's own ministry brought revival to a Russian village, he notes that over sixty "newly converted souls were examined, baptized and accepted into the church at Novo-Petrovka."[24] It was a Baptist congregation. He somewhat prosaically concludes his report on evangelistic ministries carried out in the Poltava region: "thus Russian Baptist churches were founded there."[25] Later during the revolutionary period some of the feared Makhnovtzy anarchists were converted by the preaching of people like Gerhard P. Schroeder and Jacob J. Dick. There was no exception to the established pattern: Mennonite Brethren evangelized and the new converts usually organized Baptist churches.[26]

Toward the end of the nineteenth century, the Mennonite Brethren-Baptist relationship became more complex. Both Mennonite Brethren and Old Church members were attracted to the activities of the Blankenburg *Allianz* Conference in Europe. In 1885, the conference, more liberal than its English Darbyite (Plymouth Brethren) counterpart, began and soon attracted international participation. Both its theology and leaders had a profound effect on the Mennonites in Russia. Mennonite Brethren in search of spiritual revitalization not only attended the conferences in Europe but also invited *Allianz* leaders for Bible conferences in various Russian Mennonite communities or even estates. Before long such teaching was augmented by periodicals like *Das Prophetische Wort* (The Prophetic Word) and *Botschafter des Heils in Christo* (Messenger of Salvation in Christ).

How did the *Allianz* connection impact Baptist-Mennonite Brethren relations? In a sense, it marked another stage involving outside religious influence on the spiritual development of the Brethren. Like the pietistic and Baptist literature of earlier decades, the *Allianz* material was mainly devotional (and expositional) in character and focused on the inner spiritual journey. Just as early Baptist contacts did not seriously distort indigenous Mennonite Brethren piety, so, too, the *Allianz* was generally affirming. The Brethren were not threatened by those aspects of Blankenburg theology which stressed holy living and the inner walk with God.

Other things, though, were more disconcerting. The *Allianz* advocated an ecumenicalism which argued that only two ordinances united the true followers of Jesus: baptism and the Lord's Supper. Like the English "open" Brethren, Blankenburg wished to minimize denominational differences. The baptismal mode was not a condition for church membership nor was communion celebration restricted to the known adherents of some local church. The Lord's Supper was open to all true believers.

The *Allianz*, by stressing Christian commonalities as well as the inner pilgrimage encouraged both its Mennonite Brethren and Old Church admirers to broaden their borders of tolerance. It may also have served to strengthen the growing Mennonite interest in welfare and benevolence originally inspired by pietistically inclined social advocates like Bodelschwing in Germany and George Mueller in England. In essence, the *Allianz* meant renewal in the best Christian sense. It brought revitalization to the Mennonite Brethren soul and simultaneously encouraged a holistic Christian response towards the aged, the sick, the mentally handicapped and the parentless. Regional and foreign missions, together with a broad based focus on all levels of education, were included in this new spiritual ferment.

What did this all mean for Mennonite Brethren-Baptist contacts? In one sense the Mennonite Brethren had found a new love. The Baptists had stood by their side during a period of alienation and loneliness. They had affirmed the Brethren in the early, uncertain stages and ensured stability and maturation. By the mid-1880s, the major areas of Baptist-Mennonite Brethren mutuality were clearly defined. The German Baptists had provided the emerging Brethren with a reinforcement of their salvation theology and a strong church polity. They spoke the same language of conversion, practiced immersion baptism and were strongly committed to evangelism. Both stressed informal worship, the lay ministry, and the importance of the local church.

Yet, after more than two decades, the interaction remained a relationship of "beginnings" and subsequently never really transcended that level. Towards the end of the nineteenth century, Baptist-Mennonite Brethren relations were caught in a type of time-lock. They did not keep up with the expansion of the Mennonite world in Russia. Baptists, whether German or Russian, could not participate in the secure Mennonite identity evolving in the early twentieth century. Blankenburg theology was somehow more applicable to the new religious and social quest. It did not, as was the case in the 1860s and 1870s, threaten to create a Mennonite Brethren peoplehood separated from the larger Mennonite world. The *Allianz*, if anything, created an atmosphere conducive to greater unity.

Two articles in the Mennonite periodicals of 1910 reflect something of the new spirit. When the veteran missionary, Heinrich Dirks, was asked to explain Mennonite divisions to an agent of the Ministry of the Interior, he replied that he belonged to the Old Mennonites, that the Mennonite Brethren were also Mennonites, and that the *Allianz* Brethren were new Mennonites.[27] All agreed on the basic issues regarding new life in Christ and baptism on faith. Similarly, H.J. Braun of the Mennonite Brethren argued that all Mennonites had identical views on Scripture, divorce, the oath, congregational democracy, nonresistance and adult baptism.[28] For the Mennonite Brethren, there was no longer a separate identity based on theological differences.

There had always been a segment of Mennonite Brethren identity which the Baptists could not hope to share. The issue related to the ongoing affirmation of the Brethren sense of peoplehood. The tension was there in the 1860s and continued into the twentieth century. In a sense the two groups were so near and yet so far. While theologically, Mennonite Brethren felt at home in Baptist and later *Allianz* circles, there were cultural and social dimensions which bound them to the larger Mennonite world. The things which united always remained stronger than the things which separated. A spiritual inclination towards Baptist theology stood quite apart from all the Mennonite Brethren had in common with other Mennonites. Were they not all strangers in an alien land practicing the same folk customs, speaking the same languages and participating in the annual rhythm of village life? And what of common schools and benevolent institutions? Throughout the later nineteenth century, the Mennonite Brethren joined Old Church members in a systematic colonization within Russia which not only eased population pressures in the old settlements but placed Mennonites belonging to different churches side by side on a frontier setting. Cooperation was not only essential to economic but spiritual survival as well. Joint Bible conferences, choirs, ministerial courses, and even worship services were commonplace in frontier settlements. Common mission projects and thanksgiving festivals further enhanced the sense of belonging. As religious renewal gradually permeated Mennonite Brethren and Old Church adherents early in the twentieth century, it intensified the Mennonite sense of peoplehood. Though the dawn of the twentieth century brought strong German religious and cultural forces to bear upon the Mennonite Brethren in Russia and possibly modified certain elements of their spirituality, they retained a clear sense of their ethnic identity. The Baptist connection, however important in the early history of the Mennonite Brethren, never penetrated into their innermost souls.[29]

From the start, the practice of nonresisteance was a specific area of theological divergence between these groups. The Mennonite Brethren could not forget Menno Simons and his uncompromising advocacy of the peace principle which was the most significant addition to the Baptist Confession of faith which they borrowed in 1873. In the early period of their Russian sojourn, the ideal usually meant nonparticipation in any form of civil government. By 1880 government pressure resulted in the formation of a forestry service whose cost was entirely borne by the Mennonites. State service demanded a high level of cooperation and was yet another bond in the fabric of Mennonite peoplehood. World War I broadened the application of the ideal by expanding it to include the noncombatant medical service. While the conscript came to appreciate the human and geographic breadth of Russia, he was also drawn into the existing Mennonite world in a new and vital way. In the midst of the war, Russian Mennonites stood closer to one another than at any time since 1860. Revolution and the anarchy associated with the ensuing civil war generated unprecedented cooperation. Similarly economic reconstruction and emigration concerns in the mid-l920s sustained the sense of solidarity. In the Stalinistic terror of the 1930s, it no longer mattered whether one was Old Church or Mennonite Brethren or Baptist—all suffered equally.

Yet another factor may have separated the Mennonite Brethren from the Baptists. In practical terms the issue related to the question of lifestyle as well as certain church practices. In both the Prussian and Russian Mennonite tradition all thinking in these areas was deeply impacted by Menno Simon's interpretation of what it meant to be the New Testament church or to be the people of God. Over time the demands of the Gospel were culturally and ethically institutionalized. The dissidents of 1860 lamented the resulting corruption of Christian standards and wished to reconstitute norms congruent with a visible, believers' church. There was not only an affirmation of the old piety in their concern with the oath and footwashing, but also a desire to control alcohol and nicotine addiction. The Mennonite Brethren definition of what it meant to be the people of God was generally narrower and more precisely defined than it was among their Baptist friends. Amid generally restrictive norms, Baptist tobacco smoke proved both irritating and alienating.

From time to time, the practice of local church polity also impacted Baptist-Mennonite Brethren relations. Russian Mennonites subscribed to a longstanding, if somewhat variable, form of village and ecclesiastical democracy. The mayor or elder, however assertive he may try to have been, remained subject to the good-will and support of his constituency. By contrast, the elder or minister in the German and later Russian Baptist tradition usually implied considerable authority. Somewhat ironically, the Baptists saved the Mennonite Brethren from the capricious, self-appointed authority figures of the early years through the introduction of a conference structure, yet they, themselves, remained less democratic.

A common theology of salvation, both as to process and experience, constituted the essential bond in the first decades of Baptist-Mennonite Brethren friendship. They further shared a common understanding of the meaning of baptism and the Lord's Supper, yet, in all likelihood, the Brethren arrived at some of their conclusions prior to 1860 and independently of the Baptists. The gifts which the Baptists bestowed upon the early Mennonite Brethren related primarily to a broad spectrum of church polity issues—orderly business meetings and worship, a conference structure and the immersion mode of baptism. When Mennonite Brethren organized their Russian converts, they often passed on the gifts of church polity received from the German Baptists. In later years their foreign mission efforts were completely under Baptist auspices simply because the operational framework was already there and virtually impossible to recreate within Russia.

Cooperation and friendship did not mean that German-speaking Mennonite Brethren became German or Russian Baptists. Decades of interaction could not alter a historic peoplehood rooted in Menno Simons' understanding of the New Testament and the kind of lifestyle and community it demanded. In this context, such questions as nonresistance, the oath, the nature of authority and leadership, as well as personal and congregational ethics were never minor ones. For the Mennonite Brethren, it was not a question of extreme or radical stances but of measuring and, at times, remeasuring all of life against Scripture. Their conclusions were sometimes different from those of their Baptist friends. Periodically this tradition of reading the Bible degenerated into form and legalism, which caused them to look elsewhere for correctives and inspiration. The Mennonite Brethren did so in the 1860s and again at the dawn of the twentieth century when, together with their co-religionists in the Old Church, they welcomed the Blankenburg *Allianz*.[30]

The post revolutionary period in Russia brought about the virtual destruction of all organized religion. For the Mennonite Brethren and Baptists, it was not a question of differences, but of survival. In the 1920s the churches' role in education and social welfare was severely curbed, while in the following decade the institution itself was under attack. By the mid-thirties, virtually all of the Mennonite Brethren and Old Church leaders had been exiled or executed and their churches closed. Baptist leaders and churches were sharing the same fate. Even the Baptist Union was dissolved in 1935. Formal congregational life was virtually extinct for the next two decades. The first tenuous basis for the legal existence of the evangelical cause in the Soviet Union emerged in 1944 when Stalin sanctioned the All Union Congress of Evangelical Christian Baptists. For the moment the Union offered little safety for the Russian Mennonites. Hitler's invasion of Russia had marked all Soviet Germans as potential collaborators. Their exile to Central Asia and Eastern Siberia in 1941 brought a regional, almost military style captivity which only ended in 1956. When they emerged from this setting of deprivation and dehumanization, many Mennonite believers found sanctuary under the umbrella of the AUCECB, which in some ways was now more Russian than Baptist.

It was a confusing world for the Mennonite survivors. Many of the young, cut off from their own tradition since the 1930s, heard, believed, and were baptized in Baptist churches. In the context of their experience, being Christian meant being Baptist. For them the past cultural and spiritual heritage gave way to the new realities. Yet among the older survivors there were memories of other times and other places. For some, Mennonite piety was still associated with German language and culture and possibly with a special way of reading the Scripture. Once again there were differences in Baptist and Mennonite Brethren interpretations. There were questions about a congregationally based authority and leadership, the nature of personal and community ethics, the segregation of church and state, and, on occasion, nonresistance. Here was a conscious effort to imitate earlier, historic distinctives. Many Mennonites fell somewhere between these two polarities. Perhaps the Mennonite Brethren-Baptist story in Russia will end as it began—gradually and in the midst of confusing aspirations and varying settings. The recent mass exodus of Soviet Germans of Mennonite origin appears to end the long-term coexistence of two Christian peoplehoods mutually nurturing and assisting one another on the one hand and quarreling about their separateness and distinctiveness on the other.

ALBERT W. WARDIN, JR.

Mennonite Brethren and German Baptists in Russia:
AFFINITIES AND DISSIMILARITIES

In the Russian Empire in the middle of the nineteenth century, three evangelical revival movements appeared almost simultaneously. The first group was the German Baptists in 1855, followed by the Mennonite Brethren in 1860 and the Ukrainian Stundo-Baptists, also about 1860. Although the first movement was among the German and Baltic peoples, the second almost entirely among the Germans, and the third among Slavs, all three had much in common in faith and practice and were closely interrelated. In spite of their similarities, various factors nevertheless kept them apart. To many outsiders the German Baptists and Mennonite Brethren with a common German heritage, appeared practically as one movement. Even with their affinities they could not overcome their dissimilarities and by the early twentieth century they were growing even farther apart.

THE GERMAN BAPTISTS

The German Baptist movement began on April 22, 1834. Bernas Sears from the United States baptized, by immersion, Johann Gerhard Oncken, his wife, and five others in the Elbe River near Hamburg, Germany. The small group organized a Baptist church, the first on the European continent (outside the British Isles) with Oncken as pastor. Immediately, Oncken launched a Baptist mission that became continental in scope.[1]

The new movement stressed Biblical authority and evangelical doctrine, proclaiming a supernatural work of Christ and the necessity of a conversion experience, and a regenerated life. Believers were to leave their state church affiliation, be immersed on their confession of faith, and become members of a congregation that practiced strict discipline and close communion (or closed communion as written today), inviting only individuals of like faith and practice to

97

the Lord's Table. They proudly proclaimed as their motto: "One Lord, one faith, one baptism." In doing so, the Baptists, like earlier Anabaptists, Mennonites and members of the Church of the Brethren, repudiated the territorial churches of the day with their infant baptism, sacramentalism (including baptismal regeneration), and a mixed membership of regenerate and unregenerate. The Baptists were heirs of an earlier pietist movement and a revival movement, which had begun to appear in Germany after the French Revolution. They differed from most pietists and revivalists of the time by insisting on ecclesiastical separation. German Baptists were not content as earlier pietists to be only a "church within a church," or as early German Methodists to be simply a fellowship, or, as Oncken had done in his early days, just to work with interdenominational or nondenominational mission agencies to bring renewal within the existing church structures. Instead, they would follow the path of sectarianism.[2]

With a strong ecclesiastical structure and a firm doctrinal confession of faith (adopted in 1847), Oncken molded the German Baptists into a dynamic missionary movement. Missions not only took priority in the local congregation, with each church acting as a mission society, but also in the regional association and the national Union or "Bund" (formed in 1849) to which the churches belonged. The associations and Union provided a sense of corporate unity. They gave not only guidance in doctrinal and practical matters but also combined the energies of the churches into common mission endeavors. German Baptists attempted to reach the masses through preaching, establishing Sunday Schools, distributing Bibles and other Christian literature, and appointing itinerant missionaries. With the motto, "Jeder Baptist ein Missionar" ("Every Baptist a missionary"), lay members, including women and youth, participated in mission activity. Artisans who traveled or moved to other localities also spread the Gospel message. Oncken began a training course in Hamburg in the winter of 1849-1850, which led to the establishment of a seminary in 1880. In spite of persecution that lasted into the 1850s, German Baptists experienced steady growth. Besides crossing boundaries into neighboring countries, they also found within Germany a ready field in East Prussia, which bordered the Russian Empire. It would only be a matter of time before Russia, with a large population of Germans and Protestant Balts, would experience German Baptist penetration.³ As early as 1853 the German Baptist mission in Tilsit was reporting an outreach to individuals across the Russian border. More important was the settlement in St. Petersburg in 1855 of C. Plonus, a tailor and member of the German Baptist church in Memel (now Klaipeda). He engaged in distribution of tracts, and by 1857 a group that met Sunday mornings and Monday evenings had gathered around him. German Baptists in Russia, however, marked their formal beginning as occurring on November 28, 1858, when Wilhelm Weist from East Prussia baptized Gottfried Alf and eight others at Adamow in north central Poland, followed on the next day by seventeen additional candidates. Alf made central Poland an important center of German Baptist activity and established the first German Baptist church in the Russian Empire at Adamow in 1861.⁴

It was not long before other German Baptist centers appeared. Beginning as early as 1859, migration of German Baptists into Volhynia in the Western Ukraine led to the formation in 1864 of the first two German Baptist churches in Russia proper. Volhynia, with a pioneer German population and a limited presence of Lutheran pastors, proved to be one of the most productive German Baptist fields. Farther east in the Ukraine, German Stundists, who met in small groups for devotional exercise and revival movements, helped to prepare the way for the conversion of Lutherans. Some of them eventually joined the Baptists. Two Mennonite Brethren ministers, Johann Wieler and Jakob Bekker, immersed one such a group in May 1864, in Neu-Danzig in Kherson province. The government quickly exiled the converts to Dobruja in Turkey (now in Romania), but the Baptists later revived and formed a church here in 1875. In September 1864, at Alt-Danzig, one hundred miles to the north of Neu-Danzig, a Mennonite Brethren by the name of Kowalsky baptized a second group of converts. The government immediately exiled him, though the group in Alt-Danzig survived. In 1869, along with a large baptismal service conducted by Abraham Unger, another member of the Mennonite Brethren, a Baptist church was formed there. In the following year German Baptists established a church in the important city of Odessa.⁵

German Baptists did not confine themselves to Poland and the

Ukraine but planted their witness in other parts of the Russian Empire. They witnessed among Germans in the Volga, Caucasus, Siberia, and Central Asia and among Germans, Latvians and Estonians in the Baltic. In spite of heavy migration to America, German Baptists in Russia experienced a good rate of growth. By the end of 1901, they reported five associations, 108 churches, 457 stations, and 22,244 members with 8,000 of them Latvians and Estonians.[6] In 1879 they had gained legal recognition from the government. In 1887 they formally separated from the Baptist Union in Germany by forming their own "Union of Baptist Churches in Russia," an organization that met, as in Germany, each three years.

THE GERMAN BAPTIST IMPACT ON THE MENNONITE BRETHREN

Pietistic and revivalistic impulses also affected the Mennonites in the Ukraine in both the "old" colony at Chortitza, established in 1789, and the second colony at Molotschna, which was begun in 1803 and was located about one hundred miles to the southeast. In the latter colony, the Mennonite congregation in Gnadenfeld was a center of pietism and mission interests. An important source of renewal came from Eduard Wüst, pastor of a separatist Lutheran church at Neuhoffnung, east of the Molotschna Colony. Through his dynamic preaching, which stressed the necessity of a spiritual birth, he exerted a lasting influence on a number of Mennonites in Molotschna. After condemnation by their respective churches, a number of Mennonites, who attempted to hold a separate communion for themselves, seceded from their churches. On January 6, 1860 a total of eighteen heads of families signed a document which declared that, since the Mennonite brotherhood was in a state of degeneracy, they needed to establish a church that would baptize only the regenerate, allow only members living godly lives admittance to the Lord's Supper, and exercise strict church discipline. At the same time, they declared they were still Mennonites, stating their full agreement with their founder, Menno Simons. About the same times, but independently, a renewal movement under the leadership of Abraham Unger and others emerged around 1860 in Chortitza. This group met for devotional study of the Bible and other Christian literature, some of which was published by the German Baptists.[7]

In the short period of approximately three years, from 1860 to 1863, a Mennonite Brethren Church emerged in both Molotschna and Chortitza, which was in full accord with German Baptists on the ordinances of the church. This action separated the Mennonite Brethren from their former co-religionists in the Mennonite community. The following practices became standard: 1) baptism of believers, which meant rejection of infant baptism and the automatic baptism of all Mennonite young people irrespective of their spiritual state, 2) baptism by immersion, thus rejecting the Mennonite practice of pouring or sprinkling, 3) immersion practiced by dipping the candidate backwards once, and 4) admittance to the Lord's Supper of only those of like faith and practice, which tied the Lord's Supper to baptism and introduced a form of close communion, which not only excluded the unregenerate but also believers of other communions, including fellow Mennonites. Several factors propelled the Mennonite Brethren to move so rapidly in this direction. First was the logical theological progression from the basic tenet of separation from the unregenerate. Second, their willingness to accept a new position if it appeared to be biblical pushed them in this direction. A third reason was the strong influence of the German Baptists.

In considering the third factor, Mennonite Brethren historians, greatly influenced by the work of Peter M. Friesen on the Mennonites in the Russian Empire (which appeared in 1911), have tended until only recently to understate the contribution of the Baptists. They preferred to stress the revivalistic influences of Wüst and the ability of the Mennonite Brethren to discover biblical principles on their own while also finding precedence in Menno Simon's writings. Friesen did acknowledge the German Baptist influence on Abraham Unger, the Mennonite Brethren leader in Chortitza who corresponded with Oncken, and the assistance of German Baptist visitors who helped the Mennonite Brethren in establishing a working church order. Possibly from a lack of sources and the desire to present the Mennonite Brethren as independent as possible from the Baptists, he described the ecclesiastical developments in Molotschna almost entirely as an inner Mennonite affair. When Friesen wrote his work, in spite of the fact that he had served the German Baptist church in Odessa for eight years beginning in 1888, he stressed the common roots and ties of the Mennonites. He encouraged their closer cooperation, and, contrary to the standards of the Mennonite Brethren of that time, a position of open communion. Friesen had taken this position as early as 1883. He did point out, however, that Jakob Reimer, one of the founders of the Mennonite Brethren in Molotschna, had gained knowledge of immersion from other sources including the reading of the life of Anne Judson and a Baptist tract. He did not make clear what role Reimer played in the issue of immersion except possibly to provoke debate. In fact, Friesen wrote the rather ingenious but fundamentally contradictory statement, "Accordingly, the Molotschna Mennonite Brethren Church achieved its understanding and practice of baptism, as it is now used, independently, without personal contact with the Baptists, or exchange of letters, but influenced by their writings." In any case, Baptist influence on baptism did come to the Molotschna not only through Baptist writings but also by personal contact and probably also by exchange of letters.[8]

After Johann Claassen, a member of the Mennonite Brethren group in the Molotschna, had returned in May 1860 from St. Petersburg where he defended Mennonite Brethren interests, he brought a tract which he had received from the Baptists of that city. It is almost certain that he obtained it from C. Plonus, the German Baptist who had started a tract ministry in the city. The tract came at a propitious time, since it was not long afterwards that the Molotschna congregation approved two women for baptism with Jakob Bekker authorized to perform the rite. Claassen now took the opportunity to question Bekker upon the proper mode of baptism. Bekker and Henry Bartel, after studying the booklet for themselves, came to the conclusion that not only were they not scripturally baptized with respect to mode but also they, themselves, had not been proper subjects for their earlier baptism, since both had not been converted at the time. Although Bekker had been one of the original signers of the secession statement which included the principle of believer's baptism, he and the others at the time apparently did not think of applying it to themselves but were advocating it as a policy for the future. Consequently, on September 23, after convincing themselves that Menno Simons, himself, favored immersion, Bekker first immersed Bartel, which was followed by Bartel baptizing Bekker, who then immersed three other candidates. In the meantime, Unger, in the Chortitza colony, was strongly influenced by reading the *Missionsblatt*, the German Baptist paper. His correspondence with Oncken also helped persuade him to accept the position of believer's baptism. In 1861 Unger wrote to Oncken to send a Baptist minister to immerse in Chortitza. Gerhard Wieler, already immersed by the Mototschna Brethren, however, prevailed upon him to cancel the invitation, and he and two others were immersed in the Molotschna in March 1862. The Brethren in Chortitza formed the Einlage Mennonite Brethren Church, which, as German Baptists, accepted only immersed believers into its membership, a practice which the Brethren in the Molotschna soon followed.[9]

At first, Mennonite Brethren began immersing in patterns contrary to Baptists. Initially, the Mennonite Brethren in the Molotschna first practiced trine immersion, baptizing candidates backwards three times. In 1861, Peter Ewert, a Mennonite in Central Poland, after he and another Mennonite had immersed each other following the example in the Molotschna, began to baptize candidates by requesting them to kneel first in the water and then immersing them face forward. In 1860-1861 the Molotschna Brethren corresponded with both Ewert and Gottfried Alf, the senior elder of the German Baptists in the Russian Empire. Alf was very critical of Mennonites immersing each other when a neighboring Baptist could very well do it and also condemned Ewert's type of immersion, pointing out that Baptists everywhere immersed the candidate by placing the candidate backward into the water. It was not long before Ewert and those whom he had baptized joined the Baptists, being reimmersed according to the Baptist mode. By the spring of 1861, the Molotschna Brethren were also baptizing as the Baptists did. Bekker indicates that the decision in the Molotschna was made independently of the Baptists, but in light of the correspondence with Alf it is not unreasonable to assume that Baptists may have also exerted their influence.[10]

Because of the example of the German Baptists, from its beginning the Einlage Mennonite Brethren Church in Chortitza practiced close communion. In the Molotschna, baptism and the Lord's Supper were at first independent of each other, but gradually the Molotschna Brethren also began to follow the German Baptist pattern.[11]

The German Baptists' visits to the young Mennonite Brethren movement to give counsel on public worship and the conduct of business were helpful contributions. In June 1861, a member of the Mennonite Brethren, probably Unger, made the request to Oncken: "The expenses of the journey we shall be ready to defray, and I hope you will be able to send us one or two brethren very speedily. If it is proved impossible for them to labor amongst us, we would also pay all expenses of their return to Germany."

It was not, however, until 1866, upon the urging of Unger, that August Liebig, German Baptist missionary from Catalui in the Dobruja, arrived in Chortitza to help resolve the problems of the Einlage Church. By instructing the congregation in proper parliamentary procedure, Liebig introduced order to its deliberations and reconciled the Mennonite and Baptist factionalism in the church. Russian authorities, however, cut his visit short by arresting and deporting him. In 1868 a German Baptist deacon, Karl Benzien, who settled as farm manager in the area of the Einlage Church, also brought counsel. He was even appointed to chair some of the church's business sessions. With his assistance, the church voted to elect officers, including an elder whose responsibilities were defined to include establishing regular mission stations. In 1869, Oncken, the great German Baptist leader, toured Russia, including Chortitza where he so gained the confidence of the Brethren that he was permitted to ordain Unger as an elder and Aron Lepp as minister, and thereby reinforce the church, which had already elected the men to these positions, along with two deacons. In 1871 Liebig returned, spending a year in the Chortitza area, where he was, again, a reconciling influence in the Einlage Church and where, among other things, he led in establishing a Sunday School and an hour of prayer before the Sunday morning service. Another Baptist contribution was the adoption by the Mennonite Brethren of the German Baptist hymnal, *Glaubensstimme*, which became their most widely used hymn book. A further Baptist influence was the widespread circulation of the works in German translation of Charles Spurgeon, the famous British Baptist minister of the Metropolitan Tabernacle in London.[12]

One of the most important contributions of the German Baptists to the Mennonite Brethren was Liebig's influence in establishing an annual Mennonite Brethren General Conference that began in

1872. The churches in the conference retained their congregational autonomy, but the conference, as among German Baptists, developed a strong corporate unity and promoted as its first priority home missions, which included the selection of a mission committee and the approval and support of itinerant missionaries. Liebig himself served as chairman for at least five years. It was not unusual for German Baptist ministers to attend the sessions. At the conference in Klippenfeld in the Molotschna in 1873, the delegates approved the appointment of three itinerant missionaries, two of whom were German Baptist—Eduard Leppke and Wilhelm Schulz. Earlier in the year Schulz had not only preached in Chortitza Colony but also had traveled through the Molotschna settlements where eager crowds attended his preaching, as if he were, as he reported, on a triumphal journey. In addition to his other contributions, Liebig established annual Bible courses primarily for pastors or candidates for the pastorate. His relations with the Mennonites were so good that he gratefully acknowledged their sacrificial willingness to support his move from Catalui to the German Baptist church in Odessa in 1874.[13]

In the early years their keen interest in missions enabled both German Baptists and Mennonite Brethren to reinforce each other's work and the work of the Ukrainian Stundo-Baptists. As already noted, Bekker, Johann Wieler and Kowalsky from the Molotschna, in 1864, and Unger from Chortitza, in 1869, baptized Lutheran converts at Neu-Danzig and Alt-Danzig, two locations where German Baptist churches were eventually established. Mennonite Brethren and German Baptists also began to influence the native Ukrainian population when Ukrainian servants form German households or farms or Ukrainians from a neighboring village attended German revival services. In the early 1860s Johann and Gerhard Wieler, two brothers, already mentioned as active Mennonite Brethren, worked among the Ukrainians and, contrary to law, even immersed some of them. The authorities imprisoned Gerhard for baptizing a Ukrainian convert and kept Johann under surveillance, though he continued to be active until 1886, when he fled Russia permanently. Johann encouraged the Ukrainians to form their own union for mission work according to the German Baptist-Mennonite Brethren pattern. In 1869 Unger not only baptized a large number of German converts in Alt-

105

Danzig but also bravely baptized a Ukrainian girl and a Ukrainian man, Efim Tsimbal, who had propelled himself uninvited into the baptismal line. Through this baptism Unger firmly established baptism by immersion among the Ukrainian Baptists.[14]

In the 1860s both Mennonite Brethren and German Baptists suffered severe persecution, which again reinforced their common bonds. The *Missionsblatt* in Germany sympathetically recorded not only the persecutions of German Baptists but also those of the Mennonite Brethren. When Oncken traveled to St. Petersburg in 1865, he went as a spokesman not only for his own group but also for other suffering evangelicals.[15]

German Baptists, by and large, assumed that the Mennonite Brethren, accepting also "one Lord, one faith, one baptism," were one with them. Karl Ondra, the outstanding German Baptist missionary in Volhynia, no doubt spoke for many Baptists when he wrote in 1873, at the time of attending a Mennonite Brethren conference, "Bro. Liebig's work amongst these Mennonite Brethren is everywhere visible; they are, in fact, Baptists, and so earnest and active in Mission work that they far excel our German churches." Although he admitted there were still some differences between the two groups, he went on to write, "but I hope to see a perfect union between us." In 1869, P. Friesen, a Mennonite Brethren who was probably from Chortitza, wrote a lengthy article on the origins of the Mennonite Brethren. He pointed out that, although there were differences between the Mennonite Brethren and Baptists on nonresistance and the oath, many Mennonite Brethren desired a closer union after becoming familiar with Baptists through the increasing circulation of their literature and experiencing the laudable work among them of German Baptists such as Liebig. He also declared, "The Lord may soon unite all His own into one flock" and "According to the spirit they feel themselves bound, they may now be called Baptists or Mennonites."[16]

DIFFERENCES

In spite of similar sentiments and numerous ties, the German Baptists and Mennonite Brethren could not unite. As early as 1860 with the beginnings of the German Baptist work in Kicin, Poland, the newly converted Mennonites and Lutherans engaged in heated debate, not only over the form of immersion but also over participation in the military and foot washing at the Lord's Supper. As already noted, the taking of oaths was another issue between them. German Baptists, with their largely Lutheran background, believed it was a Christian's duty to defend one's nation, while Mennonites believed that a follower of Christ should follow the path of nonresistance. In the Einlage Church, the conflict between Unger, who wished to remain as close to the Baptists as possible, and Aron Lepp, who favored disassociation from German Baptists because of their acceptance of military service and tolerance of the use of tobacco, became so intense that on Liebig's recommendation the congregation divided—one group became Mennonite Brethren and the other became Baptist—but they remained in fellowship with each other. When the Russian authorities inquired in 1873 whether the Mennonite Brethren were Baptists or Mennonite Brethren, the Einlage Church adopted (and printed in 1876) the same confession of faith as the German Baptists; however, they added an article on footwashing and one on nonresistance and the swearing of oaths.[17]

The issue of Baptist relations became particularly acute because of the agitation of Leppke, ironically a German Baptist who came from Prussia in 1872. He not only served the Mennonite Brethren as one of their itinerant missionaries but also took the extreme view that one could not be saved unless one accepted nonresistance, and he also advocated no fellowship with Baptists. With the support of Lepp, his views divided the Einlage Church again, and the issue came before the General Conference in 1876 in Molotschna where it could not be resolved and was finally dropped. After the German Baptists gained recognition from the government in 1879, the government counted the Mennonite Brethren as Baptists. The Mennonite Brethren protested, and in the following year the government recognized the separate character of the Mennonite Brethren. In any case, the Mennonite Brethren and Baptists continued to recognize each other as one in faith and maintained their fellowship.[18]

The points of contention between the German Baptists and Mennonite Brethren, however, involved more than theological differences—they touched the very core of Mennonite identity. Even though the Mennonite Brethren thought of themselves as returning

107

to the first principles of the Anabaptists, they could not completely go back since, for three centuries, they had been part of a religious movement which had evolved into an ethno-religious entity. In the Russian Empire they had not only received the opportunity of acquiring land and settling in compact communities, thereby preserving their German culture, but also they had received the concession of exemption from military service, which other German Russians in the Black Sea region did not receive. Since they were permitted to continue living in the Mennonite colonies with all privileges, any change of belief concerning government would threaten their status and bring upon them the onerous duty of serving in the Russian military. It is, therefore, not surprising that the debate concerning relations with Baptists would become particularly tense during the 1870s when the Russian government, as one of its Great Reforms, sought to require military service from all of its subjects. For most Mennonite Brethren, too much would be lost by simply becoming German Baptists.[19]

Mennonite Brethren also began to differ from German Baptist in their mission outreach, even though at the beginning they both were equally zealous. During the first decade of their existence, Mennonite Brethren made a notable record in missions, evangelizing and baptizing German converts of non-Mennonite background in the Ukraine and the Don and Volga River regions, as well as Ukrainians. As time went on, the Mennonite Brethren drew back in their outreach to both Germans and Ukrainians and increasingly found their converts from their own families or from other Mennonites. They were becoming more and more a self-contained cultural community, a status they hoped to escape in 1860. One contributing factor was the passing from the scene, either by death or migration, of the first generation of zealous missionaries, such as the Wieler brothers, Unger, and Bekker. Another situation that the Mennonite Brethren faced was that a number of their converts with Lutheran or Catholic backgrounds were more in agreement with the Baptists on military service. Even if these converts wished to become Mennonite, there was still the difficulty, if not the impossibility, of gaining recognition as Mennonites from the government. It was necessary, for instance, for Mennonite Brethren in the Don and Volga areas to become Baptists as a legal requirement.[20]

Mennonite Brethren also drew back from their earlier efforts to convert or baptize Ukrainians. In the early days in the Molotschna, Bekker recorded in his reminiscences that the Mennonite Brethren were ready to "baptize all nations limited only by . . . language restriction." The activity of the Wielers and the willingness of Unger to risk baptizing two Ukrainians in Alt-Danzig showed that even these limitations could be overcome. In 1882, on his own authority, Wieler invited Ukrainian Baptists to a conference with Mennonite Brethren in Rückenau where a mission committee with Wieler as president was formed. In the following year at a conference in Friedensfeld, Wieler insisted that a formal relationship be established between the two groups, but his efforts brought only opposition from the Mennonite Brethren leadership. For them, it was more important to retain their privileges as Mennonites than to risk the wrath of the government which would impose penal sanctions on anyone it considered to be proselyting individuals of the Orthodox faith. Only after the promulgation of the Manifesto of 1905, which brought toleration to Russian/Ukrainian evangelicals, did Mennonite Brethren again show any significant interest in reaching the native population. In 1906 the Mennonite Brethren Conference established a committee which provided support for Russian workers and the distribution of Bibles and tracts. Some Mennonite Brethren, themselves, now engaged in mission work among the Russians/Ukrainians, but their numbers were few and their support very limited.[21]

Although the German Baptists, by and large, attempted to respect the Russian ban on proselyting, they apparently, much more than the Mennonite Brethren (except for the Wieler brothers), aroused government suspicions concerning their relationships with Russian evangelicals. One need only consider the number of cases in which German Baptists were exiled and the number of references to German Baptists and their ties with the Russian Stundist-Baptists in Baptist periodicals and the *Missionerskoe obozrenie*, the Orthodox anti-sectarian periodical. In contrast to the Mennonite Brethren, German Baptists had an added advantage by being more closely allied with the Russian believers in faith and practice than the Mennonite Brethren and had greater opportunity to be in touch with them. They also developed an extensive work among Latvians and Estonians. After 1905, German Baptists supported a program of home missions among Poles, Russians, and Jews as well as a soldier's mission, a Riga Street Mission, and a tract society, besides engaging in various benevolent and foreign mission interests.[22]

Other factors, which in the eyes of the German Baptists were Mennonite peculiarities, contributed as well to the separation of Baptists and Mennonite Brethren. These resulted in making the latter appear more traditional and a people unto themselves. In 1904, Karl Bickel, head of the Baptist publishing house in Germany, visited the Mennonite Brethren in the Molotschna. He recognized that the two groups possessed many similarities; nevertheless, he noted that the Mennonite Brethren practiced foot washing, wore full beards, excluded members for the use of tobacco, and chose theologically untrained ministers as their leaders. On the other hand, H.J. Braun, a minister of the Mennonite Brethren, was very critical of the German Baptists for allowing divorce for any reason and for permitting a second marriage. Another factor which made the Mennonite Brethren appear to be separatists was their use of the low German dialect or *Preussischplatt* in everyday speech and even in some of their services. This set them apart from many Germans, such as the neighboring Swabians, who spoke a south German dialect. German Baptists were more linguistically varied and were far more scattered among the German Russian population as a whole.[23]

In the two decades before the First World War, Mennonite Brethren became increasingly drawn toward and more tolerant of the old Mennonite Church from which they had separated. This was due to personal relations within the Mennonite community itself and reform within the old church. The rule against marrying outside the Mennonite Brethren Church was eliminated. Furthermore, some Mennonite Brethren wanted to move to open communion. Mennonite Brethren participated in All-Mennonite Conferences in 1908 and 1910, which discussed the issue of military service. They were also drawn to fellow Mennonites in their participation in the government's program of Alternative Service and in their cooperation in various Mennonite educational and benevolent enterprises.[24]

The separation of the Baptists and Mennonite Brethren was further highlighted by a general lack, after the first years, of mission cooperation between them. One exception was in 1883 when, in spite of initial misgivings on the part of Mennonite Brethren in that area, S. Lehmann and John Marks enlisted Mennonite Brethren support for the German Baptist mission in the Volga region. Another exception was when the Mennonite Brethren looked to Baptists for assistance in their foreign mission work in India, working in cooperation with the American Baptist Missionary Union on the Nalgonda field from 1890 until the First World War. A number of the Mennonite Brethren missionaries on this field received training at the Baptist seminary in Hamburg. In the early twentieth century, P.M. Friesen, although recognizing the very limited relations between the two groups, was glad that not all ties had been cut. Mennonite Brethren still read Baptist literature, attended the Hamburg seminary, supported Baptist missions, and exchanged ministers. He admitted, however, this latter practice was "all too rare." By and large, these relationships, ironically, originated outside rather than inside the Russian Empire and provided more of a service for Mennonite Brethren rather than opportunities for mutual service within the Empire.[25]

In his travel among Mennonites, L. Horn, a German Baptist missionary, although greatly admiring the economic and educational activity of the Mennonites as a whole, criticized them in 1910 for living such a "completely separated life." In addition he wrote that the Mennonite Brethren Church "stands completely isolated and on the whole little is known of our work; in many cases our leading brethren are unknown." Sadly, instead of improving, the relations were apparently getting worse.[26]

In 1907, J. Heinrichs, president of a Baptist Seminary in South India, received a very cordial welcome from the Mennonite Brethren, but in 1909 he wrote to the American Baptist Missionary Union: "Indications are that relationship to us is not as intimate and cordial as formerly." One difficulty was the lack of Mennonite Brethren interest in cooperating with Baptists in establishing a seminary for Russian nationals.[27]

The isolation of the Mennonite Brethren helped to preserve their identity and special privileges but it was at the cost of significant cooperation in evangelistic and educational work with both German and Russian Baptists with whom they had so much in common. It was only after the terrors of the Stalinist period and the Second World War with the destruction of many of the Baptist and

Mennonite churches, mass deportations, and death of millions that the Russian Baptists, German Baptists, and Mennonite Brethren were again able to find their common roots and the benefits of close fellowship and cooperation.

WALTER SAWATSKY

Russian Mennonites and Baptists (1930-1990)

During the years from 1930-1990 the relationship of Mennonites and Baptists in the Soviet Union attained an intensity never equalled elsewhere. The overwhelming majority of Mennonites became fused with the Baptists into what they called "Evangelical Christian-Baptist" believers, or ECB. The history of that relationship is richly instructive for Mennonites and Baptists elsewhere, in both negative and positive terms. Many questions surface concerning the relationship of ethnicity to faith, the relative strength of an ethical versus spiritual focus for faith, and the relative merits of relationships to fellow religionists abroad. Since the shaping of developments and relationships depended almost exclusively on the larger cultural context, this analysis is a social-religious history in which the role of the state (from which both Mennonites and Baptists wished to be completely separate!) looms as the major independent variable.

The Russian evangelical movement that emerged in the second half of the nineteenth century was, to a great extent, the spiritual child of the pietistic German colonists in South Russia, including the Mennonites. The Mennonites provided initial leadership although most Mennonite colonists kept quite separate from the new Slavic evangelicals, variously known as Evangelical Christians, Stundists, Pashkovites and Baptists.[1] These new groups suffered extensive persecution at the hands of the Russian Tsarist government, encouraged by leading voices of Russian Orthodoxy. The Mennonites, in contrast, enjoyed religious toleration and great autonomy in managing their affairs. When the Bolshevik Revolution came, it ushered in an era when the Mennonites began noticing both their similarities to and differences from the other evangelicals. With the forced separation of church and state in early 1918, and the resultant widespread toleration of the sectarian groups, Mennonites found themselves making common cause with Baptists, Evangelical Chris-

113

tians and Tolstoyans in order to secure conscientious objector status for their young men. Pacifism had become the biblical teaching of these other denominations.

It was also a time of great evangelistic opportunity. Mennonites, Baptists and Evangelical Christians often banded together to support one travelling evangelist in a given area, agreeing to a common church growth strategy. Further cooperative work became possible during the famine when these church bodies were called upon to help administer the distribution of relief materials.

But the golden decade of Soviet evangelicals was a time of differentiation as well. The state insisted on loyalty declarations to the new Soviet power by church bodies and would not tolerate pacifistic churches. Both Baptist and Evangelical Christian Unions were forced to officially reject pacifism. Mennonite leaders with a much longer tradition of pacifism, and conscientized by the disastrous Self-Defense League experience (1918-1919), insisted at their last official conference (1925) on restating their demand for freedom from military service.[2] Simultaneously, major leaders for the Mennonites were working toward a broad emigration from the Soviet Union to the Americas. By 1929 when the last larger group of emigrants was permitted to leave, over 22,000 Mennonites (over twenty percent of their total) had left. With this loss the corps of individuals able to effectively lead the Soviet Mennonites was also diminished. The Russian Mennonite era essentially came to an end through abandonment and collapse. The Soviet Mennonites who tried to rebuild after World War II were a different people, as were also the Baptists and Evangelical Christians.

THE COMMON THEME OF COLLAPSE

With the promulgation of the Law on Cults of April 1929, a common levelling of all religious groups began. The law served as pretext to shut down virtually all churches. These events are now well known, although average Soviet citizens have been learning the details only during the past several years. Still, a brief sketch suffices for our purposes. Perhaps what merits more reflection, however, is reviewing the factors which explain the rapid collapse of all Christian institutions.

First, the evangelicals, including the Mennonites, were not

well organized in national terms. Evangelical Christians and Baptists, as initially the most rapidly growing bodies, set about forming regional associations but were unable to establish strong central unions. Uniting the Evangelical Christian and Baptist unions became a persistent theme but, nonetheless, proved an unrealizable one.[3] The barriers were differing understandings about polity (including Evangelical Christian disinterest in ordination), disagreements about accepting persons excommunicated by one side and now in the other union, and serious personality clashes at the highest leadership levels. While the Baptists focused on evangelism and doctrine, the Evangelical Christians concerned themselves with social ministry and fostered an evangelism which demanded an experiential conversion that was not so insistent on doctrinal formulations.

Put another way, the Baptists had developed a keen sense of denomination. In contrast, the Evangelical Christians saw themselves as part of the restitutionism fostered by evangelicals in America and on the European continent. Curiously, it was the Evangelical Christian leader, Ivan S. Prokhanov, who was most active (compared to Russian Baptist leaders) in the Evangelical Alliance and the Baptist World Alliance (after it formed in 1905). Indeed, a few years later, Prokhanov envisioned a world body of Evangelical Christians.

Mennonites found themselves in a defensive posture throughout the 1920s. They had formed regional associations (under the label of agricultural societies for development) for some coordination of effort and met in national congress with delegates. The earlier split into Old and New Mennonites, or Kirchliche and Brethren, resulted in a clear distinction between specific churchly denominational agenda versus common goals as a Mennonite commonwealth or ethnos. There was enough of a common Russian Mennonite structure to manage the forestry service, other social and mission projects, and to speak a common voice to government. Yet neither the Kirchliche nor Mennonite Brethren denominations developed an effective national church union or conference. Compared to the other evangelicals, the Mennonites were a powerful bloc because they lived in clearly defined colonies and still exercised extensive control over their public schools, though not with the degree of cultural autonomy they had enjoyed before the revolution. Yet by the end of the 1920s this capacity to control their culture through church and

115

school disappeared.

Both the initial granting of land to the peasantry under War Communism and the successive campaigns against landowners meant that the Mennonite estate owners were the first to be impoverished. Many of their number were killed, while others managed to emigrate, partly due to their newly destitute status. The Mennonite estate owners had been a major financial and intellectual pillar for Mennonite community life. They were perceived to be the reason Mennonites as a whole were regarded as being on the wrong side of the class struggle.[4] In 1929 when the major attack on the peasantry through collectivization began, the Mennonite communities were very quickly reorganized into collective farms, with Communist Party members placed in charge. In the process, many simple Mennonite farmers and tradesmen were rounded up and deported to Siberia and Central Asia as undesirable Kulaks.

This coincided with the concerted attack on religion by means of the League of Militant Godless who were independent but enjoyed powerful State and Party patronage. They demanded that school teachers be active atheists and shut down churches, removing the clergy as disloyal or as unemployed parasites. They even accused them of treason simply because they were communicating with Mennonites abroad. Thus, in the space of a few months, all the individuals still exercising leadership in the Mennonite communities were arrested. Many of these leaders returned home from prison for a short period during the mid-1930s, but they could not resume their institutional roles. The entire leadership disappeared into the camps of the Gulag after 1937-1938. The Mennonite community collapsed quickly, because it had been decapitated systematically.

The collapse of the Soviet evangelical movement as a whole was even more dramatic. The growth rate for Evangelical Christians and Baptists between 1917 and 1929 cannot be measured with accuracy. Estimates suggest an increase from about 200,000 to about three million in 1929. By the end of 1930, one leader still in office spoke of only 50,000 evangelicals. The Pentecostals were essentially a post-revolutionary movement, rising to about 27,000 and then collapsing after 1929. There were fellowships meeting in secret throughout the 1930s, but the Baptist Union officially folded in 1935. The Evangelical Christians managed to retain only one working church in Moscow. The explanation for the sudden collapse was due to the virtually complete arrest of the entire clergy and a shortage of church buildings: only about four hundred existed through actual church ownership and the rest were rented, or fellowship groups met without a fixed place of meeting. The inadequate training of leaders (excluding laity) and the lack of established traditions were also factors.

Finally, the steady aggrandizement of power in the hands of Joseph Stalin and the establishment of what is now called Stalinism, serves as a primary explanation for the collapse of Mennonites and other evangelicals.[5] The pervasiveness of Stalinism as system, especially the atmosphere of terror that reigned, caused alternative voices to fall silent. Participants have always found it impossible to communicate to others what the excesses were truly like and what it did to them.

Mennonites and Soviet evangelicals went through a common sovietizing process through the great religious purges of 1929 to 1937. All of them had their martyrs who were shot or slowly perished, and most of the leaders (with very few exceptions) were imprisoned. In many regions, there was no public practice of worship for a decade or even a decade and a half. They were also cut off from fellow believers abroad. That meant that when religious rebuilding began after World War II, Mennonites and the evangelicals shared a keen sense of commonality—a simple desire to fellowship with anyone who professed to believe.

For Mennonites and other Soviet Germans, there was a further levelling experience that produced the destruction of their culture, and which, by 1956, placed them in a dependency relationship to the more privileged Slavic evangelicals. This was the Spetskomandatura experience, the Deportation Regime that lasted from 1941 till 1956, which was only gradually abolished thereafter.[6]

THE RESHAPING OF THE SPETSKOMANDATURA YEARS

Soon after the Nazi invasion of the Soviet Union began in June 1941, the Supreme Soviet, in a secret decree, ordered all Soviet Germans deported eastward. The evacuation was sudden and traumatic. In twenty-four or forty-eight hours, the German colonists of the southern Ukraine and the Volga region were put on trains and shipped to the steppes of Siberia and Central Asia days or weeks later. Since the Nazi invasion moved forward so precipitously, large sections of the German population in the Ukraine were still awaiting trains when the German soldiers arrived and temporarily liberated them from the deportation order. German settlements in the Orenburg region and in Siberia were not moved eastward, but the settlements were forced to receive some of the German deportees. In 1943, when the German armies began their retreat, the Soviet Germans under their areas of occupation were forcibly evacuated to Poland, some also to the German Reich. Then came the collapse of Nazi Germany, and the secret treaty of the Allied Powers at Yalta went into effect. With the assistance of British, American, and French forces, former Soviet citizens were forcibly repatriated.[7] This time, however, the Soviet Germans did not return to their former colonies but were scattered across the northern and eastern frontiers of the Soviet Union to do forced labor.

The political aspect of the Nazi occupation was to leave a nearly lasting burden of guilt by association on the Soviet Germans. First, in an unprecedented style, the Soviet government condemned an entire people, instead of specific individuals, as a potential fifth column of likely collaborators with the enemy. The moral condemnation was not officially repealed till 1970, and even after that till 1985, it was still common for Soviet newspapers to equate "German" with "fascist." The Soviet Germans remained suspect after the war. Public institutions such as the media, the schools, and the factories all joined in heaping abuse on Soviet Germans as fascists. This also meant that able Soviet Germans could not rise to management levels unless they were notably outstanding, had rejected their Germanness, or were aggressively loyal to the Communist Party.

Secondly, there were two moments between 1941 and 1945 where Soviet Germans were compromised as collaborators. During the occupation, considering previous Stalinist excesses, they welcomed the invading Germans as liberators. The occupation forces established an administrative structure that relied on Soviet German administrative staff. As the Nazi racist and anti-religious policies were applied against the surrounding Ukrainian population, Soviet German administrators were forced to be executors of policies that they knew to be unwise and wrong, yet found themselves unable to resist.

When evacuated back to the Reich, Soviet Germans became part of two other actions. Polish homeowners were forcibly evacuated, and Soviet Germans were given this property in order to create a larger Reich. As the Nazi army continued its losses, forcible conscription into the army was extended more widely. Thus, virtually all able males of the evacuated Soviet Germans were forced to serve in the Nazi army. Many pacifist Mennonite males, some as young as sixteen at the time, have recounted that their options had been, quite literally, to be inducted and carry a gun or else be shot on the spot. There were also many Soviet Germans, including Mennonites, who volunteered for services with the German army, so deep was their antipathy to the Stalinist regime.

In any case, whenever actual collaborators (voluntary or involuntary) were returned to the Soviet Union, they faced severe punishment. Some were summarily shot, others received ten to twenty-five-year prison camp sentences. Their families were subjected to the usual deprivations and discrimination. A negative result was a heightened sense of German nationality and failure to assimilate with the other Soviet peoples.

A more pervasive impact came from the Spetskomandatura regime itself. Retroactive legislation of 1948 placed all deported Soviet Germans under a special command (hence spetskomandatura), a deportation regime administered for the Ministry of the Interior by the security police. The actual life experiences during the war years may have differed, but from 1945-1956 they all had several things in common. No longer regarded as Soviet citizens, the Soviet Germans were given special identity cards and required to report monthly to the local commandant. They were prevented from moving or travelling, and were even cut off from the regular mail. The authorities attempted to provide elementary education, but often this, too, was unavailable. As a result many children of those years grew up illiterate. Since most families had experienced separations due to the various vicissitudes of the war and the deportations, separated families were the rule. The average Soviet German family consisted of a mother with some children, perhaps an aunt or grandmother. The males were either dead, in prison, or in a deportation regime camp. In some cases family members had succeeded in fleeing as refugees to Germany and the Americas.

The impact of these conditions for the life of the Mennonite Christians was enormous. Where once the Mennonites had been the spiritual and cultural parents of the Slavic evangelicals, the roles were now reversed. Mennonites as Soviet Germans had undergone the loss of their culture and had lost all the institutional and physical props which undergird a religious culture. They were totally cut off from fellow Mennonites abroad. As a people, they began to develop an intense desire to be reunited with family members in what they now thought was the true homeland, Germany.

The Deportation Regime was dismantled in December 1955 in response to West German diplomatic initiatives but without any rehabilitation. At the time, individuals seeking emigration in order to reunite with families were invited to apply to the German embassy. After 40,000 applications inundated the embassy, the Soviet authorities stopped the process. They granted virtually no exit visas until the era of Detente and Ostpolitik in the early 1970s. Nevertheless, from then on, most Germans, especially the religiously active ones such as the Mennonites, began to view emigration as the first and only choice. The probability that some day they would leave for their true homeland inhibited the building up of Soviet church life and the relationship to the joint churches with Russian and Ukrainian Baptists.

COMMONALITIES AND DIFFERENCES
IN SOVIET REBUILIDNG 1945-1960

Soviet evangelicals, and the Mennonites among them, were reborn after World War II. Their recovery and expansion was uneven, due to the religious and national policies of the Soviet authorities. Stalin permitted the Evangelical Christians and Baptists to reopen some churches as a reward for patriotic service in the war. This began with the formation of a central union of the two denominations in October 1944. In August 1945 the Pentecostals were permitted to function if they would join this one evangelical union.

The arrangement of the union was the Baptist polity, but Evangelical Christians secured the most influential leadership posts.[8] The Pentecostals conceded virtually all distinctives for the sake of joining the union. The Baptist World Alliance was aware of these arrangements, but was unable to sustain any contact internationally due to the Cold War. The first serious international connection occurred in 1955 when the leaders of the All Union Congress of Evangelical Christian-Baptists (AUCECB) attended a world congress of Baptists. Formal ties to world bodies of Evangelical Christians, Pentecostals or even Mennonites came much later. In popular and governmental understandings, there existed a national Orthodox church and the national union of sectarians or "Baptisty."

The AUCECB had, however, enough unique Soviet experiences to be noticeably different from Baptists in England and America and strikingly similar to other Soviet believers such as the Mennonites. In the first place, all of them had gone through the shaping experiences of martyrdom during the Stalinist purges. Then came the suffering of the war and the years of deprivation. When government pressure on religion eased, a religious revival began that touched all evangelicals equally. There was no systematic evangelization program as in the 1920s. Christians found each other and began praying together, listening to a sermon if someone had a Bible from which to expound and the courage to risk a sermon. Gradually a corps of travelling evangelists passed secretly from group to group.

The most basic practice of these emerging groups was to acknowledge a personal conversion experience, sealed before a few witnesses through baptism. Keeping records was dangerous; therefore, the newly baptized were not necessarily entered on membership roles.

There was so little organized church activity that denominational polity and doctrine were irrelevant. Due to the widespread scattering of Mennonites and of other evangelicals through the war experiences, the new congregations were more diverse in national and denominational character. Yet there were pockets of settlement where Soviet Germans (Mennonites, Baptists and Lutherans) began to fellowship, often in secret. Though the common language was Russian, it was more prudent to speak in German.

The initial organizing phase of the AUCECB, when it was permitted to secure legal registration of congregations (1945-1948), did not affect Mennonites except those individuals able to find their way to a registered AUCECB church. When the Spetskomandatura machinery was dismantled in 1956, Soviet Mennonites began organizing their own church fellowships and faced the question of legal registration. Not having officially rejected pacifism as a denomination when pressured to do so in the mid-1920s, they also had no national denominational structure approved by the Soviet authorities. The law only permitted the registration of local societies anyway, which was done by submitting a constitution to identify the tradition and its practices. Since Soviet policy accepted only one national body of Protestant sectarians, Soviet Mennonites were expected to fit into the AUCECB structure. Some congregations that were predominantly German therefore registered as an AUCECB congregation. However, they consciously chose to think of themselves as a Brüdergemeinde (the mutually acceptable designation for Mennonite Brethren and German Baptists). In 1958, the AUCECB journal, *Bratskii Vestnik*, first reported the existence of a sub-group in the Novosibirsk ECB church, which was conducting worship in German. The writer went out of his way to emphasize this group's loyalty to the Soviet motherland.

There were Mennonite groups (Kirchliche) emerging after 1956 who attempted to organize as a denomination, but the leaders were arrested.[9] No Mennonite congregation received legal registration as an independent Mennonite church until 1966, by which time a policy of differentiation of Protestant sects suited government purposes. Indeed, the high point of Mennonite-Baptist relations came after Soviet authorities launched their second most damaging interference in church life: the Khrushchev-sponsored attack on the churches from 1959-1964. Neither the Baptist nor Mennonite story has been the same since.

MENNONITES AND THE COMPETING ECB UNIONS 1963-1989

In 1959 Soviet authorities launched a major campaign against religion, using a massive propaganda attack, tightening up legislation on religion secretly, physically harassing believers, and even enlisting the church leaders in their own destruction. For the AUCECB this reached a critical point when its central leadership was ordered to revise its church constitution so that power would reside in the central headquarters, and all missionary tendencies would be suppressed. After considering the options—to comply or be arrested—

the eleven leaders meeting in Moscow sent out the new constitution to regional senior presbyters (superintendents). Included was a cover letter that illustrated more specific actions for complying with what the Moscow leaders said was the new legislation. Some senior presbyters immediately complied. They ordered local leaders to stop special activities with youth and children, avoiding all "harmful missionary tendencies" and restricting the work of the pastor or presbyter to "meeting the spiritual needs of the members."[10] Other leaders chose to ignore the directive and waited until local government authorities applied pressure. Still others challenged the Moscow leaders by refusing to comply, by calling for a national congress to approve a new constitution, and by challenging the authority of the Moscow leadership.

Between 1959 and 1964 the AUCECB experienced a major schism, losing nearly half its members for a time to a group of reformers who by 1964 had established a competing ECB union, called the Council of Churches of Evangelical Christian-Baptists (CCECB). The story of the schism has been told in detail elsewhere, but among other consequences, the CCECB did affect the Mennonite-Baptist relationship.[11]

The reformers, first known as an Initiative Group (quickly labelled the Initsiativniki by the atheist press), circulated their position in writing by Samizdat means all across the Soviet Union.[12] Almost immediately Mennonites had to take sides, yet they could only do so individually or in small groups, and at great personal risk. If one considered the Stalinist experience, any challenge to the state by Christians was foolhardy. Yet it was evident that the generally younger generation of reformers was appealing to Soviet law itself for protection. They challenged the Soviet state to live up to its claims of permitting freedom of conscience. The authorities began arresting Initsiativniki leaders and the Initsiativniki women responded by organizing a Council of Prisoners' Relatives (CPR) that compiled a comprehensive list of prisoners of conscience, circulated it through Samizdat channels and organized letter writing appeals to appropriate Soviet authorities. Soon the materials were slipped abroad and published in hopes of influencing world public opinion negatively toward the Soviet Union precisely at a time when the Soviets needed improved trade relations.

123

Counting the role of the Mennonites in the West, we can summarize the responses four ways: 1) some joined the reformers' challenge to the state to stop interfering; 2) the majority sought accommodation to the AUCECB; 3) about a third of the Mennonites withdrew into a consciously Mennonite de facto denomination to make its separate peace with the state through securing registration; 4) Mennonites outside the Soviet Union gradually intensified their efforts to assist through supporting all options, eventually also appealing to Soviet authorities on behalf of Mennonites.[13] In the process, the North American Mennonites, in particular, found themselves working closely with Baptists through the Baptist World Alliance.

The CCECB option was a serious challenge to those Mennonites who knew their history, for the parallels to the sixteenth-century Anabaptist radicals was striking. Even atheist scholars recognized the similarity. Most Mennonites supporting the Initsiativniki were themselves only vaguely aware of that history, but they knew that their forebears had been persecuted for claiming to "obey God rather than men." Of course, this passage from Acts 5:29 could be modified by the scriptural injunction of Romans 13:1-6 to submit to the authorities. AUCECB and CCECB leaders used such passages on one another with passion and apparent conviction, as did the Mennonites. Neither Baptists nor Mennonites developed a carefully considered philosophy of the church-state relationship. On most of the principles of their faith, however, such as separation from the state, the autonomy of a local congregation, or the authority of Scripture, all parties were in agreement. They differed in emphasis, though. To complicate matters, in the heat of a pressured moment before authorities, individuals often had to take action or make decisions alone. Thus, the power of group support or group consensus was greatly diminished or made impotent. The KGB interrogators and the media also sowed suspicion by releasing false reports of betrayals.

Almost from the beginning, a key leader of the CCECB was Georgi Vins, a young man from Kiev. His paternal grandfather, Jacob J. Wiens, had shifted from the Russian Mennonites to the Baptists by throwing his lot in with the intrepid evangelists of late Tsarist Russia.[14] Vins, after his deportation to America in 1979, discovered Mennonite relatives. He also associated initially with some Mennonite churches, then joined more closely with independent fundamentalist Baptist churches.[15]

Kornei K. Kreker of Novosibirsk, long a member of the national CCECB presidium, was more typical of the Mennonites who joined the CCECB. He identified with Mennonite ethnicity and language but the only meaningful spiritual and theological category was to be Baptist. Thus for him, as for the noticeably disproportionate number of ethnic Mennonites on the lists of prisoners of conscience, the issue was simply one of either being faithful to the Gospel and making it known to all nations, or pretending to be more faithful to the biblical injunction of submitting to the authorities. The conduct of individual Initsiativniki Mennonites put off other Mennonites who observed a spiritual arrogance or a combative style. The local situations differed widely, so that the choices were never simple or constant.[16]

With the schism spreading, AUCECB leaders appealed to the authorities to permit calling a national congress in order to restore unity. The authorities consented, apparently not having expected serious and organized dissent. They hoped to bring all the Baptists back under a single structure, even if they needed to make concessions to the AUCECB churches. As the first congress since 1944, the unity congress of October 1963 was significant enough. Delegates from across the Soviet Union came, even if delegate selection depended heavily on KGB approval. They approved a revised constitution that borrowed heavily from the one proposed by the Initsiativniki. But the schism was not yet healed and the AUCECB needed some positive achievement that fit their unity theme. Without consulting other Mennonites, Heinrich Allert of Karaganda, not an acknowledged leader of the Mennonites, requested the assembled delegates to accept the Mennonites into the union. So it was announced.

At the 1966 congress, with seventy-six persons of Mennonite background attending, a formal statement of union was approved.[17] The official explanations have set the tone for the relationship ever since. Theologically or spiritually, Mennonite and Baptist spokespersons claimed, there had never been any difference between them, even considering differing practices on "non-essentials" such as footwashing and military service. The concessions to the Mennonites joining were cultural and administrative in nature only. They were permitted retention of German language in services of worship, and a separate structure of German leaders where deemed appropriate. So as to allow this new ethnic group of German Mennonites a voice in the national structures of the AUCECB, two persons were elected to the council. Viktor Kriger had remained in Moscow after completing his military service and already in 1964 became a special AUCECB staff member for Mennonite concerns.

During the years 1964-1985 the German Mennonite role in the AUCECB grew into an influential and highly respected one. AUCECB General Secretary Alexander Karev, in a speech to European Baptist leaders shortly before his death, explained the broad historical tradition and vision he saw in the Mennonite-Baptist relationship.[18] He stressed the common Anabaptist origins by recommending Menno Simons as a father of the faith for Baptists, in spite of Menno's baptism by effusion. It was the witness of Mennonites that stimulated Baptist beginnings in Russia, and Karev spoke with appreciation of their gifts to the united brotherhood. Indeed, Karev wanted his European colleagues to consider the Soviet union of Mennonites and Baptists as a model to emulate. The Mennonite leaders within the AUCECB did have the advantage of being able to read German theological literature if any could be found. They also received some personal tutoring by older Mennonite leaders (once they had been released from prison) who had some biblical training, and perhaps the organizing flair of Germans. Later, a new generation of leaders coming to power in the 1970s outranked these Mennonite leaders in general secular education. This was a time when Germans were still more restricted in educational opportunities.

Two major developments since 1986 have cast a pall on Mennonite-Baptist relations. In that year, Jacob Fast, long time Mennonite spokesperson and AUCECB Presidium member, as well as deputy superintendent for the vast RSFSR union of churches, was disgraced through a sexual indiscretion and removed from all offices. His successor, Emil Baumbach, lasted a year, but he too was removed on a similar charge. There were other able and highly respected Mennonites leaders[19]—as Fast and Baumbach had been—

but both the central union leaders and the Mennonites themselves now began to feel that the Mennonite leaders were no better than anyone else and would have to live down the disgraces. To complicate developments, the liberalization of Perestroika finally reached the Soviet Germans in early 1987 when they were permitted to emigrate to West Germany in ever growing numbers. By 1991 over 40,000 Soviet Germans of Mennonite origin, perhaps over half from the AUCECB churches, had left. That included all prominent leaders, although Franz Enns, special Mennonite representative on the reorganized UECB council of 1990, remained in the Soviet Union.[20]

The third option had been to withdraw from the Evangelical Christian-Baptist conflict in favor of rebuilding a separate Mennonite denomination. This was a necessity, in any case, for Kirchliche Mennonites, who, in spite of a letter to all churches from the AUCECB Presidium in 1964 that urged acceptance of fully born again Mennonites into communion fellowship, were prevented locally from taking communion or from election to leadership. It has been difficult to determine whether it was the Baptists or the Mennonite Brethren who were more zealous in insisting on immersion baptism as the only acceptable form. The Kirchliche Mennonites of Novosibirsk and those of Tokmak, Kirgizia obtained registration as local autonomous Mennonite churches in 1966 and 1967 respectively. There were probably three political reasons why this became possible. First, in 1964 Soviet Germans had been officially rehabilitated from the charge of collaborating with the Nazis. Second, in 1965 the governmental agencies for regulating the Orthodox and the other religious bodies united into one council and the state religious policy, adjusted to suppress and isolate dissent by making concessions to moderate religious groups, meant that additional Protestant denominations would be tolerated. Finally, the constitution and statement of belief that these Mennonite churches submitted with their application for legal registration excluded the traditional pacifism clauses. Local congregations now declared their loyalty to the Soviet Union by implicitly rejecting pacifism.[21]

This emergence of the Kirchliche Mennonites as legally recognized congregations was gradual, with the state resisting efforts toward another national Mennonite denomination. By 1985, however, a younger set of leaders (i.e., persons in their forties and fifties) began a de facto system of monthly consultation. When a Mennonite World Conference representative, visiting in 1988, reported that the governmental Council for Religious Affairs was ready to offer national denominational recognition to the Mennonites, the new emigration fever had taken away both the means and the desire to organize.

There were some independent Mennonite Brethren congregations that also chose the withdrawal option. Centered in the Kazakhstan mining city of Karaganda, after the established ECB church was closed for a time during the Khrushchev years, Mennonite Brethren believers began meeting separately in households. The Karaganda Mennonite Brethren church was blessed with educated leaders (former school teachers). They were able to emphasize a clearer sense of historic uniqueness. In 1967 they secured independent registration.[22] Up to four congregations affiliated with this staunchly German and independent congregation.

Mennonite Brethren in the former Orenburg colonies also claimed to be separate from the AUCECB. This was contradicted by functioning in full unity with Russian and mixed congregations in the region, and by always sending delegates to AUCECB congresses. Apparently, their insistence on being independent of the national union was an effort to be dissociated from the AUCECB's membership in the World Council of Churches (WCC). Influenced by fellow ethnic radio broadcasters from America, these Mennonites and fellow Russian and Ukrainian Baptists thought the WCC was a sign of apostasy.

In 1989 the Soviet Union entered a "process of evangelization," to cite an oft-heard phrase, but it was also the bicentenary of the Russian/Soviet Mennonites. For the first time since 1925, Mennonites organized several national celebrations with governmental approval. Yet, instead of using the anniversaries for sharpening self-identity for the task ahead, the ceremonies seemed like a time to bid goodbye to the Soviet Union before leaving for Germany. After relatively brief presentations on the history of the Mennonites, the Baptists transformed the ceremonies by leading evangelistic rallies. Thus it seems that the ongoing history of Mennonites in Russia would be swallowed up in that of the Baptist movement.

It would be more accurate, however, to regard Mennonites as

having been swallowed up into the larger amorphous evangelical movement, for the denominational arrangements of the Khrushchev years remained in a confused state. The most active group of churches, the autonomous ECB churches (formerly CCECB members), have preoccupied themselves with mass evangelism in an interdenominational style, refusing to form a church union. While the remnant left in the CCECB has become more separatist, the AUCECB's role has declined at the expense of the nationalist ECB unions. In some of them, the union of Evangelical Christians and Baptists may not survive the competing pressures for emphasis on doctrine versus service. The Pentecostals officially left the AUCECB in 1989 with governmental blessing. Mennonites, for as long as they intended to stay in the USSR, stayed with the arrangements of the past.

REFLECTIONS ON THE BAPTIST-MENNONITE RELATIONSHIP

It has become a truism that Christian faith could not be persecuted out of existence in the Soviet Union. Soviet evangelicals, including Baptists and Mennonites, left behind a line of martyrs to the faith, some of whose stories are already part of a common oral tradition. Others will be recovered and recorded as the struggle to know their own history is intensified. What seems more surprising to some observers is the degree to which ethnic identity persisted in spite of the systematic sovietization of the country, and the degree to which identity with the ethnos preserved the faith.

For Soviet Mennonites, the ethnic aspects of being German and Low German Mennonite became a vital survival technique. Such qualities also prevented them from ever fully joining with the Russian and Ukrainian ECB faith families, though their doctrines and practices essentially became the same. The Mennonites, to a greater or lesser degree, viewed themselves as aliens and sojourners, who would eventually move home to Germany. When that did happen, they still could not answer the question of whether to be Mennonite or Baptist and have persisted in using all the options of their Soviet context.

If the Mennonites and Baptists as believers' churches believed in an integration of faith and works, of both a spiritual and an ethical focus, then during the strictures of the Soviet experience, the ethical emphasis became privatized. A ministry of charity to the poor was forbidden. Therefore, the Soviet Mennonites did not experience the recovery of a strong social service and mission commitment that has characterized the Mennonites of the West, nor did they engage in active peacemaking that has distinguished Mennonites from Baptists to some degree. With the Mennonite Brethren in the majority during the post-war period (compared to the Kirchliche Mennonites), a movement emerged more identified with the spiritual renewal of nineteenth-century Pietism than with the sixteenth-century Anabaptist ethical themes. It is not surprising, therefore, that Soviet Baptists, whose beginnings are also in the nineteenth-century Pietist movement, and Mennonite Brethren find themselves uncomfortable in the new post-Perestroika time of opportunity to make a Christian contribution to social questions.

During the period in question, the state often restricted Soviet Mennonites and Baptists from developing serious associations with fellow believers abroad. At all the major moments of decision, such as 1930, 1944, 1957, 1963-1966, Western partners were usually uninformed and unable to offer assistance. Mennonites, primarily through joint action in Mennonite Central Committee, resumed fraternal visits after 1956, but until the mid-1980s they were either part of a Baptist delegation (for the sake of getting a visa) or officially hosted by the AUCECB and permitted to relate to independent Mennonites only at the AUCECB's discretion. An alternative approach regularly repeated since 1958, was to travel as private tourists, although MCC was the official sponsor. However, the travel restrictions were only one way that the heavy, interfering hand of the state hindered relationships. The most extensive and sustained joint Baptist-Mennonite activity has been the preparation of a multi-volume Bible Commentary series in Russian translation, from 1979-1992. Significant in itself, the regular meetings with the AUCECB partner became the opportunity for a deepening intimacy in internal church life with them. These contacts also deepened a sense of fraternity between leaders from the Baptist World Alliance and Mennonite Central Committee.

The Mennonite-Baptist relationship in the Soviet Union from 1930-1990 was more extensive and intensive than anywhere else. Always the heavy-handed interference of an unfriendly state shaped the story of these churches seeking to be separated from the state. Even in 1992, as this relationship is in the process of dissolution through emigration, or through heightened denominational competition, one can detect an intensity of feeling among Soviet and Western Baptist and Mennonite leaders about that relationship—some negative, others positive. What the participants have in common is that they care deeply about the matter.

PETER PENNER

The Russian Mennonite Brethren and American Baptist Tandem in India (1890-1940)

It is generally known that the Mennonite Brethren, during the first two decades of their emergence in Russia (1860 to 1880), accepted help from German Baptists in marking out their distinctives within the larger Mennonite community. Yet, given the persecution they received from the Mennonite civil authorities, they did everything possible to establish their identity as Mennonites and to rid themselves of the Baptist "tag." Ironically enough, once that was achieved, the Mennonite Brethren formed an enduring partnership with Baptists, American no less, in order to do mission work in India.[1] There was no precedent for such a relationship, and none would recur once it had run its course. Though it was always theoretically possible to restore the partnership, this never happened. By 1918 the Russian Mennonite Brethren in India were completely cut off from their churches by the Russian Revolution and were content to continue within the Baptist Union.

How the purposeful affiliation with the American Baptist Missionary Union (ABMU) in 1888 became a formal partnership by 1905 is indeed an intriguing story. Owing to unforeseen circumstances, in 1914 the partnership turned into a Baptist takeover in 1914 to prevent closure of the mission work.

Given the outworking of this relationship over the decades, a persisting question has been raised by recent researchers: why was the Russian Mennonite Brethren work not taken over by the American Mennonite Brethren Mission (AMBM)? Since 1899 they had also worked among the Telugus. Various persons, for years, have wondered about what seems so logical in hindsight—the two MB missions should have merged.[2] Why didn't they? A careful use of previ-

133

ously under-utilized archival materials, reveals that it was quite unavoidable for the partnership to become a merger with the Baptists. Moreover, there is no proof that there were "strong efforts" by American Mennonite Brethren to form "one missionary society" with their Russian coreligionists. In fact, American Mennonite Brethren made an unerring search for complete independence, which ushered in an 1898 decision not to subordinate themselves to other societies.[3]

To clarify these issues this chapter is divided into two parts, identifying each with a foremost leader of the Molotschna Mennonite Brethren working in the Nizam's Dominion of Hyderabad. The sources clearly suggest that, at Nalgonda, Abram J. Friesen and Cornelius H. Unruh, in succession, were the recognized leaders. Friesen, as "superintendent," brought out six other couples and four single women, and took the relationship through the first three stages. The years from 1890 to 1915 may rightly be called the Friesen years. The Unruh era succeeded in 1915 and lasted until 1940.

THE ABRAM J. FRIESEN YEARS: 1890 TO 1915

Friesen, the son of a well-to-do mill owner from Einlage, Chortitza, was born on May 15, 1859. His family was among those who went over to the new Mennonite Brethren church, initiated in January 1860. Though clearly designated by his father as his successor in business, Abram chose to answer an unmistakable call to missionary work. While attending the Baptist Seminary of Hamburg Horn, Germany (1885-1889), he offered himself for missionary service under the ABMU among the Telugu-speaking peoples of India. His suggestion to the Mennonite Brethren congregations in Russia that they should affiliate with this "Anabaptist-minded missionary society" with its headquarters in Boston was accepted. Meeting at Rückenau, Molotschna, the Brethren gave their undivided support for this venture together with the ABMU.[4]

Abram and Maria (Martens) Friesen arrived in India in late 1889. Following language study in Secunderabad, they took over an existing Baptist mission at Nalgonda at the end of October 1890 and chartered their first congregation on June 4, 1891. His father, Johann A. Friesen, came to visit in September 1893 and provided much-needed financial assistance. After their second furlough in 1905, they took Katharina Reimer back with them. When both Katharina and Maria became ill in 1908, the Friesens returned home to Rückenau. After some years as a missionary "not in active service," Friesen returned again in 1913-1914 for a personal visit. He had been the undisputed leader of the Mission and also the founder and editor of *Das Erntefeld* (*The Harvest Field*), a monthly publication, 1900-1914, designed for Russian Mennonite readers. Moreover, during his first furlough he had influenced American Mennonite Brethren to activate their missionary zeal in the direction of the Telugu people.[5]

Friesen was the key figure in the development of the second stage—the constitutional partnership with Boston. Already in 1895 he was negotiating with Samuel W. Duncan of the ABMU about accepting more missionary candidates on the same basis as he had been accepted. Additional prospective candidates, he explained, already examined by the Molotschna Mennonite Brethren Conference before they left for Hamburg studies, were keen to enter the Telugu field. He was trying to head off the interest among both Russian and North American Mennonite Brethren to think of going to a West African colony. Friesen did not think the small number of Mennonite Brethren in Russia were ready for their own mission. Though overjoyed when the ABMU encouraged further applications for service in India, his analogy for the partnership was unflattering: "Our churches would . . . 'rather be the tail of a rat than the head of a mouse' in mission work."[6]

Friesen continued to press the ABMU in a matter that had engaged him since 1898: the guarantee of Russian Mennonite Brethren salaries in India. The Molotschna churches were giving a disproportionate amount to the building of stations and churches in the Nalgonda district. Yet, it was still essential to have this guarantee from the ABMU because of the nature of the Russian giving. It was entirely voluntary and not the result of a levy. If a satisfactory compromise could be worked out with the ABMU, Friesen was certain that the Molotschna conference, and especially his friends, would continue to give as long as they saw their work in Nalgonda district placed on a solid footing. If the present negotiations failed, Friesen knew there would be a growing feeling of independence and alienation.[7]

These negotiations, quite protracted, led to a working agreement in a Stockholm, Sweden, meeting in 1904 between the ABMU secretary Thomas S. Barbour and Friesen. At a time when many donations were coming to Friesen from Russia as "specifics" (designated gifts), they agreed to share costs as refereed by an India-based ABMU committee. Friesen would try to persuade the Russian treasurer to send all monies through the office in Boston.[8]

The year 1905 had not ended before Friesen came back with a firm, and successful, request for amendments to the agreement. Evangelism would be a Russian responsibility, salaries would be shared, but all educational and medical work would have to be guaranteed by the Union. After all, there were only about four thousand Mennonite Brethren in Russia (his figure) compared with the many, many more Baptists in America. At issue, too, in Friesen's mind was the matter of concentrating their forces. He did not want any recruits from Russia sent to a Union station outside the Nalgonda district, though he knew that some Baptist colleagues in India feared that Mennonite Brethren wanted to concentrate their efforts so that when they were strong enough, they would break away or offer themselves to the AMBM.[9]

In any case, in line with the above agreement, the Molotschna representatives at Rückenau drew up a constitution for their relationship with the ABMU. Heinrich J. Braun, an estate owner and publisher, served as secretary-treasurer for many years.[10]

The years from 1898 to 1905 were crucial in another sense. While Friesen, supported strongly by Abram Hübert, was working out these mutual responsibilities, the American Mennonite Brethren were making decisions about a mission to India. Friesen used this development to prod the ABMU into a satisfactory partnership. If not, his people would prefer to work under what he called the newly-formed "American MB Mission Union." This was the period when Nicolai and Susie Hiebert from Minnesota went to Nalgonda for language study in preparation for their own work among the Telugus. While the Hieberts, because of illness, had to retire from India even before completing language study, Friesen entertained the strong hope, until well into 1902, that N.N. Hiebert's favorable impression of the ABMU might lead the Americans to join with the Baptists. Friesen asked "The Rooms" (a name frequently used to designate the ABMU) on June 28, 1901, "Will the constitution of the ABMU permit a union with the [American Mennonite Brethren]?" Though such a union did not materialize, the answer to this was affirmative. The arguments for a working relationship among these three entities were summed up in a letter from Suryapett dated October 22, 1902 signed by Friesen, Abram Hübert, and Heinrich Unruh. This was also about the time John and Maria Pankratz arrived to take up their language study at Secunderabad. Though there was some disappointment that the American brethren decided to go it alone, Friesen was encouraged by gifts from Kansas and Colorado, earmarked for "spirit-filled [indigenous] evangelists." Friesen wrote that although the Americans organized independently, these gifts, while not urgently needed, were a promise that we "have not been forgotten by our friends" and, what is most important, "we have their prayers also."[11]

Between 1898 and 1905 more Russian Mennonite Brethren missionary candidates had been found, screened, sent to Hamburg, and then to India. The couple associated with the second station, Suryapet, were Abram J. and Katharina (Penner) Hübert. They arrived in India in 1898. Despite many objections from Muslim officials in this Nizam's Dominion, they built up a magnificent station over a long period of years.[12] They stayed "down in the plains" most years. They had only two furloughs in thirty-eight years—one in order to acquire Canadian citizenship in the 1920s. They retired in the Nilgiri Hills at Ootacamund in 1936.[13]

Two brothers followed the Hüberts. Heinrich and Cornelius Unruh came from a well-known family in the Spat-Schöntal congregation. Having completed his studies in Hamburg, Heinrich married Anna Peters. They arrived at Nalgonda in 1899 and eventually settled and built at Jangaon. Eminently a practical man, he too built what was called a "showcase" station.[14] Shortly after returning from their furlough, Heinrich came down with typhoid fever and died on November 20, 1912. Franz and Marie (Warkentin) Wiens recorded the last days and words of Heinrich Unruh for posterity in *Das Erntefeld*. They turned his tragic death into a powerful appeal to the Molotschna Mennonite Brethren to send more missionaries and to undergird the work with fervent prayers.[15]

Cornelius Unruh met his wife Martha Wottmann, a trained nurse, in Germany. They took over the work in Nalgonda when the

Friesens left in 1908 and remained there, except for several furloughs, until their retirement to Kitchener, Ontario, in late 1939. Among their vicissitudes was a brief internment in Germany in 1914-1915. Caught there by the war in August of 1914, the ABMU managed to use the US State Department to free them for a return to India.[16]

Besides Katharina Reimer, three other single women: Anna Epp, Anna Peters, and Aganetha Neufeld, worked for brief periods in India. Epp arrived for language study in 1904, only to marry during the next year the widower Daniel Bergthold of the AMBM.[17] Peters sailed with Franz and Marie Wiens in 1909 and worked as a nurse at Suryapet under the auspices of the Women's American Baptist Foreign Mission Society. Because of tuberculosis of the spine she returned to Russia in 1912.[18] Neufeld went out in 1913, perhaps to replace Peters, accompanied by A.J. Friesen on his last trip to India. Though little is known about her, she seems to have carried on until 1923.[19]

Johann G. and Helene (Hildebrand) Wiens went to India in 1904 in the company of Cornelius and Martha Unruh. Following language study at Nalgonda, they were asked to take charge of various stations, among them Hanamakonda (which was also an ABMU medical center), Suryapet and Jangaon. At first, Wiens himself had difficulty obtaining medical clearance, but it was the "long illness of our little Elizabeth" that cut short his career, forcing a return to Europe for a cure. This prevented him from accepting a call to teach at the ABMU's seminary at Ramapatnam. Living in the Crimea at Tschongraw, Wiens founded a Bible institute in 1918. When he applied to the ABMU in 1922, the Union could not make any appointments. In consequence, when the Wiens family migrated to Canada in 1925, Johann helped to found (with A.H. Unruh and Gerhard Reimer) the Winkler Bible Institute.[20] These all, guided by Abram Friesen, concentrated their energies in Nalgonda district, building up the three stations Nalgonda, Suryapet, and Jangaon.

Relations between Friesen and The Rooms became strained in 1909. ABMU assistant secretary George B. Huntingdon seemed all too ignorant of the partnership forged, and of the way in which the joint venture had developed over the past eighteen years. Friesen, at home in Rückenau, protested most forthrightly, and proved to his satisfaction that it was Boston that was in arrears to Rückenau, and not the other way around. Two years later he warned, again, that some disillusionment was setting in among Molotschna supporters. All this occured at a time in 1911 when foreign secretary Barbour actually visited Nalgonda and, according to Cornelius Unruh, praised Friesen for his magnificent accomplishments there.[21]

Six days after Hübert cabled news of the death of Heinrich Unruh at Jangaon (November 20, 1912), Friesen reminded The Rooms of what the twenty-three year relationship meant. He seems to have emphasized a dimension that proved unsettling in Boston, but which encouraged the newest missionary, Franz Wiens, to think in terms of greater Mennonite Brethren ownership. Friesen asserted that as long as Russians supplied missionaries and money in the proportion they had been doing, the three stations concerned "shall be considered as belonging to our churches." It was the principle of concentration on Nalgonda and offshoot stations, he insisted, that had served to keep Russian interest high and monies flowing as required.[22]

One may infer that this ever-increasing desire for concentration and ownership by the Russian Mennonite Brethren helped persuade the Baptists to retain control of the Nalgonda district stations. During Friesen's last visit to the field (1913-1914), he and Franz Wiens carried that wish too far. Franz and Marie (Warkentin) Wiens came from Siberia and the Molotschna, respectively. He prepared for missionary service at St. Chrischona, Basel, and she in Berlin for hospital work. They were commissioned at Rückenau in the presence of the Friesens and the Hüberts. In 1909 they proceeded to Nalgonda and, when Heinrich Unruh died, served at Jangaon until the cool season of 1913-1914. Just about the time Friesen was hoping, on his last visit, to place one village church entirely under the name of the Mennonite Brethren, Wiens allowed the following to be published in *Das Erntefeld*: "If only we in India would not have to divert funds into 'strange quarters,' if only we could administer such funds ourselves." Going even farther: "if we worked '*against the rules*' of the Union to which we are subservient, we could show the world to what extent the Molotschna could carry this magnificent work."[23]

Though some letters are missing in the Franz Wiens collection, one must conclude that those in Boston perceived this as having gone far beyond the agreement of 1904-1905. The following scenario seems likely: soon after, Wiens regretted these statements, realizing how they would be interpreted by The Rooms. He then wrote a letter of regret, sending it first to J. Heinrichs at the Baptist Seminary, Ramapatnam. Alerted by Heinrichs, The Rooms chose to accept that letter as a form of resignation. Huntingdon wrote Wiens on December 26, 1913 that he would not be permitted to return as a missionary under the ABMU once his coming furlough was over.[24] This disappointment aside, it was also clear they could not return to Russia because of the impending war. Therefore, they decided to make their home in America.[25]

It was fortunate, therefore, for the Jangaon station that the last couple to be sent before the Great War—John A. and Anna (Nikkel) Penner—could take over in 1914. They prepared for service in Germany. He studied in Hamburg and she in Berlin and Riga. They went to India in 1913 and stayed through four terms. John proved to be a gifted craftsman, and demonstrated that when given the right tools he could teach people to manufacture many useful items on a mission station.[26]

Coinciding with this critical point in the Mennonite Brethren-Baptist partnership was the Great War. In 1914 Heinrich Braun, the Rückenau treasurer, gathered $1,500, but could not send it out of the country. Then Friesen, Hübert, and C. Unruh combined to petition the Society to help Rückenau for the duration of the terrible times into which the war with Germany threw them. Could the ABMU send that amount to Nalgonda immediately and, if necessary, underwrite them until the crisis had passed over? In response, secretary Baldwin in late 1914 made a special appeal to his board, saying that these Molotschna Mennonites, "'Baptist in all but name', have had the most cordial relations with our board, and, if this Board should refuse the request, it could not help having a most unfortunate effect.... They would feel that they were not trusted, that their fidelity through these years has amounted to nothing and the influence which American Baptists through the Board have been able to have upon them would be lost."[27]

Over this issue and in these circumstances Friesen backpedalled and acknowledged to "Brother Baldwin" that, yes, "legally," these stations "belonged to the [ABFM] Society."[28]

At this crucial moment, misunderstandings notwithstanding, it was clear that the ABMU wanted to retain these three stations. The efforts of the Friesens, Hüberts, and the two Unruhs, commanded respect in Boston. The exemplary appearances of their stations, in a very arid part of the Deccan, as well as their success in winning a large church among the Telugus in a mere quarter century were well known. Baldwin and his peers had the highest respect for these missionaries who not only had learned Telugu, but a passable English as well.[29]

During all this time, the relations between the Molotschna Mennonite Brethren and the American Mennonite Brethren were cordial and mutually supporting. In fact, Nalgonda served as an hospitable starting place for the earliest American Mennonite Brethren. A warm welcome in a strange land awaited them. Friesen provided a language teacher, as well as the first indigenous preachers, as they began to branch into other areas: N.N. and Susie (Wiebe) Hiebert to Hughestown and John and Maria (Harms) Pankratz to Malakpet (both in Hyderabad city), Daniel and Tina (Mandtler) Bergthold to Nagarkurnool, and John and Maria (Epp) Voth to Deverakonda, a field given to them by the Baptists. The Pankratzes, particularly, received much moral support early when Muslim resistance to their work became most fierce. In his eulogy of Heinrich Unruh, J.H. Voth told of the latter's great interest in the American Mennonite Brethren efforts. Unruh had expressed hopes for close working relationships in education and other endeavors.[30]

There is no reason to believe that these fraternal relations did not continue. There is no surface evidence that the American Mennonite Brethren ever asked for or expected to be given the fields built by their Russian counterparts.[31] The ABMU was not prepared to take advantage of the impossible situation into which the Molotschna was thrown by war, revolution, and then famine. Besides, the ABMU stations were all far from Secunderabad and Hyderabad cities. Under the general comity of missionary societies, the AMBM chose to build nearer to or within these cities, and then branch out to the south and south-east.

In addition a very practical question must be raised: could the American Mennonite Brethren have afforded these three stations in

1914? The ABMU was willing to give up Deverakonda, an unfinished station in 1910, but Nalgonda? Even at the time of the sale of Mahbubnagar by the ABMU to the Hillsboro board in 1936, the latter asked a very low price based on the tremendous contributions made by the Russian Mennonite Brethren toward the buildup of the work among the Telugus.[32]

THE CORNELIUS H. UNRUH YEARS, 1915 TO 1940

Though The Rooms did not speak of Cornelius Unruh as a "great general" until 1932,[33] he certainly took over the leadership in the Nalgonda district, in this fourth and last stage during the beginning of the Great War. Long before that, however, he had served notice that he had the same toughness as Friesen when it came to asking questions of Boston secretaries.

While the Friesens were occupying Nalgonda (1905-1908), Cornelius and Martha Unruh had charge of Palmur (later Mahbubnagar), a station built by Edward Chute of the ABMU at the turn of the century. Their work blossomed here because of the revival of 1906. This had its origins in Keswick-type meetings at Coimbatore, in the Hills, attended by Johann Wiens, Abram Friesen, and Abram Hübert. Because of this, Unruh needed more preachers to open more outstations in this rapidly enlarging work. When he felt he was being cut back in the appropriations promised to Chute earlier, Unruh gave vent to some sharpness of which he proved quite capable. He considered that an agreement had been made, and if it was not kept, his preachers would die for lack of nourishment. "They can't board in heaven and work in Palmur field." Though still a junior missionary, only three years on the field, he stated his conviction that even God was above the ABMU and he was responsible to God.[34]

While Unruh sounded like Friesen, he early took a different approach concerning the use of funds originating in Russia. Noting that some of these had dried up quickly when Friesen "resigned" from the Mission in 1909, and convinced that he would not be able to command as many well-to-do "friends" in Russia, Unruh threw himself on the ABMU more than Friesen had found it necessary. Later in the year he said that he did not like this "specifics busyness" at all, and that he preferred to have all designated gifts accounted for in the Boston office. All the same, he did not want to hear of any cutbacks, least of all for Nalgonda which, after all, had been like a "first-born" to Abram Friesen.[35]

Although Cornelius had this aggressive edge in his character, he commanded respect at the American headquarters. The person serving as foreign secretary during much of Unruh's time was Joseph C. Robbins, a native of Nova Scotia. Robbins proved helpful in many complex situations in the interwar period. Because the Unruhs, Hüberts, and Penners were enjoying such fruitful years, despite frequent famines in the Nalgonda district, he took them into his confidence. Beginning just after the Great War, Robbins annually informed them of the theological tensions within the Northern Baptist Convention (NBC). He explained the reasons for the removal in 1920 of the Society's headquarters from Boston to Manhattan. He also shared his vision of what the NBC could do with the large amount of money given to it by John D. Rockefeller.[36]

Robbins' assistance was particularly crucial during the years 1922 to 1925 when furloughs for the Penners at Jangaon, the Hüberts at Suryapet, and the Unruhs at Nalgonda overlapped. The vital question of citizenship preoccupied each family. Now that they were completely cut off from Russia and virtually stateless, they longed to attain citizenship elsewhere, preferably in the United States. To their dismay, they found they could not bypass the five-year residence rule. When it was discovered that they could gain their citizenship in Canada within a twelve-month period, Unruh took a leading role in making possible a change in residence to Canada and the realization of Canadian citizenship for all three families. Robbins as a former Canadian was particularly helpful in facilitating the process toward citizenship. The Canadian and then British immigration officials had to be persuaded to allow former Russian citizens, working under American sponsorship in India, to fulfill residence requirements in Canada during the usual furlough time, and then return to a British colony in a state of unrest. John A. Penner spelled out the poignancy of the situation—for the sake of their children they needed a country they could call their own.[37]

Never did Cornelius Unruh show his genius for getting things done for his extended family and others as he did during this furlough in 1923 to 1925. These years coincided with the beginnings of the migration of about 21,000 Mennonites to Canada from Communist Russia. While the Cornelius Unruhs were in Waldheim, Saskatchewan, he took up the cause of his brother Heinrich's family. He had earlier ensured that Anna Peters Unruh with her six children would be cared for in Russia. Since Anna had died in 1922, Cornelius, with the help of his brother Benjamin in Karlsruhe and the Canadian Colonization Board in Rosthern, contrived to bring all of his nieces and nephews to Canada. They arrived in 1924 while the Unruhs were waiting for their Canadian citizenship papers. Having arranged housing and schooling for the eldest children, Cornelius and Martha adopted John C. and Elizabeth.[38]

Because of this activity, Unruh helped the Hüberts bring together two young people who went to India as missionaries of the ABMU: Katie Hübert and Jacob P. Klahsen. After marrying they went to India in about 1930.[39] They were, so to speak, the eighth Russian Mennonite Brethren couple.

Upon the Unruh's return to Nalgonda from furlough, they reflected on the many ways in which Robbins had helped them. Unruh wrote Hermann Neufeld at the *Mennonitische Rundschau* that, though limited to appropriations from New York, they "could not have fallen into better hands" than those of the ABMU under foreign secretary Robbins. The ABMU had treated them "more nobly and generously than any other." Indirectly, he seemed to be suggesting that they might not have fared as well had they been taken over by the American Mennonite Brethren in 1914. Except for the ABMU the Russian Mennonite Brethren could very well have faced closure of their stations and personal unemployment. Unruh asserted that if tomorrow the clock could be turned back in Russia, the ABMU would gladly revert to the former partnership.[40]

Unruh chose to take the inference one step further. It became evident during the overlapping furloughs, when the Baptists ran the stations of Nalgonda district instead of the Mennonite Brethren, that some support from American Mennonite Brethren for the Russian Mennonite Brethren work had been diverted to the AMBM. Upon which Unruh wrote that "it was not a good policy to take bricks from your neighbor's broken-down house in order to build your own." John Pankratz at Malakpet took offence at this, but when Unruh apologized, the problem was cleared up quickly and the good relations between them, built up since 1904, continued.[41]

The visit of secretary Robbins and his wife to Nalgonda in 1929 demonstrated for all how pleased the ABMU was with that work. Conversions and baptisms among the outcaste Malas and Madigas had reached such revival proportions that Unruh could pronounce, to all intents and purposes, that these "backward classes" could be considered evangelized. At Nalgonda the Unruhs had ninety-three preachers and Bible women working in about seven hundred villages, and had a church of nearly six thousand members, including about fifteen thousand children.[42] If the corresponding figures for the other two stations were added, the results would be impressive.

Robbins proved most helpful when it came to choosing a university for the Unruh's two surviving sons, Cornelius Charles and Henry Cornelius. After they had completed their studies at Breeks Memorial School, Robbins, himself a graduate of the Baptist school, Acadia University, in Wolfville, Nova Scotia, suggested that they should send their sons there. Three years later, at Acadia's spring convocation in 1933, Henry and Cornelius graduated with B.Sc. degrees and their father, on his last furlough, was given an honorary doctorate in recognition of his eminent services in India.[43]

During his last term in India, which coincided with the worldwide depression, Unruh articulated his views on indigenization. He rightly judged that it was now time to concentrate on reaching the Sudras (farmers). This caste element was needed for long-term success in their implementation of indigenization and self-support. He was not in favor of turning mission properties over to Indian Christians so that they could use them as a substitute for overseas funding. He blamed such thinking among Indian Christians on what he called "this mindless ministry of handouts" elsewhere. They should learn to stand on their own to provide for their needs. In the midst of his initiation of the first self-supporting field associations, he was the "great general" of the Mission.[44]

In 1934 Unruh and Hübert tried to persuade the ABMU to retain Secunderabad for its centrality to the work in Hyderabad state. Since the balance sheet in New York continued to be plagued by the depression, Unruh seemed to accept the sale of the old Palmur field (Mahbubnagar and Gadwal) to the AMBM in 1936, especially if

145

this meant that John A. and Anna Penner could be transferred to Suryapet in the Nalgonda district. Robbins gave Unruh the details of the sale and spoke favorably of Henry W. Lohrenz, the MB leader with whom he had been negotiating.[45]

These trustful relations with Robbins continued until the Unruhs retired in 1939 to Kitchener, Ontario, where they joined the Mennonite Brethren Church. Unruh was especially pleased that Nalgonda was left in the hands of the Karl Erich Frykenbergs, who had taken charge during their 1933 furlough. Following Unruh's death in 1941, a secretary in New York wrote Martha Unruh in terms that would have pleased Cornelius: Nalgonda's mission compound "with its cleanliness and order and peace had somehow made its impression upon the entire community."[46]

The Russian Mennonite Brethren and American Baptist tandem ended with the retirement of the Penners to Kitchener in 1950 and the Klahsens to London, Ontario, in 1953.[47]

CONCLUSION

It is clear from the successes in the Nalgonda district under the leadership of Abram Friesen and Cornelius Unruh, in partnership with the ABMU, that these all but forgotten Russians complemented the great Baptist missionary tradition developed since the 1860s.[48] Besides, they were an early inspiration to American Mennonite Brethren who came after them to work among the Telugus. In many ways they facilitated the easy acquisition of former Baptist stations by the American Mennonite Brethren. That, however, is another story.

CLARENCE HIEBERT

Mennonite Brethren-Baptist Relations in the United States

"We are similar to Baptists" is a frequent response Mennonite Brethren use in describing themselves. Explanations on distinctive concepts and practices, like the peace emphasis, are often included to qualify this comparison to Baptists.

This Baptist association is logical. After 1860, when the Mennonite Brethren had seceded from the mainline Mennonite body, known as the "Kirchliche Mennonites"[1] in South Russia there was some Baptist influence. In South Russia, an association with the Baptist "sect"[2] tended to generate intense feelings among many of the traditional and powerful in Russia's Mennonite "establishment." Mennonites, after three centuries of persecution for their faith, had been socialized to regard themselves as "a holy remnant" in the larger world. Their stance of nonconformity to the world made them leery of contacts with any "outsiders." This is one reason why contact with Baptists made them suspect.

Fourteen years after the Mennonite Brethren began in Russia, some began to relocate to North America. Their first fourteen years in Russia were intense years. The barrage of changes instituted, processes experienced, interpersonal interactions, emotions felt by joiners, rejecters, observers, critics and analysts were deeply engraved on all involved. Relocating to America did not clear the slate of this past. It was an indelible part of the participants in the new American setting.

America was a new arena in which the next stages would develop. New personal and circumstantial variables offered opportunities for other outcomes and emphases to surface. The Baptist input introduced in Russia was significant. It was, in fact, so significant that Mennonite Brethren in North America continued to be dubbed

147

as "Baptists" or "Mennonite Baptists,"³ often in a derogatory way, by their fellow Kirchliche Mennonite settlers.

When these immigrants came to North America the Baptist—Mennonite Brethren relationship in Russia was still in flux. The Baptist—Mennonite Brethren connections in Russia had become both valuable and threatening particularly because of the extensive contacts with the German Baptists Ministers' Seminary in Hamburg-Horn, Germany. Baptist minister August Liebig's contact seems to have been the most helpful and least problematic.⁴ His mild-mannered, pastoral and devout love for Mennonite Brethren and involvement in their struggles seems to have been precisely what this first generation needed as they worked through the agendas that faced them.

The Baptist contribution to Mennonite Brethren development in Russia that the nineteenth century immigrants brought with them can be summarized as follows: (1) they aided them in understanding and adopting the immersion mode of baptism; (2) they ordained some of the first leaders; (3) they helped them in establishing church polity; (4) aspects of both the content and style of worship were adopted by Mennonite Brethren; (5) they offered direction and expertise in missionary and evangelistic outreach; (6) they helped broaden Mennonite Brethren ecumenical horizons in recognizing each other's baptism as valid and participating in each others' communion services; (7) they offered compatible, worldview-broadening educational opportunities through their Hamburg seminary; (8) Mennonite Brethren accepted and later continued to use much of their hymnody; (9) they modeled Sunday schools, itinerant ministering, church periodical production, choral workshops and Bible conferences.

Between 1874 and 1884 approximately eighteen thousand Mennonites from Russia settled on the plains from Manitoba to Kansas. Kansas received more than any other region. Their arrival was part of a much larger German immigration. By 1880 there were two million German born people in America, plus 250,000 German-speaking immigrants from Russia. The 1890 census revealed that there were seven million German-speaking people in America. Subsequently German Americans were considered the largest minority in the United States, numbering some thirty-five million. Reportedly, one out of every six Americans had German ancestry.⁵ Nearly 120,000 German-speaking Russians came to America between 1870 and 1920. About half of them settled in the North-Central United States (Kansas, Nebraska, the Dakotas, Minnesota, Missouri and Iowa). Approximately twelve percent of these were Mennonites. Only a small minority were Mennonite Brethren. The Mennonite Brethren settled in the midwest frontier alongside their Kirchliche Mennonite neighbors and among many other German-speaking immigrants from Russia. Roughly two-thirds of the non-Mennonite immigrants were Lutheran; the other one-third were Roman Catholic and other smaller Protestant groups.⁶ Included were also other renewalist-oriented groups. Some had been neighbors to Mennonites in Russia, and some of them had already become Mennonite Brethren or Baptist.⁷ The mindset of these other Russian-German immigrants is crucial to an understanding of Mennonite Brethren development in relation to Baptists in the United States.

Some of these traditionally non-Mennonite, Russian-German settlers had associated with the Mennonite Brethren in Russia and had already experienced or begun to be involved in spiritual renewal. They too had become weary of their own religious traditions and had been influenced by renewalists and enamored by reports of awakenings elsewhere. Some of these Lutheran, Reformed and Roman Catholic neighbors had also been influenced by Edward Wüst (a German minister who itinerated among Mennonites) the Stundist movement, and reports of pietism and reawakenings in Europe and North America. All of the nearby fellow Russian-German immigrants, often nominally Christian, were regarded by Mennonite Brethren as potential converts just as they had been in Russia.

The "revolutionary" 1860 Mennonite Brethren reawakening in Russia represented a radical institutional breakthrough. The Mennonite Brethren secession seems to have been among the first to actually result in a new denominational structure. Contemporary Baptist historians in Russia still consider this 1860 event a major contributing factor in the founding of the Baptist Church in Russia.

Upon coming to the United States it was natural that the Mennonite Brethren would initially find it desirable and profitable to seek Baptist relationships—the kind they had experienced with Germany's Baptists. Within two decades after their coming, however, they found themselves with some second thoughts about Baptist connections, much as did their Russian brothers. Though they were united with Baptists on some basic doctrines, they were fundamentally different on one important matter—the issue of nonresistance. Because of this, both education and missionary endeavors would be profoundly affected. Mennonite Brethren appreciated Baptist assistance and emphases in areas like evangelism, polity, education, missions, music and congregational life. They simply could not, however, agree to capitulate to their stance on nonresistance. Nor did they like the perceived threat that Baptists were "swallowing them up" in schools and missionary programs.

In the New World, with its radical religious pluralism, some of those who had recently joined Mennonite Brethren congregations in Russia now found other renewalist groups more appealing. They felt that affiliating with some of these other churches was socially less demanding. Adjusting to "Mennonite ways" seemed to be assumed in joining the Mennonite Brethren. Often the Mennonite cultural ways were so closely entwined with their religious ways that Mennonites could not readily differentiate between the two.

The theological differences, nonresistance aside, among these renewal-minded groups were not always that significant. What they shared in common was a strong desire to retain their German traditions. In Russia they had all lived in rather isolated settings, largely among "their own kind." Among the new immigrants, of whatever theological persuasion, the reflective questions were frequently the same. Will the "family" or "tribal magnet" survive? Will there be enough of us to make life socially amiable? Will the dialect (low German for Mennonites) that offers us close relationships and warmth be useable in this new setting? Will we find compatibility with others who worship and fellowship like we do? Will we be able to sing the old songs and preach the old sermons? Will we truly become established here? Is there a future for our children in this new environment?[28]

In the 1860s the frontier for immigrants was primarily Michigan, Texas and Minnesota; in the 1870s it was Kansas, Nebraska and the Dakotas; in the 1880s it began to move toward the Pacific Coast. The renewalist-oriented Mennonite Brethren and former Kirchliche Mennonite immigrants did not fraternize easily with each other upon coming to America. The reasons are not hard to recognize. The Kirchliche frequently carried with them a disdain for the 1860 "defectors" from the mainline body in Russia. Many Kirchliche viewed them as unstable, regarding them as Baptists rather than Mennonites. The rigid stance on immersion baptism which Mennonite Brethren advocated was not practiced by the Kirchliche groups, most of whom ultimately joined the General Conference Mennonite Church in North America. Some Mennonite Brethren also displayed a posture of spiritual superiority to those from whom they had seceded. They were slow in noting the growing spiritual sensitivities evolving among their former Kirchliche neighbors. General Conference historian C. Henry Smith's 1941 description of Mennonite Brethren is probably typical:

> Being strict immersionists, they fraternize freely with the Baptists, preferring Baptist theological seminaries to all others for that reason; and have lost some members to them. Because of their emotionalism, their religious credulity, and their craving for new religious experiences continually, they have been more readily victimized by unhealthy religious movements of various kinds than have the more stable and composed General Conference groups. In certain localities they have lost heavily to the Adventists and other more or less fanatical sects."[9]

There were other differences between the Mennonite Brethren and the Kirchliche immigrants of the 1870s. Mennonite Brethren insisted that baptism be limited to those who could testify to a definite "conversion experience." The Kirchliche, though increasingly agreeing on the need for a personal spiritual awakening, tended still to base baptism on a satisfactory learning and acceptance of the catechism. This meant that Kirchliche joining the Mennonite Brethren had to be rebaptized by immersion.

Style of worship and fellowship also were clearly different. One of the points of Mennonite Brethren protest was the lethargy of the songs used in Kirchliche Mennonite worship. Mennonite

Brethren opted for the more pietistic evangelistic and celebrative Gospel songs of North America rather than "*die alte, schlepende Lieder*" ("the old dragging songs"). They soon chose Baptist hymnals produced in Germany, like the *Glaubensstimme*, as their own. Mennonite Brethren gatherings, likewise, were more informal: sharing of testimonies, intercession for one other, discipling, informal singing, Bible studies (often with lay leadership) and prayer meetings.

MENNONITE BRETHREN BAPTIST RELATIONSHIPS IN MARION COUNTY, KANSAS

In 1874 nine baptized Mennonite Brethren arrived in Marion County, Kansas. Eight of the Mennonite Brethren had once been Kirchliche; one had been Lutheran. These nine became the nucleus of the Ebenfeld congregation, America's first Mennonite Brethren Church. Ebenfeld had a stormy beginning and early development. The story reveals some common aspects of Mennonite Brethren development. The surge of immigrants coming to the Marion County frontier in the final quarter of the nineteenth century was anything but homogeneous. Before Hillsboro developed as an important commercial center for Mennonites, a number of smaller settlements had formed in the area. They were one-street villages similar to the Russian past. Most of the immigrants came to Kansas from rural, isolated, provincial settlements. There was a kind of social "brittleness" in each unit. Surrounding Ebenfeld were numerous such units, each ready to defend its own tradition. Beginning in 1873 Bruderthal, a small community of Kirchliche farmers, was founded some eight to ten miles north east of Hillsboro. Its members spoke primarily high German. Johannesthal was located about four to six miles west of Bruderthal. This settlement of Polish settlers was from Deutsch-Wymyschle and Deutsch-Kazun. They lived in the French Creek community and were clearly identifiable by their "Polish dialect" of low German. It was in this Kirchliche community that the Hillsboro Mennonite Brethren Church was born. The "French Creek revival" of 1881 and 1882 became the nucleus for this congregation.

The Lehigh area, about seven to fourteen miles north, had another clearly distinguishable community of Polish-Russians strongly influenced by the Michaliner Pietism of Würtenberg, Germany. The Springfield Krimmer Mennonite Brethren was formed three to six miles south of Lehigh. Though compatible with Mennonite Brethren in most doctrines and practices, and cooperative in many endeavors, they were a distinct community. They had emigrated from the Crimea of Russia.

In the Goessel area further south there was a large community of low German Kirchliche who, to this day, are still referred to as "the Alexanderwohlers." They were Molotschna Mennonites who had also been influenced by renewals in Russia. Though they did not secede and become Mennonite Brethren they were sympathetic to their concerns. Alexanderthal, just two miles southwest of Hillsboro was a community of low Germans evolved largely from ex-Kleine Gemeinde Mennonites who relocated to Kansas from Manitoba, after joining the Church of God in Christ, Mennonite, or the "Holdeman" Mennonites.

Gnadenau, the Krimmer Mennonite Brethren village three miles south of Hillsboro, gained the most notoriety in the press. In 1874 this low German-speaking group came to America as an entire congregation under the leadership of the well-known elder, Jacob A. Wiebe. The first few Mennonite Brethren families arriving in Marion County from Russia in 1874 attempted to assimilate with this congregation. Their different emphases, however, soon resulted in a separation. In the next two years, additional Mennonite Brethren immigrants arrived to swell their ranks, including many former Lutherans who had joined them in Russia. Farther east, about eight to twelve miles from Hillsboro, was a community of high German Mennonite Brethren. This congregation, under the leadership of Jacob Ehrlich, an elder, was made up mostly of Volga German ex-Lutherans. In 1900 this congregation and the pastor affiliated with the German Baptist Conference.[10] The Ebenfeld community was located about five to eight miles southeast of Gnadenau and west of the Ehrlich congregation. The Ebenfelders had a more heterogenous mix of persons from a diversity of backgrounds than any of these other communities. Several different German dialects were used.

The nine baptized Mennonite Brethren who formed the 1874 nucleus from which Ebenfeld formed vacillated between worshipping separately as a Mennonite Brethren group or with the Krimmer Mennonite Brethren. By 1884 this small nucleus was joined by ninety-four more who had been baptized and became Mennonite

Brethren already in Russia. Among them were at least fifteen who came from the Chortitza Colony and brought with them the strong Baptistic influences of elder Abraham Unger. About forty to fifty were from Molotschna. A total of 580 persons belonged to the families of these 103 members. Between 1874 and 1884, eighty-seven were baptized at Ebenfeld after coming to America. Of the 190 total members there were 104 ex-Lutheran, six ex-Roman Catholic and eighty of Mennonite background.[11] A different accounting of the Ebenfeld membership indicated that there were 253 members in 1888 of which roughly half were of Mennonite background and half of different religious traditions.[12]

Though they viewed each other as a united body of converted and baptized adults, it soon became evident that there were points on which they were not united. They increasingly realized how much their ethnic, social and ideological differences separated them. Each used their own German dialect when they were with "their own kind." High German, a more formal and much less used language generally, generally was spoken in church gatherings. Distinctive food preferences, socializing styles, clothing and other cultural practices from each tradition reinforced the differences. The other groups seemed especially touchy in relation to those coming from the Molotschna. It was the Molotschna leaders who were regarded as founders of the Mennonite Brethren in Russia. Therefore the Molotschna leaders tended to assume that responsibility for shaping Mennonite Brethren thought and emphases; determining acceptable practices seemed to be their prerogative. Those who dared to challenge the "Molotschna-acceptable" ways may have been particularly rejected by that group. Issues like the "sister kiss" or the "sin of making music" (i.e., instrumental music) brought about heated confrontations.[13]

Contention also surfaced with regard to millennialism and predestination. The mode of baptism, whether kneeling and forward (Krimmer Mennonite Brethren) or standing and backward (Mennonite Brethren) also triggered debate. The advocates for more Baptist cooperation or even merger were strongly opposed by those who already regarded the congregation as being too pro-Baptist. Religious options already introduced to them in Russia attracted particularly some of the newly converted from non-Mennonite traditions—

especially to Seventh-day Adventists and Baptists. Included in the mix were some who had been influenced by the kind of pietism known among the Kirchliche prior to 1860 in Ohrloff, Gnadenfeld and Alexanderwohl. They believed that experiencing the gift of God's grace and love would bind them together as they fellowshipped and prayed. Nothing else mattered. All issues would be resolved through this kind of corporate experience.

The inter-relation of the traditionally Mennonite and ex-Lutheran who had come from the Don River area and the Kuban focused on another aspect. They had lived side by side with people of various traditions and tended to emphasize evangelism and discipling. Being busy with this task would minimize other agendas.

Most of those coming from a non-Mennonite background tended to be lumped into the category of "Volga People." Though the first Ebenfeld chroniclers frequently listed them this way, more careful analyses have been made since then. They have established that though they were from non-Mennonite settlements they were primarily from the Volga area.[14] Most came from the Black Sea area. They resided considerably closer to the Chortitza and Molotschna Mennonites than the Volga location farther north.

The early leaders of Ebenfeld were equally diverse. Peter Eckert, though initially active and even aggressive in seeking to bring the Ebenfelders together, was their leader for a relatively short time. He could not guide them to stability. Within a few years he sold his farm, withdrew from the Ebenfeld congregation, moved to Hillsboro to establish a business there, and never joined another congregation. He asserted that he felt most at home with the Baptists. No church, he declared, emphasized enough "freedom." Peter M. Friesen, historian of the Russian Mennonites, commented on Eckert, his work and emphasis, suggesting that Brother Eckert and those who went with him did not bring anything healthy with them when they came from the Volga. They caused the destruction of the first Mennonite Brethren Church in America. Then, "by the gracious leading of God, Abraham Schellenberg came."[15]

Eduard Leppke was briefly the unofficial leader at Ebenfeld. He had been a Baptist before joining the Mennonite Brethren in Russia. He advocated for the nonresistant position so strongly that others dubbed him a "Hyper-Mennonite." At Ebenfeld and at some early conference sessions he proposed totally discontinuing relationships with Baptists. He vacillated between Krimmer Mennonite Brethren and Mennonite Brethren membership. At one point he even attempted to form a new separatist group apart from either of these. In the end he left the Mennonite Brethren and became a Seventh-day Adventist.[16]

Peter Gaede, while still in the Kuban Colony in Russia, is usually referred to by historians as one whose presence, ideas and style always fomented dissent. He arrived in Ebenfeld in 1879 where he also influenced others to be agitators. He was particularly successful in doing so among the increasingly disillusioned ex-Lutheran "Volga people." In 1886, he, along with ten other Gaede family members and some Ebenfelders, joined Hillsboro's Seventh-day Adventist Church.[17] Hillsboro's German Baptist church elder, Leohnard A. Jaenicke, also reaped some of the Ebenfeld harvest among discontented immigrants from the Volga and Don River. During Eckert's failing leadership he was successful in his concerted efforts to persuade some how right the Baptists were. The German Baptist Conference reports of 1884 noted that "In Hillsboro, Brother L.A. Jaenicke has successfully thrown out the net of the Gospel."[18] Those reports also make it clear that Jaenicke was aggressive in "taking advantage" of the deteriorating situation at Ebenfeld while they were in a crisis of leadership and theological emphases and practices. It appears that Jaenicke in 1881 established the Hillsboro German Baptist Church because of this crisis. Its emergence was also part of a larger pattern of blossoming German Baptist mission stations in Kansas. By 1887 it reached a peak membership of approximately 150. Though they managed to erect both a church facility and parsonage in Hillsboro, they were never able to fully support a pastor. John A. Pankratz, a Rochester Seminary graduate and ex-Mennonite Brethren, served as the pastor in Hillsboro from 1900 to 1902 and in Marion from 1914 to 1920. The church ceased to function around 1928. No extant church membership or minute records for this congregation have been located.[19]

The Ebenfeld problems were acute in these early years. Three important Mennonite Brethren leaders—Abraham Cornelsen, Johann Foth and Abraham Schellenberg—were significant in bringing about greater stability. In 1879 Cornelsen, with his family of ten sons, emigrated from the Don River settlement to Ebenfeld. He had been one of the eighteen seceders from the Kirchliche in 1860 and authored the first draft of the 1860 document of secession. For doing so he was driven out of his colony. He relocated to the Don River settlement where he served as an elder in a Mennonite Brethren congregation comprised of members from both Mennonite and non-Mennonite moorings. His premature death in 1884 permitted him only a short time as leader in Ebenfeld.

Meanwhile a Prussian-born 1883 immigrant, Johann Foth, also began to assume leadership at Ebenfeld. He was converted at the Don River settlement where Cornelsen had served as his minister. In 1879, after Cornelsen immigrated to America, Foth was asked to lead the Don group. Shortly after his arrival in America he assumed leadership in Ebenfeld because of Cornelsen's ailing condition. Ebenfeld called him to be their leading minister in 1884; he was ordained as an elder by Abraham Schellenberg in 1885 and served the church in that capacity until 1916.

Under Johann Foth's leadership the congregation stabilized. The Ebenfeld congregation and the Ebenezer congregation thirty-five miles to the west proceeded in a more secure and firmly established fashion. They came to be regarded with greater respect and confidence by others in the neighboring Mennonite communities. Elder Abraham Schellenberg provided strong and authoritative leadership for both as well as for other early immigrant congregations.

In turning to three established leaders to center the fledgling congregation Ebenfeld gained leaders who might refocus the meaning of 1860 and bring needed correction. They also secured leaders who had dealt with Baptists from Germany in Russia and knew how to navigate between the two traditions.

The Ebenfeld story raises the larger issue of many disillusioned people who never assimilated into any Mennonite Brethren congregation. A sizeable number became Baptist, Krimmer Mennonite Brethren or Seventh-day Adventist. At issue was the ability of fledgling Mennonite Brethren congregations to assimilate differing kinds of peoples. It may have been the most serious reason for the defection of Mennonite Brethren to the Baptist (and other) denominations.[20]

During the first half century in the United States this problem of assimilating those of non-Mennonite background into Mennonite Brethren congregations occurred frequently. Those who spoke German were the only natural and accessible pool of potential converts into their congregations. Many German-speaking people from Russia resided around them. Success in assimilating them is not evident, especially in locales where German Baptist congregations existed. Upon examination of the Ebenfeld roster of members in the first decade it becomes apparent that only a few of the most common forty to fifty family names representing those from non-Mennonite roots remained active among the Mennonite Brethren. Those who remained Mennonite Brethren include Seibel, Ollenburger, Hagen, Hein, Just, Prieb and Resiwig. What happened to families like Nazarenus, Pelz, Hard, Stiebing, Bereth, Schoenhoff, Schaeffler, Daehn, Zeih, Tomsen, Dilger, and Freitag? Their names have simply disappeared from church records.

Similar attrition is noted in other congregations where sizeable numbers of persons from non-Mennonite moorings had initially joined. Extinct Mennonite Brethren congregations in the following locations illustrate the same phenomenon: Marion, Dorrance, Durham, Herrington, Tampa, and Mingo in Kansas; and Culbertson, McCook, Sutton, Hastings and Eldorado in Nebraska. Similar, though shorter lists could be made for other states as well.

A glance at the lists of conference delegates represented at Mennonite Brethren conference sessions in the first forty years in America reveals a pattern similar to Ebenfeld. Other names are missing from continuing Mennonite Brethren membership: Brehm, Benke, Buchholtz, Burkart, Ehrlich, Fuchs, Fruechting, Glanz, Haelzer, Hager, Heiser, Heizenreider, Hergert, Karbs, Kiehn, Kiesau, Kleiber, Laubach, Lesser, Mohn, Nippkau, Orbach (Urbach), Popp, Riffel, Reischer, Ross, Rusch, Schwalk, Sattler, Sittner, Spohn, Trieber, Traut and Weber. Where there was a mix of people of non-Mennonite background with those of Mennonite background, many seemed to have experienced the inability to socially assimilate. In a few Mennonite Brethren congregations persons of non-Mennonite Brethren heritage flourished, notably Harvey, Sawyer and Velva in North Dakota; and Lodi, California.

Mennonite Brethren represented only one of the renewalist options for German-Russian emigrants coming to America's midwest. In Russia Mennonite Brethren had been in the forefront as a renewalist denomination. Upon their arrival in America, some who had joined in Russia found other available options more to their liking or with whom they found it easier to assimilate. These were German-speaking Baptist, Methodist, Evangelical United Brethren and Congregationalist churches.

Where Mennonite Brethren intermarried with those of other groups, assimilation seemed to be more successful. It was probably easier to assimilate by marrying a Mennonite male because the traditional family name was retained. A Mennonite Brethren female, marrying a non-Mennonite name probably became less assimilable.

Some of the more assertive non-Mennonite joiners did well in ministry and became widely accepted. Notable leaders of this kind carry family names like Just, Hein, Seibel and Ollenburger.

It is crucial to recognize that those who had historic Mennonite connections with Molotschna or Chortitza tended to be the most readily eligible candidates for leadership positions. In the early years Elder Abraham Schellenberg's authoritative style of leadership was broadly recognized. He came from Russia's Mennonite Brethren "nerve center" at Ruckenau. Subsequently Mennonite Brethren in Kansas were often referred to as "the Schellenbergers."

Those coming from the less powerful non-Mennonite pool, however, probably felt intimidated. One can understand how hesitant they might have felt in dialogue with those in power. Being an advocate of ideas or practices other than the traditionally Mennonite, would have taken considerable courage. At Ebenfeld, for example, the "Volga folks" who advocated practicing the "holy kiss" among all genders were blamed for the divisiveness this triggered. These newcomers to the Mennonite Brethren argued vigorously for literally practicing a New Testament directive (cited five times in Paul's letters) to "greet each other with a holy kiss."

Russia's Mennonite Brethren, however, remembered all too well the excesses that developed between 1862-1865 when such practices led to wild antinomian ways. Those most familiar with Mennonite Brethren beginnings assumed a dominant position toward these "outsiders" seeking to remedy this problem. This implied not only giving them the right answers, but also offering the right processes for dealing with those who came from non-Mennonite ways. John F. Harms, P.M. Friesen and Abraham Schellenberg seemed to agree that dealing appropriately with the "Volga people problem" meant bringing order according to the Molotschna Mennonite interpretation and way.

What might the Ebenfeld story sound like if one could understand the perspective of the newcomers, those from the Volga, Don River or Belowesch? Was the Mennonite Brethren concern one of discipling and "re-theologizing" these newcomers to the Anabaptist/Mennonite view of the church, or was there another agenda—that of attempting to re-socialize these newcomers to Mennonite cultural ways?[21]

The deterioration of meaningful relationships during these tensions, leading to membership loss at Ebenfeld, is evident. Though available information is inadequate, sufficient clues exist to make some deductions. It appears that in this volatile situation the urgency to "win arguments" resulted in experiences of rejection by many.

Could other ways have been used to process differences more pastorally, sensitively and beneficially in this heterogenous Ebenfeld mix of newcomers? To do so would have called for unusually sensitive leadership skills. As newcomers to Mennonite emphases each faction wrestled with its own worldview, logical processes and decision-making styles. Was there any process of Anabaptist mutuality and consensus building that allowed for developing an understanding of each other? Did this include a concern for discipling them? It is evident that not only "correct theology" was needed. Acceptable, God-pleasing methodology to go about discerning theology and applying it was also required.

Frustrated with understanding the Mennonite Brethren doctrinal stance on nonresistance coupled with social assimilation problems caused some to find a new church home among the German Baptists. Baptist congregations were accustomed to accept a more heterogenous social mix than Mennonite Brethren and in this respect modeled a better view of the church. In Nebraska there was a greater tendency for those from non-Mennonite traditions to join the evangelically-oriented German Congregational churches. In the earliest years after immigrating to America a sizeable number lined up with German-speaking Seventh-day Adventists. Some Mennonite

Brethren were attracted to this group's strong millennial interests and more literal and legalistic following of biblical directives.[22]

MENNONITE BRETHREN-BAPTIST RELATIONSHIPS IN MISSIONS AND EDUCATION

By 1885, ten years after the Mennonite Brethren came to America, their membership totaled about 1,200. In Russia the Mennonite Brethren mother church numbered about 1,800. By 1885, America's German Baptist church membership stood at 12,193—ten times the size of the Mennonite Brethren. They were baptizing about one thousand each year. In addition to strong relationships with the English Baptists in America, they were already involved in missionary outreach and produced Baptist periodicals.

The missionary expertise of Baptists was well known. It dated back to the widely-read and exciting accounts and accomplishments of William Carey and Adoniram Judson. Baptists had efficient, organized agencies in place—not only to process potential workers, but also to send them abroad. They established schools to provide theological education for pastoral work and overseas missionary education. In several countries experienced Baptist missionaries aided new missionaries in language studies, developing cultural sensitivity, introductions to national leaders, and assisted with obtaining travel and legal documents.

In 1885 Abraham and Maria Friesen became the first Mennonite Brethren missionaries from Russia to go abroad. They prepared for missionary work by attending the German Baptist seminary in Hamburg. According to P.M. Friesen, Mennonite Brethren attended a variety of theological schools in Western Europe: the Barmen Missionshaus, Johanneum, St. Chrischona, Basel Seminary and University, Neukirchen and the Berlin Allianz Bibelschule.

Following the Russian model of attending the Hamburg German Baptist seminary for missionary preparation, Mennonite Brethren in America similarly chose the German Theology Department of the Baptist seminary at Rochester, New York. In 1852 Rochester established a German department to educate leadership for German-speaking Baptist congregations in America. Between 1885-1915, at least twenty Mennonite Brethren studied at Hamburg, while between 1883-1927 some forty to sixty enrolled at Rochester.

Some of the first American Mennonite Brethren missionaries and leaders were among these: John Pankratz, John H. Voth, David Dyck, John J. Franz, Peter H. Wedel, Frank J. Wiens, Henry F. Toews, Frank A. Janzen and Peter C. Hiebert. In the 1905-06 academic year, eleven out of the total of thirty students enrolled were Mennonite Brethren.[23]

Bethel College (established 1893) and Bluffton College (established 1898), two German-language Mennonite colleges in existence at that time might have provided an appropriate educational context. Since they were institutions established by the General Conference Mennonites whom many Mennonite Brethren identified with the Kirchliche group in Russia, they were probably deemed inappropriate for the kind of pietistic, conversion-emphasizing, mission-focused schools they desired.

The Rochester experience represented more than preparation for missionary work. Mennonite Brethren students experienced broadened, Americanizing horizons in this Baptist institution.[24] This totally non-Mennonite setting provided a different outlook on life for these erstwhile relatively isolated *Stillen im Lande* ("quiet in the land"). Returning to their more provincial Mennonite communities seems to have been difficult, at least for some. It is not surprising to note that those who experienced this exhilarating different social and academic environment would have favored closer relationships with Baptists.

The training of these missionaries in both Russia and the United States, commencing in 1885, led to parallel missionary involvements in both countries. The first Mennonite Brethren missionary festival in Russia took place in 1867. From the beginning, both in Russia and America, the Mennonite Brethren pursued an evangelistic outreach among their German-speaking neighbors. Offerings were received for itinerant evangelists in both.

Into the 1890s there were forums for Mennonite Brethren and Baptists to discuss missions. The developing Mennonite Brethren congregation under the leadership of Jakob Ehrlich illustrates these connections. The congregation that met in a school house on his farmyard was formed largely by Russian immigrant converts from a non-Mennonite background, similar to the Ebenfelders. The problems that had plagued Ebenfeld also led to a major exodus from this congregation to the Seventh-day Adventists and Baptists. Ehrlich, however, declared himself fully in line with the Mennonite Brethren Church during that 1879-1880 upheaval. Nonetheless, in 1900 Ehrlich and his entire congregation affiliated with the Baptists. In the years surrounding the turn of the century Ehrlich instituted an annual two- to three-day spring missions festival together with the Baptists, which attracted up to 1,500 visitors. It took place in the open country close to Ehrlich's farm near Marion, Kansas. In a tent, filled to overflowing, participants listened to spirited missionary sermons and reports by both Baptists and Mennonite Brethren. Music was an integral part of these meetings. Congregational singing, choirs, ensembles or quartets furnished special music. A few excerpts of reports from the Baptist periodical *Sendbote* by Baptist pastor John A. Pankratz, a former Mennonite Brethren who had attended Rochester, offers interesting perspectives on Baptist—Mennonite Brethren relationships. In 1898 Pankratz reported

> Because the *Sendbote* is not so narrow in its perspective that it does not include some things that come from their other branches and is not directly from our Baptist circles I would like to request that you receive this brief report I am submitting. A number of our fellow preachers from the Kansas Association were invited to attend and participate in the May 26-30 yearly mission festival of the Mennonite Brethren (actually Baptists) at Marion, Kansas. . . Some may have referred to this as a Mennonite-Baptist fest because there were more of our fellow preachers present than Mennonite Brethren. It was a meeting of the Lord. God was with his people.

In June of 1899 Pankratz reported that a tent large enough to seat 1,500 people was erected, which seemed far too small to accommodate the visitors. Speakers included Abraham Friesen, the Russian Mennonite Brethren missionary to India, Dr. Clark, Secretary of the Missionary Union from Boston, and E.R. Suevern of Berlin, the director of the mission in the Cameroon. Pankratz noted that

163

> Maybe our dear Lord will grant us grace that through festivals of this kind, more and more of that separating wall between Baptists and Mennonite Brethren will be broken. That is the way it should be. It should not be the way it has often been and is now. This is not of the Lord. O people of the Lord, let your light shine effectively, be faithful in your work and strive so that all of the differences between the true children of God will fall away.[25]

Eduard Schewe, director of the Berlin-based Cameroon mission, visited Mennonite Brethren during his 1895 trip to America. He found their interest in mission strong and reported:

> [The Mennonite Brethren] are a valiant people, piously holy (*gottgeheiligt*) and zealous for mission, particularly mission to the gentiles. The large and wonderful mission gatherings in special mission tents set up in open fields were like a bubbling fountain of blessing which I shall remember as long as I live. Just imagine the endless fields of corn as far as the eye can see, having no more than three homes in view and the huge, white tent standing in their midst. Horsedrawn carriages loaded with people were rolling in from all directions. Within a short time the tent was surrounded by a literal barricade of one hundred to one hundred eighty wagons drawn by some three hundred of the finest horses.
> More than one thousand people attended the meetings which began at nine o'clock in the morning and lasted until ten o'clock in the evening. Between the three major gatherings people met in smaller groups for singing and prayer to praise God. Both noon and evening they served a simple meal . . . The moving of the Spirit was evident throughout these meetings. While the programs

were edifying in nature, the primary theme always focused on "The Mission in Cameroon." We spent five weeks with the Mennonite Brethren and I am grateful to the Lord for allowing me to become personally acquainted with these our zealous partners in mission. Our missionaries Wedel and Enns are from this fellowship.[26]

Schewe was impressed, but Mennonite Brethren were not always equally satisfied with his work. At two conferences in the 1890s these Baptist relationships became central topics of discussion. Schewe's tactics in recruiting personnel and raising money for Baptist causes was apparently a concern. In 1892 a Baptist minister, A. Sievers from Kansas City came to the Mennonite Brethren Conference at Goessel, Kansas asking for an audience "to bring greetings from his conference and to discuss ministries in the West, especially Nebraska" with the delegates. He was refused a hearing until all other business matters were completed.

In a closed session, without Schewe present, Johann Regier, an elder from the Henderson, Nebraska congregation, openly expressed his complaints about the way the Baptists were "working the area" where Mennonite Brethren had been involved. He referred to Hastings, Sutton and Henderson. The Baptists were concentrating their work in these areas with excommunicated and discontented Mennonite Brethren. Regier contested both their focus and style.

The lengthy dialogue that followed revealed a growing uneasiness and dissatisfaction with Baptist-Mennonite Brethren relationships. Some recalled the history both in Russia and in America and reiterated what distinguished Mennonite Brethren from Baptists. Some attempted to clarify and bring resolution to unfortunate relationships in different communities. By this time most of the leaders were concerned about involvements with Baptists in missionary work.

In looking more closely at the circumstances surrounding this critical discussion, one dimension not included in the conference minutes contextualizes the grievances that triggered this emotionally charged discussion. Claus Regier, a former Mennonite Brethren immigrant to Henderson, attended Rochester Seminary from 1882 to

165

1884 and was listed by the Baptists as being active in the Sutton and Hastings area from 1889 to 1891. Later his ministering services are linked to South Dakota, but primarily to Bessie, Oklahoma (1899-1915). It appears that he was a disgruntled Mennonite Brethren, who as a Baptist-trained, ex-Hendersonian was seeking to undermine the Mennonite Brethren. Or he may have been so thoroughly persuaded that Baptist beliefs and ways should or would replace those of the Mennonite Brethren that he was attempting to speed up the process.[27]

There was also discussion about an assumption that Sievers had come to propose a merger with the Mennonite Brethren. This also caused friction in the constituency. Some contended that the Baptists were determined to "swallow up" the Mennonite Brethren. If, in fact, there was to be a merger, the entire Mennonite Brethren constituency needed to be appraised of the issues involved. Furthermore, if there was to be a satisfactory decision, a discussion of these matters needed to include an open and free dialogue of leaders from both denominations. This discussion on the 1892 Conference floor set the direction for the important decisions of 1896 that led to becoming independent from the Baptists in missionary endeavors.

Frank C. Peters regards the 1892 Conference as the critical clarification point establishing Mennonite Brethren-Baptist relationships. Peters summarized the issues and the discussion:

> 1. When members of the Mennonite Brethren Church are disciplined, they invariably leave before discipline is completed and join the Baptists. It seems that Baptist churches accept them without inquiry into their previous record.
> 2. When evangelism has been carried out by Mennonite Brethren in outlying areas, those saved are quickly proselyted by the Baptists, making the establishment of a Mennonite Brethren Church in that area impossible.
> 3. The Mennonite Brethren Church adheres to such principles as nonresistance, abnegation of the oath, footwashing and forbidding of divorce. The Baptists would not endorse these practices.

4. Various practices such as the use of tobacco, attendance at theaters and circuses is forbidden by the Mennonite Brethren Church.

After listening to this report, Sievers agreed that the Baptist churches would recognize the Mennonite Brethren Church and would accept only such members of the church as could present a letter showing that they had been in good standing. The Conference then declared that it would continue to support missions through Baptist channels; yet in all other matters they wished to maintain autonomy.[28]

A second dialogue about Baptist missions relationships took place at the 1896 conference at Ebenfeld when Heinrich C. and Maria (Ewert) Enns of Bingham Lake, Minnesota requested Mennonite Brethren support for their going to Cameroon under Baptist sponsorship. They were not the first to apply for such joint sponsorship. When Abraham and Maria Friesen went out as the first Russian Mennonite Brethren missionaries they did so under Baptist sponsorship. Closer to home was the experience of a highly respected young Mennonite Brethren working in Cameroon under Baptist auspices. Peter H. Wedel, a young Mennonite Brethren from Kansas attended Rochester Seminary with the support of a local *Schulverein* (school association), in the hope that he would return and help establish a Mennonite Brethren school. His brother, Cornelius H. Wedel, became the first president of Bethel College, a General Conference Mennonite school, when it opened in 1893. But a Mennonite Brethren Conference school was not in the offing in 1888 so Peter became the Conference evangelist and continued in that work until 1895. Feeling called to missionary work he privately negotiated an appointment with the Baptists and went to Cameroon. For most Mennonite Brethren the Peter Wedel decision was a disappointment. After hoping he would become their leading educator and then being a successful evangelist he apparently made the decision to join the Baptists without consulting his fellow Mennonite Brethren. Heinrich and Maria Enns had attended Rochester for the six years previous. Heinrich had been a student colleague of four other Mennonite Brethren at Rochester: Johann Berg, John A.

167

Pankratz, John H. Pankratz and Peter H. Wedel. While at Rochester he had developed considerable interest in the German Cameroon colony and felt called to go there. Opportunities in Cameroon had been highlighted through contacts with the Baptist Mission for West Africa agency headquartered in Berlin. The peoples of Cameroon were responding well to the Gospel. Some missionaries, however, had already died giving their life for this cause, victims of tropical African diseases. Replacements to bring the Gospel were urgently requested.

Heinrich Voth, in introducing the Enns candidates to the Ebenfeld conference, indicated that he had always hoped that such young people could be missionaries under Mennonite Brethren sponsorship. Some of the delegates argued that it was not feasible or possible for Mennonite Brethren to establish their own mission program. Others argued for the establishment of missions independent from the Baptists. The discussion revealed intense sentiments in both directions. Dietrich D. Claassen, one of the founders of the Ebenfeld congregation, noted that the delegates were expressing two opinions and that the two lines of thought were leading them further apart. Some felt that this Baptist involvement was breaking up the conference; others did not share that perception.

John F. Harms, the *Zionsbote* editor from Hillsboro read a letter from a Baptist missions director named Scheve. The writer indicated that he did not view the Mennonite Brethren as Mennonite but as Baptists. Other delegates responded that the confusion was the result of Mennonite Brethren not having their own schools. The resolution of what the Enns couple should do—whether to go as Baptists or await the development of a Mennonite Brethren mission program— was finally left to them and their home congregation to decide. The conference agreed to support them with only two hundred dollars for the interim year as well as agreeing to send one hundred fifty dollars to Abraham Friesen in India and to Peter H. Wedel in Cameroon.[29]

Less than a month later, on November 10, 1896, the Ennses departed from their Minnesota home. In the Baptist weekly, *Der Sendbote*, a two part, lengthy report is given about their trip. Nothing is included about any farewell in their home Mennonite Brethren congregation at Mountain Lake, Minnesota. There are some descriptions about their departure. They expressed mixed feelings about going, wondering if they would ever see their homes again. They were exuberant, however, about finally moving toward their long-felt desire to serve in Cameroon.

The most noticeable feature of these lengthy articles, in contrast to their Mennonite Brethren connections, was the delight they expressed about being among Baptist friends again in Chicago, Cleveland, Rochester (which he refers to as "his second home"), Hoboken and New York City. In each of these settings they met friends, were welcomed, prayed for, and sent on with God's blessings to their anticipated ministry in Cameroon. The friends they learned to know and met enroute were a source of special joy to them. They expressed themselves in ways that would make one assume that they were Baptists rather than Mennonite Brethren. The Rochester contact, one surmises, endeared them to a host of cherished friends, perhaps more cherished and meaningful than those that mark his own Mennonite Brethren past.

The year 1896 must be regarded as the turning point for Mennonite Brethren missions in developing their own independent agency apart from the Baptists. Though they were inexperienced in mission administration, they soon managed to deal with recruitment, financial management, field administration and other needed procedures. Their frustration in feeling themselves to be a tool for Baptist ministries, and thereby gradually losing their own Mennonite Brethren distinctives, was resolved. In 1899 they launched out on their own when they sent their first missionaries, N.N. and Susie Hiebert, to India. A year earlier, in 1898, they created their first, functioning mission board. In 1899 a special consultation on missions brought together sixty ministers and lay people to launch their own missionary work. Fortunately Abraham Friesen, the Russian Mennonite Brethren serving under Baptist auspices in India, was present to guide them through the many questions that surfaced. It was he who suggested that an independent mission field could be established adjacent to where the Russian Mennonite Brethren served. This assembly also decided that they would commission their own missionaries, that women missionaries were acceptable, that a constitution should be drafted and that educational arrangements should be made for missionary preparation. McPherson College (a Church of the Brethren institution in McPherson, Kansas) became that school for awhile, instead of Rochester's Baptist Seminary. Special concern was raised about allowing continued access of recruiters or financial solicitors to Mennonite Brethren.[30] Prior to this time Baptist solicitors for funds and missionaries had been making increasing appeals to American Mennonite Brethren congregations.

Hans Kasdorf's study of Mennonite Brethren mission development concludes the discussion about Mennonite Brethren-Baptist relationships by citing both the actual reasons and the apparent underlying reasons that finally led Mennonite Brethren to establish their own mission agency:

> Whatever theological motives there may have been for the establishment of an independent Mennonite Brethren mission field among the "pagan peoples," the extensive and intensive debate at the 1896 Convention in Ebenfeld, Kansas, suggested several other than theological and biblical reasons for independency.
>
> (1) There was an overwhelming desire on the part of the Mennonite Brethren to retain and employ their own missionaries. . .
>
> (2) There was an implicit fear of being absorbed by the Baptists.
>
> (3) There was the perpetual drain on the mission treasury without the existence of an Mennonite Brethren mission field. . . Whatever happened, one thing was clear: the Baptists should no longer be permitted to exploit the good will, the financial treasury, and the human resources of the Brethren.
>
> (4) The counsel of the Russian Mennonite Brethren missionary Abraham Friesen of India had a decisive impact on the decision of the Brethren in America. . . Friesen stated: "If either all or the majority of the brothers and sisters in America are of the opinion to build up their work at home on their own, they should do likewise with regard to gentile mission. There is enough work among the many thousands here in India." Friesen went on to

indicate that India had many unoccupied fields where no one was working; he was prepared to assist the American Brethren in finding a suitable area for their own work.[31]

As the missions involvements with Baptists tapered off during the 1890s so also did the educational ties. Shortly after the 1896 cessation of mission collaboration with German Baptists, the question of schooling for leaders in various church-related vocations again became a central issue. Disagreements about the location and type of school Mennonite Brethren wanted seemed to keep them from moving ahead. Trying to retain Russian and German models of schooling and the Rochester experience both ended in frustration. The older generation still seemed intent on preparing their children for basically rural and farm occupations and, at most, having only their religious and educational leaders attain "higher education." The younger generation had their own schooling interests in mind as they became increasingly Americanized. The older leaders tended to regard the American "liberal arts" model as threatening. The resources for equipping such a school with Christian faith-oriented faculty seemed out of reach. Yet this was exactly what their children seemed to be seeking.

McPherson College, a liberal arts, Christian college of the Church of the Brethren, was located twenty-five miles west of Hillsboro, Kansas. That school's administration invited area Mennonite Brethren and Krimmer Mennonite Brethren congregations to take over the German Department. They offered use of some class rooms for instructing Mennonite Brethren students in the curriculum of their choice. Students were also free to enroll in any of McPherson College's regular classes.

The Mennonite Brethren Conference was not willing to fully endorse that kind of a venture. They did, however, endorse having a central Kansas nucleus do so and promised to offer finances to support this venture. This curriculum was not as distinctly focused on theological leadership training as that of Rochester and so it appealed to a wider diversity of Mennonite Brethren young people. It was in a desirable location for most of the Mennonite Brethren at that time. John Funk Duerksen, the major professor, was the most highly trained leader among the Mennonite Brethren immigrants. They felt secure in the pastoral concern he would offer.

Between 1898 and 1905, when the Mennonite Brethren operated the German Department, nearly 250 Mennonite Brethren students attended McPherson. This is at least five times more than the total attending Rochester. Among these were a number of persons who subsequently became significant leaders among Mennonite Brethren. Included were Daniel F. Bergthold, A.P. Epp, John J. Franz, Bernhard J. Friesen, Peter C. Hiebert, Henry W. Lohrenz, Abraham L. Schellenberg, Henry F. Toews, Peter R. Lange, Leonard J. Franz and Franz J. Wiens. During this same time period there were at least seven students (Peter E. Penner, H.V. Wiebe, P.V. Wiebe, Henry H. Adrian, David Harder, Frank J. Baerg, Henry Shenkofsky) who attended the other nearby Mennonite College—Bethel College in North Newton, Kansas.

With the establishment of Tabor College in 1908, under the leadership of thirty-year old president Henry W. Lohrenz, a Mennonite Brethren institution existed that attempted to meet as many of the youth and church needs as possible. Though only a recent B.A. graduate from McPherson College, Lohrenz enjoyed the confidence of the constituents.[32]

The German Baptists never established a Christian liberal arts college of this kind in the United States. With Tabor's establishment in 1908, some of these German Baptists began attending there. No official denominational ties were ever established with these North American Baptists. Since the mid-1960's however, they have had a board member serve on its Board of Directors. Tabor has officially been named by their leadership as one of three recommended colleges for their youth. At Tabor, Baptists have usually comprised the second highest number of enrollees in denominations represented. Between 1971 and 1991 Baptists students annually constituted between twelve to twenty percent of the student body. The largest number of Baptists comes from North American Baptist constituency.[33]

Through the years some Baptists have also served as faculty members at Tabor or as special lecturers in the yearly Bible Conferences. Tabor faculty members and students have frequently served their nearby congregations in pastoral functions or in giving choral or Christian educational leadership. A sizeable number of Mennonite Brethren who have continued their theological education beyond that available in Mennonite Brethren institutions also have chosen Baptist institutions. For about two decades the Rochester connection continued to attract a few seeking advanced theological training. At mid-century the most popular Baptist school was Kansas City's Central Baptist Theological Seminary. By 1965 at least twenty-five persons had received graduate degrees there. Others attended the Los Angeles Baptist Theological Seminary and Western Baptist Theological Seminary in Portland, Oregon. More recently the Southern Baptist Theological Seminary in Fort Worth, Texas has attracted most of those seeking doctorates from a Baptist school.

Before 1950, the ratio of teachers and pastors having graduate degrees from a Baptist School would have been higher than is the case today. Most of the pastors attended a Northern Baptist or non-denominational Bible Schools or Colleges. Between 1955 and 1991, of the thirty-five professors who taught at the Mennonite Brethren Seminary in Fresno, California, ten received at least one of their graduate degrees from a Baptist seminary; eighteen received at least one graduate degree from a non-denominational seminary; ten from a Mennonite seminary.[34]

APPRAISALS OF MENNONITE BRETHREN-BAPTIST RELATIONSHIPS

There was a kind of "glue" that initially bonded Mennonite Brethren and German Baptists in America. Both groups sought freedom, often shared family connections, were German-speaking, conversionist/immersionist-oriented, desired abandoning their former "tired" religious traditions, searched for farm lands for large families, were fellow-adventurers confronting America's frontier, and were zealous in their interests for missions and an education for their children. In these associations some Baptists influenced Mennonite Brethren significantly. Though less so since 1900 than in the earlier years, some Mennonite Brethren continued to regard Baptists as the most compatible among America's various denominations. This tended to be more evident among laity than conference leadership. Mennonite Brethren leadership has traditionally and increasingly leaned again more into Mennonite associations than Baptist.

In developing various associations in America most Mennonite Brethren have continued to be aware of their Anabaptist-Mennonite emphases rather than swimming full-stream with other groups. Most Mennonite Brethren insisted on retaining the cardinal emphases of their Anabaptist-Mennonite tradition. Some Baptist associates advocated that they abandon their historical teaching of nonresistance, the practice of footwashing and the refusal to swear an oath. This they adamantly refused to do, since they regarded those doctrines as central to their faith position. Another dividing emphasis was the Mennonite Brethren practice of conference covenant making as opposed to having independently autonomous congregational relationships like the Baptist polity.

It was relatively easy, particularly for the early Mennonite Brethren immigrants in North America, to join the German Baptists. For the historically isolationistic Mennonite Brethren the broadened horizons offered through Baptist contacts were attractive, particularly for the young. Baptists also represented an opportunity to enter a more American-oriented, popular, mainline body rather than continuing to identify with a small, struggling, "heretical" minority body that appeared to have little future. In a lay ministry denomination the opportunities to be in a professionalized and salaried ministry was attractive to some potential leaders. Some Mennonite Brethren tended to advocate moving towards a merger with the German Baptists. They viewed them as a compatible body with which they could readily align. They were attracted to some of their already established schools, missions and publishing programs. This seemed more appropriate than to go through the throes of initiating their own identity in religiously pluralistic America.

Historically Mennonite Brethren owe a debt of gratitude, mainly to the German Baptists (now North American Baptist Conference) for their significant influences. Both in Russia and in America, German Baptist theology and methodologies were catalytic in stimulating new ways of thinking with regard to worship, church governance and relations to the world. Mennonite Brethren relationships with Baptists opened the doors to a broader world than their isolationistic past had encouraged. Baptists offered a new, trusted avenue for Christian relationships beyond the relatively closed Mennonite circles. Useful, creative and innovative ways modelled by Baptists were attempted, though they sometimes led to undesired consequences.

The early missionary and educational endeavors were modeled by Baptists. Once Mennonite Brethren dissociated from the German Baptists in these areas, they surpassed them in both. Particularly in missions abroad. Roughly twenty-five percent (200,000) of the 1992 world Mennonite population belong to the Mennonite Brethren. The North American (German) Baptist world-wide census is less than half that number.

Nonresistance has continued to be the main distinctive separating Mennonite Brethren from the Baptists groups that were closest to them. America, the new homeland of immigrants was world-renowned as a land of democracy and freedom. To those not schooled in a more intense Biblical understandings of "nonresistance" this position seemed highly illogical in America. They found it relatively easy to change their church membership in order to become truly "mainline American." Nonresistance narrowly understood as an obligatory, wartime issue, was applied only to qualified, healthy males of a given age group. Those who adhered to the New Testament nonresistance teachings through the years knew its more inclusive dimensions, and saw the implications for all of life in much more penetrating ways.

The Mennonite experience of holding to this position had, for three centuries, been a life and death issue. Their forebears had been persecuted, harassed and exiled for believing and practicing this nonresistance. They regarded it as a Christ-centered worldview and lifestyle that penetrated all of life. Theoretically, nonresistance had to do with how one regarded one's own total life. It had implications for the meaning of property, the nature of earthly citizenship, relationships to others (believers and unbelievers) and even to family dynamics. It had to do with what one regarded as ultimate authority, how to deal with feelings and actions toward those generally seen as personal, social, national or international enemies.

Nonresistance was linked to evangelism and missions. Priority was to be given to God's "love agenda" with all people, not only one's own human evaluation or feelings about others. Mutual aid, a simple lifestyle, refusal to avenge evildoers, an emphasis on reconciliation in all situations, were cardinal. Living a Christ-disciplined life with and through fellow believers—the Church—was the way one expressed Christ-surrenderedness. In its deepest implications, then, it was linked to one's view of the church, the world, and all of one's existence. The directives from the Bible on being a "separate" people of God, not conforming to the world, and out of step with unbelievers, were integral to this nonresistance stance. Those faithful to Christ were expected to be misunderstood, rejected, hated and persecuted for such humanly illogical attitudes and behaviors. The response to evildoers was even more puzzling: to bless, to give generously, to love, to pray for them—"to be merciful to them even as God is merciful"(Luke 6:35).

When those who did not understand the implications of this position narrowly related nonresistance only to war issues in their new American setting, this teaching seemed ridiculous. Logically argued, America's protections for freedom of religion were regarded well worth military defense. Wars conducted to preserve a country like America should, according to that logic, be regarded as "holy wars," something pleasing in God's sight. In America the Baptists were loyal patriots, valuing their religious freedoms and regarding participation in military service appropriate when called to do so by government.[35]

In a world increasingly violent and militarily dependent it is likely that this polarization will increase. Mennonite Brethren who are eager to become evangelically mainline, as in the past, may continue to abandon this life-encompassing worldview and become Baptists or members of some other Evangelical group. Meanwhile, some Baptists, more prepared to investigate this long-held Mennonite orientation from out of a "pilgrim/stranger" stance are drawn to its biblical underpinnings. The posture is one of self-denial and cross-bearing. Unfortunately, America's lures to mainstream pursuits have often distracted both Mennonite Brethren and Baptists from the best of their traditions. Both, when faithful to their historic callings, provide inspired moments of Christian faithfulness.

ABE J. DUECK

Baptists and Mennonite Brethren in Canada

In 1980, *Baptists in Canada: Search for Identity Amidst Diversity* was published.[1] The subtitle could have served equally well for a book about Mennonites in Canada and, one suspects, about Mennonite Brethren in Canada. If the search for identity amidst diversity applies to both groups, then it is obvious that an investigation of the relationship between the two groups is not likely to lend itself to easy analysis or result in unqualified conclusions.

A quick review of the literature on Mennonite Brethren history in Canada does not suggest that much of significance about Mennonite Brethren-Baptist relationships will be discovered—certainly nothing like that which pertains to early MB history in Russia or the later experience in the Soviet Union. The index to John A. Toews' *History of the Mennonite Brethren Church* does not contain any references to Baptists in Canada.[2] Several volumes by Frank Epp on Mennonites in Canada are also void of significant references to Baptists.[3] Peter Penner's recent study of Mennonite Brethren church planting in Canada, on the other hand, contains several references to Baptists, some of which are pursued in this essay.[4] In general, little attention has been given to this topic.

The literature on Baptist history in Canada does not contain many references to Mennonites, let alone Mennonite Brethren. The most definitive recent publication has several brief references to Mennonites, but none specifically to Mennonite Brethren.[5] Other works, recent or earlier, also prove disappointing.[6]

MENNONITE BRETHREN IN CANADA

Mennonite Brethren were among the last of various Mennonite bodies to arrive in Canada and only arrived in larger numbers in the 1920s, whereas in the Unites States they had already established a significant presence as a result of the migration of the 1870s.[7] The beginnings in Canada actually came as a result of missionary efforts by Mennonite Brethren from the United States among other Mennonite groups already established in Manitoba. The first Mennonite Brethren church was organized near Winkler in 1888. Growth at first was slow, but by 1907 small groups were meeting in Winnipeg and the first urban church was established in 1909. In Saskatchewan, the first church was organized in Laird in 1898 and soon small congregations emerged in other rural areas of Saskatchewan. In the other western provinces and Ontario, however, MB congregations were not established until the major wave of immigration of the 1920s, which came in the aftermath of the Bolshevik Revolution in Russia.

The significance of the relatively brief sojourn of Mennonite Brethren in Canada needs to be understood at the outset. The larger Baptist groups in Canada have had a much longer experience in Canada and are also largely Anglo Saxon in origin. As a result there was a major linguistic and cultural gap which kept the two communities apart even though theological compatibility might have allowed them to work together in many areas. Mennonite Brethren in Canada, by and large, only made the language transition from German into English in the 1950s or later and have only recently entered the mainstream of Canadian life. Therefore the potential for significant relationships has been quite limited.

A detailed history of the two groups in Canada cannot be provided here. Nevertheless a brief identification of the major Baptist groups in Canada will help set the context for an investigation of the relationships between Mennonite Brethren and Baptists. An attempt will then be made to evaluate the nature of the relationships to discern whether there are some unique and significant dimensions. Unfortunately, there is no adequate comparative framework for this study. No similar study of Mennonite Brethren relationships with other denominations has been done and therefore conclusions will be very tentative. A comprehensive theoretical framework for understanding denominational relationships still needs to be developed.

BAPTISTS IN CANADA

The largest Baptist denomination in Canada is the Canadian Baptist Federation (CBF), which in turn has four member bodies.

These are: 1) The United Baptist Convention of the Atlantic Provinces, 2) Union d'Églises Baptistes Françaises au Canada, 3) Baptist Convention of Ontario and Quebec, and 4) Baptist Union of Western Canada. The CBF is a coordinating body of the four groups, with a total membership of over 133,000.[8] Each group has a distinctive history that has its implications for our study. The major theological institutions are Acadia Divinity College in Wolfville, Nova Scotia and McMaster Divinity College in Hamilton, Ontario. There are also leadership education or training institutions in Whitby, Ontario; Calgary, Alberta; and Montreal, Quebec as well as Carey Hall, a residential center associated with Regent College on the campus of the University of British Columbia in Vancouver.

The second largest Baptist group is the Fellowship of Evangelical Baptist Churches in Canada, a loosely associated body of Baptists from various regions. Organized in 1953, it had a membership of about 58,000 by 1991.[9] The Fellowship churches are the product of a schism among Baptists in Canada and the fundamentalist-modernist controversy of the 1920s. McMaster University (earlier Toronto Baptist College, which combined with Woodstock College and moved to Hamilton in 1930) was at the center of the controversy.[10] Thomas T. Shields of the Jarvis Street Baptist Church led the fight against McMaster and, in protest, left to create his own seminary, Toronto Baptist Seminary, now Toronto Baptist Seminary and Bible College (TBS). Many churches left with him and eventually became the core of the Fellowship Baptists in central Canada. Shields, as well as the Jarvis St. Church, eventually became isolated when the Dean of the TBS, W. Gordon Brown, was dismissed. He led in organizing the Central Baptist Seminary in Toronto in 1949, which remains one of four seminaries controlled by the Fellowship Baptists. The others are: London Baptist Bible College and Seminary in London, Ontario; Northwest Baptist Theological Seminary (NWTS) in Langley, British Columbia (formerly in Vancouver); and Seminaire Baptiste Évangélique Canadien (SEMBEC) in Montreal, Quebec. The Toronto Baptist Seminary created by Shields still operates today as a school of a small Association of Regular Baptists (Canada).

Other Baptist bodies in Canada include the North American Baptist Conference that originated as the German Baptists. In 1989 they had a membership of over 17,000.[11] It operates the North American Baptist College and Divinity School in Edmonton and has a cooperative arrangement for transfer of academic credit with Tabor College, an Mennonite Brethren liberal arts college in Hillsboro, Kansas. Another Baptist group, the Baptist General Conference of Canada, was originally a Swedish body. It has a membership of over six thousand and operates the Canadian Baptist Seminary in Langley, British Columbia (formerly Vancouver Bible College).[12] In addition, the Southern Baptists have become established in Canada and there are numerous smaller groups such as Free Will Baptists and independent Baptist churches. A few may be of local significance for Mennonite Brethren churches.

MENNONITE BRETHREN-BAPTIST RELATIONSHIPS

The three Baptist groups with the most significant Mennonite Brethren relationships are the CBF, the Fellowship Baptists, and the North American Baptist Conference. Historically, various Russian Baptist groups, now absorbed into the larger denominations, also had important connections. All of these relationships have interesting regional variations.

Ontario

In Ontario, contacts between various Baptist groups and Mennonite Brethren seem to have been minimal. Few Mennonite Brethren have studied at the Baptist institutions. Although a number of Mennonite Brethren have studied in the Religion department of McMaster University (now a provincial institution), the Divinity School has not attracted many, despite its location close to a large MB population and despite its solid academic reputation. Its reputation as a "liberal" school may have deterred some.[13] In recent years, with the appointment of theologians like Clark Pinnock and William Brackney, the school seems to have embarked on a conservative course which may make it more attractive for Mennonite Brethren.

Mennonite Brethren have enrolled in greater numbers at Central Baptist Seminary in Toronto. These include David Ewert (B.D.) and George Shillington (M.Div.).[14] Theological compatibility may well have been a factor, Toronto Baptist Seminary has also attracted several Mennonite Brethren. In the past two decades at least seven Mennonite Brethren or former Mennonite Brethren studied at TBS.[15]

The present (1990) Registrar, Rudy Wiebe, and his wife are former members of the Leamington Mennonite Brethren Church. David Ewert has been invited to teach summer schools at the seminary occasionally, most recently in 1986.

A survey of Mennonite Brethren pastors and leaders in Ontario does not generally point to strong relationships with Baptists, although there has been some cooperation in ministerial associations and in other areas.[16] In towns with a concentration of German Baptists, as in Kitchener, there was more interaction. The Kitchener Mennonite Brethren Church and the Central Baptist Church belonged to a German speaking *Allianz* that sponsored cooperative services.[17]

While Heinrich H. Janzen was in Kitchener, he also ministered frequently among various Russian groups, especially Russian Baptists.[18] In 1943 Deyneka of the Toronto Russian Gospel Association and Oswald Smith of the Toronto People's Church asked Janzen to begin a Russian Bible Institute in Toronto. Janzen accepted and taught there (commuting from Kitchener) until 1946 when he moved to the Mennonite Brethren Bible College (MBBC) in Winnipeg. Most of the students came from Russian Baptist churches. Janzen also preached in many Russian Baptist churches, both in the United States and in western Canada. Others like Franz C. Thiessen, Jacob Thiessen, David B. Wiens, Abraham H. Unruh, and Abram Huebert (from Leamington) also ministered among the Russians.[19]

In Kitchener itself, the Benton Street Baptist Church and the Kitchener Mennonite Brethren Church operated a joint Daily Vacation Bible School (DVBS) program in 1965. There were also frequent joint "Fireside Services" for youth, cooperative efforts in major crusades and Sunday School conventions and Baptist participation in the Kitchener Mennonite Brethren "Celebration Choir." The Kitchener "Sacred Song Quartet" served in many Baptist churches and in 1964 a Sunday School outreach program in the Puslinch Lake area was turned over to the Preston Baptist Church.

In Virgil, the Mennonite Brethren Church worshipped in the Creek Road Baptist Church from 1937 to 1941 after a fire had destroyed its own building. From 1968 to 1970 a young Mennonite Brethren couple, Rudy and Marlene Wiebe (nee Reimer), assisted a new pioneering Baptist Church in Leamington. The group was using the old Mennonite Brethren church building. Later Rudy attended TBS, pastored Faith Baptist Church in Oakville, and eventually became a faculty member at TBS. In Orillia, cooperation with Baptists was ongoing. In the mid-1940s, several students from TBS were in charge of the DVBS work that was connected with the Christian Fellowship Chapel.[20]

The flow of members between Baptist and Mennonite Brethren churches does not reveal a strong movement in either direction. Eden Christian College, the only Ontario Mennonite Brethren educational institution of recent years, has had few Baptist students.

Prairies

The Baptist churches on the prairies did not experience the degree of turmoil that the Baptists in Ontario experienced. The histories of several institutions were nevertheless strongly affected by the conflicts of the 1920s. In Manitoba, Brandon College, which later became Brandon University, was a Baptist college and was subject to similar criticism as that directed against McMaster. Although T.T. Shields and others added their voices of protest against the college, most of the criticism came from British Columbia. The controversy led in 1926 to a complete break in British Columbia. About a third of the churches left the Baptist Union of Western Canada to form a separate Convention of Regular Baptists of British Columbia, now a part of the Fellowship Baptist churches.[21]

In Alberta, a phenomenon closely tied to the radical politics of the province had a profound direct and indirect impact on Mennonite Brethren. William Aberhart, the founder of the Social Credit movement in Alberta and long-time premier of the province, came to Alberta in 1910 from Ontario. In Ontario, as a Presbyterian, he had come under the influence of the Niagara Prophetic Conference with its radical dispensationalism and pessimistic apocalypticism.[22] Aberhart's experiences in the Presbyterian Church and frustration with the religious establishment partially prompted his move to Calgary, Alberta. In due time, he became supply pastor at the Westbourne Baptist Church, a mission of the First Baptist Church. His style and radical views, however, led to conflict with mainline Baptists (he was also not immersed until 1921). In the 1920s he became involved in the fundamentalist-modernist controversy, including criticism of Brandon College. By 1925 he founded Calgary Bible Institute, later named Calgary Prophetic Bible Institute. A number of Mennonite Brethren, including John A. Toews, later attended this school. Aberhart also conducted a popular radio ministry, later assumed by Ernest C. Manning, and a correspondence Sunday School of the Air. The degree of influence of all of this on Mennonite Brethren, while difficult to measure, was undoubtedly considerable.[23] Mennonite Brethren in Alberta were strong supporters of both Aberhart and Manning, more because of religious factors rather than political issues. That support may have been easier because the Baptist identity of both Aberhart and Manning and their institutions was tenuous. The Baptist Union expelled Westbourne and subsequently Aberhart founded a Bible Institute Baptist Church.

The schism did not end there. In 1929 the Westbourne congregation split and in 1934 Morley Hall, assisted by Lesley E. Maxwell, formed a rival Bible institute,[24] which became Western Baptist Bible College in Calgary. At least one MB, David B. Wiens, attended this college and graduated in 1939. Several years earlier Wiens had been converted as a result of contacts with a Baptist minister and was baptized in the Drumheller Baptist Church by Mennonite Brethren minister, Heinrich Klassen.[25] Regular Baptists in British Columbia supported Hall, and in 1945 the college moved to Port Coquitlam near Vancouver and was renamed Northwest Baptist Bible College. This institution eventually fed into the stream of the Fellowship of Evangelical Baptist Churches in Canada.

The Mennonite Brethren in Alberta presently have no educational institution within the province, although at one point there were several Bible institutes; the province also jointly sponsors Bethany Bible Institute with Saskatchewan. At least three present pastors have received considerable theological education at Baptist schools and at least one other pastor has previously held a pastoral position in a Baptist church. In the early years, before Mennonite Brethren were formally established in Edmonton, there was concern that they were joining Baptist and Alliance churches.[26] Noteworthy, however, is the fact that North American Baptist College in Edmonton has a Mennonite Brethren faculty member in the music department (Mel Unger) and that another Mennonite Brethren, Ron Dyck, regularly teaches a psychology course at the college.

Mission and outreach efforts on the prairies brought occasional interaction with Baptists. Peter Penner cites an interesting incident in Blaine Lake, Saskatchewan in 1934 that resulted in a mutual statement of Mennonite Brethren and Baptists condemning war.[27] In Pierceland, Saskatchewan, a former Baptist minister served as pastor of the Mennonite Brethren Church from 1971 to 1974. In Regina some Mennonite Brethren worshipped in a German Baptist church before an Mennonite Brethren church was organized. In Lloydminster, many Mennonite Brethren worshipped in a Baptist or Alliance church before a Mennonite Brethren church was organized. A report specified that eighty percent of the Baptist church council in 1978 were former Mennonite Brethren. One of the early church workers there, Eric Penner, was a graduate of Northwest Baptist Seminary (NWBS) in Vancouver.[28] Bethany Bible Institute, an Mennonite Brethren school in Hepburn, Saskatchewan, has had few Baptist students. A few faculty members, however, have received some of their education at Baptist schools.

In Lindal, Manitoba, a non-ethnic Mennonite Brethren church transferred its affiliation to a Baptist church in 1939. In Ashern, Mennonite Brethren began a missionary effort in about 1945, but after the work ceased in about 1959,[29] the believers were advised to join the Moosehorn Baptists.

Special attention needs to be given to the Winnipeg setting. The early history of the Mennonite Brethren Church in Winnipeg is closely linked with the German Baptist Church. German Baptists had already established a congregation in Winnipeg by the end of 1889 before there was any MB presence there.[30] When the first Mennonite Brethren immigrants arrived in the early part of this century, a number joined the German Baptist Church.[31] A number of Mennonite family names appear in the records of the First German Baptist Church.[32]

In 1913 a more organized Mennonite Brethren effort began under the leadership of William J. Bestvater. The group first rented the basement of a mission chapel on the corner of Manitoba and McKennzie St. from the German Baptist Church. This arrangement continued for three years. From 1919 to 1929 there were many joint activities, especially relating to youth and music, Peter Penner of the

German Baptist Church was the choir director of one of the major musical events and Ben Horch of the Mennonite Brethren was also frequently involved in joint musical events.

A recent study of the McDermot Avenue Baptist records revealed that at least nine transfers of membership took place between 1913 and 1935 from Mennonite Brethren churches to the Baptist church.[33] Several are from the Winkler Mennonite Brethren Church. The reasons for the transfers are not clear, although it appears that Mennonite Brethren felt a very close cultural and theological affinity with the German Baptists and that the feelings were mutual. This is demonstrated by the fact that Mennonite Brethren ministers and faculty members of the Mennonite Brethren Bible College were frequently invited to preach at the German services of the German Baptist churches. Some years ago Martin Durksen organized a German Alliance that included Mennonite Brethren, General Conference Mennonites, and German Baptists. One of the purposes was to encourage pulpit exchange. Prayer meetings, crusades, and German schools have been other forms of cooperation. The Rowandale Baptist Church and the McDermot Avenue Baptist Church have been involved most extensively in these relationships.

The two Mennonite Brethren schools located in Winnipeg both of which originated in the mid-1940s, have had a large number of Baptist students throughout their history. The Mennonite Brethren Collegiate Institute (MBCI) has had an average of thirty-eight Baptist students each year in the past fourteen years. The number has increased gradually over that period so that the average from 1985-1990 was seventy. During the 1989-1990 year the Baptist students were divided about equally among three major organizations: North American Baptist Conference (German Baptists), Baptist Union (CBF), and Baptist General Convention. MBCI has also employed several Baptist teachers.

Mennonite Brethren Bible College has also had a significant number of Baptist students from various parts of Canada. The average during the 1980s was approximately thirteen. Baptists constituted the largest non-Mennonite Brethren group. A number of faculty members have received some of their education at Baptist schools. These schools include Central Baptist Seminary in Toronto, Southern Baptist Theological Seminary in Louisville, Central Baptist Theological Seminary in Kansas City, McMaster Divinity School, Southwestern Baptist Seminary in Fort Worth, and Bethel Theological Seminary in St. Paul. In addition Baptist speakers, including Jarold Zeman and Clark Pinnock (both of the CBF), have been featured at special occasions.

British Columbia

British Columbia afforded considerable opportunity for interaction between Mennonite Brethren and Baptists. Northwest Baptist Theological Seminary (NBTS), formerly Northwest Baptist Bible College of Alberta, is part of the Associated Canadian Theological Schools on the campus of Trinity Western University in Langley. It and its predecessors have been training institutions for many MB leaders both from British Columbia and elsewhere. In the four years from 1985-1989, an average of fourteen MB students enrolled at NWBS.[34] In a 1989 survey of Mennonite Brethren pastors, six out of thirty respondents received some education at NWTS or its predecessors. Nick Dyck, long-time Director of Home Missions in British Columbia, and Herb Brandt, a prominent leader in British Columbia and North America, are among those.

Carey Hall is the Baptist institution on the campus of the University of British Columbia. Operated by the Baptist Union of Western Canada, it is well known among Mennonite Brethren. Dr. Roy Bell, Professor of Family Ministries, is a frequent speaker at Mennonite Brethren gatherings. In 1984 he addressed the Canadian Convention meeting in Clearbrook. Regent College has also been the locus of significant contact between Mennonite Brethren and many other denominations, including Baptists. Prior to his appointment at McMaster, Clark Pinnock was on the faculty at Regent and was well known and respected by MB students.

Vancouver Bible College, which is now Canadian Baptist Seminary in Langley, has also been a training institution for at least one Mennonite Brethren pastor. Ray Bystrom, who pastored the Killarney Park Mennonite Brethren Church for a number of years and is now on the faculty of the Mennonite Brethren Biblical Seminary in Fresno, received a B.Th. degree from the school in 1966.

Columbia Bible College (formerly Columbia Bible Institute), a college sponsored jointly by Mennonite Brethren and the Conference of Mennonites in British Columbia, has strong Baptist connections. During the 1980s an average of seven or eight Baptist students attended Columbia Bible College (CBC). Two of the present faculty members received some of their theological education in Baptist schools. Perhaps the most stormy phase of CBC's history came during the brief presidency in 1978-1979 of Samuel Mikolaski, a Baptist (CBF). The decision to invite Mikolaski may have been motivated by a desire to enter the mainstream of North American evangelicalism and to elevate CBC's academic status. Mikolaski did bring a solid academic reputation.[35] While personality factors may have been at the root of the crisis that developed, the issue may also point to deeper differences between Mennonite Brethren and Baptists. Differing leadership styles and concepts of peoplehood were also part of the struggle.

The Mennonite Educational Institute (MEI), in Clearbrook, has no detailed record of the number of Baptist students. During the 1980s, MEI employed at least two Baptist teachers.

The history of several British Columbia MB congregations includes significant Baptist elements. Peter Teigrob began an Mennonite Brethren mission work in Hope in the early 1940s. Mennonite Brethren, frequently under suspicion as Germans during World War II and not wishing to expose their identity, decided to join the Baptists.[36] The Ruskin Mennonite Brethren Church, which began as a result of a Daily Vacation Bible School outreach program in 1955, was turned over in the same year to the Baptists.[37] In Kitimat, a church was begun in 1960 but due to various difficulties it dissolved in 1967, and the majority of members joined a nearby Baptist church.[38]

Mennonite Brethren settled in the Victoria area and students attended the University of Victoria long before Mennonite Brethren established a church there in the late 1960s.[39] In the intervening years, many Mennonite Brethren went to Baptist churches and churches of other denominations. Helmut Janzen, an MBBC graduate, pastored the Central Baptist Church in Victoria for a number of years. Later he returned to work in the Mennonite Brethren conference.

In Burnaby, the Willingdon Mennonite Brethren Church had a large influx of people from the Faith Baptist Church. The Killarney Park Mennonite Brethren Church has had several pastors with Baptist background. The first was an articulate Baptist from Britain, Bob Roxburgh, who became pastor in 1971 and captured the attention of Mennonite Brethren across Canada. He came to Killarney Park after serving as pastor at Killarney Baptist Church in Calgary and left the Mennonite Brethren scene almost as suddenly as he had arrived.

Quebec

Among the newer churches in eastern Canada, the Quebec developments were unique. The various evangelical bodies are still small and relatively young. Quebec society itself has undergone revolutionary changes in the past several decades.

The Union of French Baptist Churches of Canada has a history which dates back to the middle of the nineteenth century. Yet, contrary to what we might expect, in 1971 it had a total membership of only 398 in eight churches.[40] By 1991 it had increased to 2405.[41] In 1982 the Union established the Centre d'Études Théologiques Évangéliques (CETE) as a theological training institute in Montreal. The school has obtained academic recognition through Acadia University.

The Fellowship Baptists have also been active in Quebec, especially since the mid-1950s. A theological training school was established in 1974 in Montreal (Seminaire Baptiste Évangélique Canadien—SEMBEC). Martha Wall, a Mennonite Brethren, worked as secretary during its early years.

Mennonite Brethren beginnings in French Canada date to 1961 when returning missionaries from the political turmoil in Zaire, came to Quebec. Ernest Dyck was the pioneer Mennonite Brethren missionary in the province. Because of the nature of the work in Quebec, cooperation between various evangelical bodies was essential and developed quite naturally. The "Quebec Every Home Crusade," a tract distribution ministry, included Plymouth Brethren, Fellowship Baptists, and Mennonite Brethren. Institut biblique Bethel in Sherbrooke was another interdenominational venture, supported especially by the same three groups. Several Mennonite Brethren missionaries to the Congo earlier studied French at Bethel. Later, Ernest Dyck taught some courses at Bethel and also became a Board member. Fellowship Baptists were strongly involved until the 1974 establishment of SEMBEC.

Youth and Sunday School work were areas of considerable cooperation between Fellowship Baptists and other evangelical and fundamentalist groups. Plymouth Brethren, Baptists and Mennonite Brethren sponsored two or three rallies a year in the 1960s and early 1970s, organized by provincial youth committees. For several years, Jean Théorêt, presently President of Institut biblique Laval (IBL—a Mennonite Brethren school), was chair of the Youth Committee, which organized highly successful Sunday School conventions and sponsored cooperative crusades. Ernest Dyck and Martha Wall were prominent in these efforts.

Cooperation between Union Baptists and other Mennonites was less enthusiastic. The membership criteria of the Union Baptists were too open and were under some theological suspicion. Ernest Dyck felt that Fellowship Baptists had a strong emphasis on evangelism and were more successful in planting churches. In addition, Fellowship Baptists also were not open to cooperating on committees with Union Baptists and, hence, Mennonite Brethren essentially had to choose between the two Baptist groups. By policy, Union Baptists were not invited to participate on committees.

A number of matters have changed in recent years. With the creation of more institutions of their own, the various groups appear to be less interested in cooperation with others. There have been some exchanges of faculty members between IBL and SEMBEC, but recent years have witnessed more educational cooperation with the Union Baptists. Denominational identity and loyalty in all groups still seems weak except at the leadership level. Members of the various denominations enroll in any of the institutions, often basing their decisions on pragmatic factors rather than on denominational loyalties. Likewise, members in each denomination transfer to other denominations with relative ease. A broad evangelical identity supercedes denominational identities.

The Maritimes

In the Maritimes there is still only a small Mennonite Brethren presence. Some Mennonite Brethren who moved to the Maritimes joined Baptist churches because there were no other options. Peter Penner refers to Siegfried and Margaret Janzen who joined a United Baptist Church in the Annapolis Valley in Nova Scotia, but who continued to think of themselves as Mennonites.⁴² Other Mennonite Brethren also worshipped with Baptists, while a number of Baptists joined the Mennonite Brethren churches that were eventually established there.

CONCLUSION

Are there then some general observations that can be made concerning Mennonite Brethren-Baptist relationships in Canada? The extent of Baptist diversity makes it difficult to generalize, yet some tentative assessments can be made.

1) Mennonite Brethren-Baptist relationships appear to have been more extensive than MB relationships with any other non-Mennonite denominations. Peter Penner's study of MB church planting, for example, makes many more references to Baptists than to any other non-Mennonite denomination. It is also clear that more Mennonite Brethren have studied at Baptist schools than at schools of other non-Mennonite denominations (excluding inter- or non-denominational schools). In terms of transfer of memberships, the evidence indicates that there has been significant movement of Mennonite Brethren to Baptist churches and of Baptists to Mennonite Brethren churches.⁴³

2) Theologically, Mennonite Brethren in Canada currently see considerable compatibility between themselves and Baptists.⁴⁴ Mennonite Brethren pastors and church leaders see two major differences between the denominations in two areas: first, peace and nonresistance, and second, ecclesiology. In relation to ecclesiology, the factors mentioned most frequently were the concepts of peoplehood, local church autonomy, and the concept of leadership. Mennonite Brethren view Baptists as having a stronger leadership style with a greater emphasis on local church autonomy.

Other theological issues cited frequently were the Calvinist theology of Baptist churches (e.g., eternal security) and the rigid orthodoxy, fundamentalism, legalism, or dogmatism of Baptist churches. These factors suggest that Mennonite Brethren have had their closest connections with Fellowship Baptists and other conservative Baptist groups instead of with the CBF, at least at the local level. Sometimes, the opposite factors emerged (e.g., liberalism), which suggests an acquaintance with segments of the CBF.

It would appear that to a considerable extent Mennonite Brethren consciousness of the fundamentalist-modernist schism at the local level came via the Baptists. No other denomination in Canada was affected by this schism as much as the Baptists. Mennonite Brethren who came to Canada in larger numbers during the 1920s did not directly experience the controversy and initially were kept from entering the North American religious mainstream by the German language barrier. Gradually, an awareness of North American issues grew, and their Baptist connections tended to move them more toward the fundamentalist wing—both toward radicals like Aberhart and the more moderate Fellowship groups. In contrast, many Mennonite Brethren remained critical of the dogmatism and exclusiveness of Baptists.

3) In some instances Mennonite Brethren have clearly felt a greater degree of compatibility with Baptists than with other Mennonites. Perhaps Ontario and Quebec illustrate this most clearly. Mennonite Brethren in Ontario did not even share a common ethnic and cultural heritage with most other Mennonites in that area, who were mostly of Swiss-South German origin. At the theological level Mennonite Brethren often found more in common with Baptists—perhaps reflecting their history in Russia.[45] Other Mennonites were often considered theologically more liberal or culturally more conservative.

In Quebec the pioneer Mennonite Brethren missionaries clearly felt that they had more in common with Baptists than with other Mennonite groups who were also active in the vicinity. Their more "evangelical" or "fundamentalist" identity was the attractive quality.

On the prairies, Mennonite Brethren related more to General Conference Mennonites than to Baptists, both because they shared a common heritage and because frequently they lived in the same rural communities. Baptist connections were most frequently in areas of church planting, in theological institutions, and, sometimes, in urban areas where there were German Baptists who shared linguistic and cultural traits.

Although this essay concentrated on direct relationships between Mennonite Brethren and Baptists, it should be noted that there has been significant interaction at broader levels. The Believers Church Conference in Winnipeg in 1978 involved mostly Baptists and Mennonites, including many Mennonite Brethren. Similarly, the Mennonite Central Committee has cooperated with Baptists on a variety of issues and projects. The Canadian Foodgrains Bank, which began under MCC auspices, now involves a partnership of various groups, including MCC and the Canadian Baptist Federation. The Evangelical Fellowship of Canada brings Mennonite Brethren together with many Baptists and evangelicals of other denominations. The prospects appear to be bright for more dialogue, understanding, and cooperation in the future as Mennonite Brethren increasingly see themselves as a significant part of the larger evangelical community in Canada. The challenge will be for them to see such interaction as an opportunity to share their vision of the church and discipleship while opening themselves to the contributions which Baptists and others can make to their own faith and witness.

Augustus H. Strong: Baptist Theologian for the Mennonite Brethren

When the Mennonite Brethren describe the theological influences that have shaped their tradition they customarily refer to the impact of movements like German Pietism, American Fundamentalism and Dutch-Swiss Anabaptism. Well known names accompanying these movements are Eduard Wüst, J. Gresham Machen, and Harold S. Bender. Much less familiar is the unexpected name of Augustus Hopkins Strong, the leading North American Baptist Conference theologian, educator, and author. In some ways an unlikely candidate, Strong turns out to be a more significant Baptist connection than the Mennonite Brethren students of that generation might have imagined. The impact of this (Northern) Baptist theologian on Mennonite Brethren theology is both varied and important.

A PROFILE OF STRONG AS SYSTEMATIC THEOLOGIAN

Augustus H. Strong was born in 1836 in Rochester, New York. He graduated from Yale (1857) and Rochester Theological Seminary (1859), and studied a year at the University of Berlin. As an ordained minister, he served in two pastorates. He was active in the life of the North American Baptist Conference serving as president of its Missionary Union and of the national convention. Strong was president of Rochester Theological Seminary for forty years, from 1872 to 1912. During a major part of that long tenure, his influence extended to the broader American religious culture. He died in 1921 in Rochester.[1]

Strong's mature thought is most comprehensively reflected in the 1907 edition of his *Systematic Theology*, the three-volume work for which he is best known.[2] In it, he sought "to maintain traditional orthodoxy within the Calvinistic framework while adopting both evolutionary thought and biblical higher criticism."³ His deep conviction that conservative, orthodox theology must engage modern thought led him to attempt a "synthesis of historic Christian faith and personal idealism." He sought to undergird a biblical theology with contemporary philosophical themes that have roots in Platonism.⁴ As a result, he gradually came to the conviction that a singular, integrative view of reality (monism) that makes room for the transcendence of God and the separate human personality. That understanding recognized the ethical issues posed by the great problems of modern philosophy and theology—freedom, responsibility, sin, and guilt.⁵

Over time he shifted from a Reformed Federal theology to an ethical monism.⁶ The "radical immanence of Christ in creation became his key for balancing [the] tension" between orthodox and modern thought. His "views of creation, providence, inspiration, human sinfulness, divine justice, atonement, and world missions were shaped by this principle."⁷ Significant disagreement exists as to how successful Strong was in attempting this 'new' synthesis between theological orthodoxy and modern thought, or whether such an endeavor was even possible. Yet, Strong's efforts towered above most theologians of his generation.

Of historical importance is the fact that Mennonite Brethren theological education intersected at several points with Strong's theology. Before World War I, a significant number of American MB church leaders studied under Strong at Rochester Theological Seminary. After World War II, about a dozen Mennonite Brethren studied at Central Baptist Theological Seminary in Kansas where Strong's *Systematic Theology* was widely used. Undoubtedly Mennonite Brethren studying at other conservative seminaries were also exposed to Strong.⁸ His *Systematic Theology* was also used as a text in courses at the Mennonite Brethren Bible College (MBBC) in Winnipeg, Manitoba; at Tabor College, Hillsboro, Kansas; and at the Mennonite Brethren Biblical Seminary (MBBS) in Fresno, California.⁹ Its use at the MB Bible institute level was minimal. At Mennonite Brethren Bible College, however, it was a primary theology text for more than two decades.

THE USE OF STRONG AT MENNONITE BRETHREN BIBLE COLLEGE

Since Mennonite Brethren Bible College was the main center

of theological training for leadership and laity in the Mennonite Brethren Church in Canada, the extensive use of Strong for a generation of theological education is significant.[10] A series of prominent Canadian Mennonite Brethren churchmen used Strong in their systematic theology courses at MBBC.[11] Considering the major role Mennonite Brethren Bible College graduates have had on the theological ethos of the Canadian conference of Mennonite Brethren churches and its other training institutions, this Baptist connection is most significant.[12]

J. A. Toews' Use of Strong's *Systematic Theology*

Strong's influence at Mennonite Brethren Bible College came largely through the instruction of John A. Toews. Born in Russia and educated in Canada and the United States, Toews taught at MBBC from 1947-1967 and again from 1976-1979. He also was president from 1956-1963. He served the Mennonite Brethren church nationally and internationally through his preaching, writing, boardsmanship, and leadership as moderator at the provincial, national and general conference levels.[13]

During his long career at Mennonite Brethren Bible College, he taught a wide spectrum of courses in Bible, history, theology, and practical ministries.[14] *Systematic Theology* was the course he taught most frequently. He taught one of the two sections virtually every quarter. Toews' use of Strong's three-volume *Systematic Theology* for almost two decades represented the most sustained use of Strong in MB theological education. Combined with the fact that Toews left over 300 pages of single-spaced, carefully handwritten (and often typewritten) notes, there is ample data for a case study of Baptist-Mennonite Brethren connections.

Whether Toews was fully aware of Strong's place and purpose in the broader theological arena, or even in his own Baptist denomination, is uncertain. What is more clear, however, was his actual engagement with Strong's *Systematics*. At times it reflected a straightforward, uncritical embrace of central facets of Strong's position. At other's it showed a guarded critique of aspects of his thought; and, on occasion, Toews seemingly rejected outright, sections of Strong's theology.

Toews' extensive set of lecture notes on Strong begin with

some preliminary observations.[15] He offered an evaluation of Strong's *Systematics*, expressing the difficulty in choosing an appropriate text, and cited the positive and negative features of Strong's text. Positively, it was comprehensive, logically organized, and provided a philosophical analysis that related theology to world views. Negatively, it was coldly intellectual (lacking an experiential approach), compromising with contemporary speculative thought (yielding to evolution and higher biblical criticism, and compromising the biblical doctrines of creation, inspiration, and election.)

Toews then discussed the various problems and approaches to theology, showing keen awareness of some of the issues related to theological epistemology. He expressed concern regarding the lack of theologizing in the Anabaptist-Mennonite tradition, permitting, for example, Mennonite Brethren leaders to rely too much on Lutheran and Baptist theologies. There is a touch of irony here in view of Toews' heavy reliance on the premiere Baptist theologian of the day. Yet his point regarding the lack of theological resources and sustained theological reflection in the Mennonite Brethren tradition remains valid. He used Strong to fill that void.

Toews' lectures had the express purpose of helping the student find direction through "general principles and patterns" as outlined in Strong's systematics. He provided a careful summary and analysis of each of the eight sections that make up the three-volume systematics: (1) Prolegomena, (2) Existence of God, (3) The Scriptures a Revelation from God, (4) The Nature, Decrees, and Works of God, (5) Anthropology, or the Doctrine of Hu(man)ity, (6) Soteriology, or the Doctrine of Salvation through the Work of Christ and of the Holy Spirit, (7) Ecclesiology, or the Doctrine of the Church, (8) Eschatology, or the Doctrine of Final Things. He followed Strong closely throughout the duration of his course, yet freely supplemented, expanded or replaced Strong's material from other sources. Significantly, Toews omitted the subsections on the revelation and inspiration of Scripture and the ordinances of the church, and entirely left out the last section on eschatology.[16]

The impact of Strong on MBBC students was heavily filtered through the lecture materials, personality, and style of J.A. Toews. Yet one must not underestimate the influence that came through the discipline of mastering the Strong text and Toews' supplemental lectures. The students who studied under Toews were tested twice each semester on their understanding of Strong. There is an extensive set of examinations (midterms and finals) on all the materials in Toews' lecture notes and Strong's volume as taught in several courses over a period of two decades. The first exams consist of a long list of "true or false" questions that tested the student on the specifics of Strong's theology. The second set of questions asked students to define, discuss, and analyze or evaluate. The questions reflect an intention to master Strong's material, and to inculcate his perspective, more than to critically evaluate.

In the late 1950s and early 1960s Toews introduced materials relating to neo-orthodox theology. He also increasingly focused on methodological issues regarding the aim and purpose of theology and the task of the different disciplines (e.g., relationship of Old Testament and New Testament, hermeneutical principles used in interpretation, and the respective tasks of biblical and systematic theology). His exams questioned all these issues as well as prolegomena issues (epistemological and metaphysical) relating to God's existence.

Toews' exams tested the student on general theories about various doctrines and the significant persons or historical movements associated with them. Not only were Strong's views tested, but also the views of others, as represented by Strong. Periodically, Toews provided questions that reflected his critical stance toward a view and which asked students to substantiate it (for example Strong's view of election). In later exams, he asked for more critical evaluations, involving basic issues such as analyzing philosophical assumptions underlying Strong's view of regeneration. However, Toews did not use exams to question Strong's basic approach in any major way, rather he designed questions to permit distancing and rejection of certain theological specifics.

Reflections on Toews' Use of Strong's *Systematic Theology*

Toews followed Strong with remarkable care and affinity in most areas of Christian doctrine. Although he felt some reservations regarding classical systematic "methodology," Toews extensively used the broad resources of Strong's systematics in placing the full range of doctrinal issues before the student. In his presentation of Strong, Toews offered varying degrees of affirmation and reservation regarding three major areas of Strong's theology.

Epistemology. Toews followed Strong closely in presenting the classical epistemological and metaphysical issues about the existence and knowledge of God (clearly expressed throughout the first three major sections of his work). Toews would define, however, the nature and role of theology more relationally and practically than Strong. Noticeably, he departed from Strong on the doctrine of inspiration. Strong's epistemology relative to Scripture was so unacceptable to Toews that he omitted it altogether.

This omission is not insignificant since, as James Garrett points out, Strong "gave considerable attention to the doctrine of inspiration."[17] As early as 1880, according to Garrett, Strong "refuted both the mechanical dictation theory of inspiration and the theory that God inspired only the general ideas of authors." Instead, he used the analogy of the Spirit-filled preacher to advocate "a mediating position concerning inspiration, namely, 'the whole-souled movement of the man under the influence of the indwelling Spirit.'"[18] Garrett points out how Strong not only refuted the dictation, intuition, and illumination theories of inspiration in *Systematic Theology*, but also he "more favorably advances the 'Dynamical Theory,' according to which inspiration is 'supernatural, plenary, and dynamical.'"[19]

Strong, however, was reluctant to defend any theory of inspiration. Scripture records special revelations of God. Revelation, thus, was a corrective to human ideas and was essentially trustworthy and sufficient for its religious purposes.[20] Carl Henry states that for Strong "no one theory of inspiration is necessary to the Christian faith, although whatever theory is framed 'should be the result of a strict induction of the Scripture facts, and not an a priori scheme to which Scripture must be conformed.'"[21] Thus, for Strong "inspiration may retain every imperfection consistent with truth in a human composition, for it presents divine truth in human forms."[22] Henry says that for Strong "inspiration guarantees inerrancy only in things essential to the main purpose of the Scripture, and can accomplish its purpose through writings in some respects imperfect. It did not generally involve 'a direct communication . . . in the words.'"[23] Strong said:

> Despite imperfections in non-essential matters, the Bible furnishes "a safe and sufficient guide to truth

and to salvation." The presence of historical and scientific errors does not involve the necessity of error in morality and religion. For "as in creation and in Christ, so in Scripture, God humbles himself to adopt human and imperfect methods of self-revelation." The unity and authority of the Bible are "entirely consistent with its gradual evolution and with great imperfection in its non-essential parts."[24]

Strong accepted historical and scientific imperfections as consistent with a dynamic view of inspiration. He allowed for composite authorship at different times and dramatic compositions of later dates (e.g., Jonah, Daniel, Isaiah).[25]

Undoubtedly, Toews had difficulty in presenting such a view of Scripture in the context of MB education. To be sure Toews' presentation of Strong's ideas represented a standard, conservative, evangelical, if not fundamentalistic, reading of Strong. However, in the theologically partisan world of the mid-twentieth century, Toews found it necessary to omit entirely Strong's section on inspiration. He was convinced that Strong, in comparison to the Mennonite Brethren, had drunk too deeply at the well of modern thought on this most critical theological issue.[26]

Yet it was precisely in Strong's doctrine of inspiration and revelation that Toews might have been able to integrate his increasingly explicit Anabaptist historiography with a more accommodating and mediating, orthodox epistemology. That he did not pursue that possibility reflects a certain ambiguity and tension in Toews' mind regarding the relationship between tradition and history. That tension, however, was increasingly resolved as Toews progressively affirmed the Anabaptist roots of his tradition. Nonetheless, Toews' use of Strong represented a continuing dilemma for him, personally, and a symbolic one for the Mennonite Brethren tradition. The theology of Scripture, the relation of Scripture to theology, and the relationship of theology and history is an enduring problem for the Mennonite Brethren tradition.

Theology. The second area relates to "theology" proper. In the classical debate, Toews followed Strong's position regarding the organization of the attributes of God. Since Strong retained the distinction between substance (i.e., divine essence) and attributes, Toews emphasized the invariability of God's holiness, a fundamental characteristic which required propitiation. He, likewise, followed Strong in his trinitarian formulations. Toews departed, however, most noticeably from Strong on the doctrine of the decrees of God. He concurred, with Strong, that they involve fruitless speculation. While Strong quoted extensively from philosophical theists, Toews felt, no doubt, that biblical support was lacking regarding the decrees theology. In contrast, Strong provided more direct biblical warrants for the trinitarian position he took. Toews also questioned Strong's doctrine of creation (a work of God) which he felt was too accommodating to modern thought. For Strong the doctrine of creation was not bound to the phrase "creation out of nothing," which he thought a philosophical rather than a biblical notion. He preferred the phrase "without use of preexisting materials." Thus the "new conception of 'nature as the expression of the divine mind and will' should make creation more comprehensible . . . than the old conception of the 'word as substance capable of existing apart from God.'"[27] This formulation, reflecting the influence of the new dynamic immanentism on Strong, emphasized the positive, divine agency in creation.[28] Clearly, Strong believed in a theistic evolution.

For most conservative evangelicals, including Toews, such a view represented too great a concession to the evolutionary drift of modern thought. In Anabaptist-Mennonite theology, God's continuous willing leaves room for human freedom, responsibility, sin and guilt. Toews, for example, affirmed the freedom of the human will. Regarding the doctrines of creation and the decrees, however, Toews distanced himself. He also avoided what he considered the more speculative and modernistic aspects of Strong as well as his Calvinistic tendencies.[29]

Soteriology. Strong's anthropology and Christology were soteriologically oriented. Toews closely followed Strong's understanding of human nature and its relation to the saving activity of God. Although he questioned Strong's conception of the relationship between the human and divine (a theistic evolutionism), Toews generally affirmed Strong's doctrines of human nature and sin. They seemed to agree with Toews' Anabaptist-Mennonite proclivities in theological anthropology. Thus he endorsed Strong's concepts regarding human freedom, will and intellect. Likewise, Toews adhered to Strong's modified, kenosis Christology and the centrality of Christ. Strong's emphasis on substitution alongside that of sharing—substitution (external) as also sharing (internal)—seemed to fit well with Toews' believers' church soteriology. It deemphasized the external, mechanical implications of, for example, the Anselmic commercial theory, or the federal headship view of the atonement in Princeton theology.[30]

However, Toews' most sustained critique was of Strong's doctrine of election. Toews faulted Strong for emphasizing divine sovereignty more than human freedom. In essence, Toews found Strong's doctrine of sin too Augustinian and his doctrine of salvation too Calvinistic. Toews, more than Strong, focused on the dimensions of faith and human response. He saw the Bible emphasizing God's sovereignty in terms of divine initiative rather than decrees. In turn, human response came through regeneration, conversion, justification, sanctification, and perseverance—to use Strong's terminology—which resulted in a dynamic union with Christ.

THE MEANING OF STRONG FOR MENNONITE BRETHREN THEOLOGY

Strong's (Reformed) Baptist theology significantly shaped the mind of Toews. One cannot teach the comprehensive system of a major theologian for two decades without being shaped by the interaction. It is equally certain that Toews' long-term instruction of Strong had a cumulative effect on the theological orientation of the students and their subsequent roles in church leadership and ministry.[31] The precise nature of that impact becomes clearer when both Toews and Strong are placed in the larger historical and theological currents of Mennonite Brethren history.

Theological Education at MBBC in Historical Perspective

In the essay, "The Changing Role of Biblical/Theological Education in the Mennonite Brethren Church," Abe J. Dueck locates major transitions in theological education which took place among Canadian Mennonite Brethren since World War II. Against the backdrop of Mennonite Brethren origins in Russia, Dueck traces the development of two, parallel, theological streams. Both had their roots

201

in the old world. The one stream, originating in the Baptist Theological Seminary of Hamburg and in the Blankenburg conferences in Germany, introduced into Mennonite Brethren theology "a distinctive (dispensational) system of biblical interpretation."[32] This theological stream was reinforced, in varying degrees, by North American fundamentalism, and mediated in Canada by leaders like Jakob Reimer and William J. Bestvater. It promoted a dispensationalist-fundamentalist hermeneutic and made deep inroads into the Canadian Mennonite Brethren churches.

The second stream focused not only on biblical interpretation but also on broader theological issues. It was also "more involved in the study of issues pertaining to Mennonite history."[33] Abraham H. Unruh, the first president of Mennonite Brethren Bible College, was the individual most responsible for mediating this stream in Canada. Unruh was a man of "considerable depth and learning, and had a 'liberal' concept of higher theological education."[34] His theological orientation was more mainstream and moderate.

Thus the emerging identity of Canadian Mennonite Brethren was forged out of an ongoing dialectic (existing since its beginning) between a dispensationalist-oriented theology that provided grounds for fundamentalist influences, and a moderate and more expansive theology that reinforced (and was reinforced) by mainstream Mennonite and Evangelical proclivities. Both were strengthened by movements emerging, or already established, in North America.

It was out of the second stream that Mennonite Brethren Bible College was founded, and its identity forged. In the post-war period, Mennonite Brethren found themselves groping for theological identity in the context of a dynamic religious process where the original fundamentalist movement divided into two movements (evangelicalism and separatist fundamentalism) together with the rediscovery of the Anabaptist vision.[35]

From the late 1940s into the 1960s, John A. Toews became an influential leader and teacher in Canada. He significantly shaped Mennonite Brethren theological identity and epitomized the best of that development. The new Evangelicalism (relating to methods of biblical scholarship) and the new Anabaptism (as defined by Harold S. Bender in relation to history, theology, and ethics) were at the heart of his thinking.

Therefore, Toews' use of Strong must be understood in the context of this marriage of the new Evangelicalism and the new Anabaptism. Although Toews mediated the more conservative Strong, his interpretation of Strong nudged the Mennonite Brethren theological debate into broader classical Christian (albeit Reformed-Baptist) issues. Strong's more expansive and mainstream theology moderated the more constrictive impact of fundamentalist dispensationalism during this generation. Thus Toews' and other Mennonite Brethren Bible College faculty's use of Strong made an important, if not decisive, contribution in providing a more moderate tone and furnishing a more expansive theological agenda.[36]

Strong and the Problem of Historical Consciousness

To understand the significance of the Mennonite Brethren relying heavily on a Baptist like Strong, we need another perspective. We must locate the meaning of Strong's theology in a broader religious milieu.

In *Augustus H. Strong and the Dilemma of Historical Consciousness,* Grant Wacker contends that Strong's life spans a major intellectual transition from orthodox rationalism to historical consciousness in western culture and religious thought.[37] Wacker seeks to understand the meaning and impact of Strong's theology in terms of the glacial confrontation between orthodox rationalism and historical consciousness in American culture. His thesis is "that Strong is best understood as a tragic figure, forced to choose between incompatible yet, in his judgment, equally cogent conceptual worlds."[38]

Strong's dilemma was not unique but became paradigmatic for a whole generation of Protestant ministers trained in the Strong tradition. For Wacker "the conflict between orthodox rationalism and the modern world was not basically a dispute about doctrine, but a dispute about underlying epistemic assumptions."[39] He observed:

> Most Protestant conservatives and virtually all fundamentalists . . . rejected the whole business with scarcely a second thought. Yet there were a few conservatives, such as Augustus H. Strong, who took these questions with utmost seriousness be-

cause they knew that they had no choice. At the same time they clung to the conviction that the truths—or at least the essential truths—summarized in the great creeds of Christendom had somehow eluded the grip of historical process."[40]

Wacker then tries "to show how modern notions of social and cultural process slowly, almost imperceptibly, undermined the elaborate framework of orthodox rationalism that (Strong) had inherited and used to uphold his philosophical and theological system."[41] In the end, Strong's theology contained a deep ambivalence. On the one hand, he wanted to affirm the historical process and method. On the other, he continued to affirm the changelessness of God's truth.[42] This theological ambivalence kept him "strung between the poles of doctrinal regularity and historical awareness."[43]

Wacker makes a persuasive case that Strong's efforts were "to wed tradition and modernity," but that "was not what most persons were looking for. . . . No one seems to have believed that Strong offered the solution."[44] Both liberals and conservatives liked to use him but in the end neither really claimed him as their own.[45]

Historical Consciousness and the Tale of Two Men

Strong tried to find a mediating position just as the boundaries were being drawn for the major theological battle of the twentieth century. Toews, half a century later—and in the midst of an ethnoreligious tradition being introduced to modernity—found himself to be one of the prime leaders in bringing the Mennonite Brethren tradition into its own historical consciousness. Thus, Strong and Toews (and MBBC), in very different ways, played comparable roles in their respective denominations.

Wacker concedes that ultimately Strong patched together a workable synthesis between inherited doctrine and modernity. It was, however, an accommodation, a forced marriage without romance or genuine attraction. "In the final analysis his work is . . . best described as an uneasy and . . . tragic effort to hold incompatible worlds together."[46] Yet, for Wacker, Strong's continuing relevance was precisely because of the tension between tradition and modernity.

Toews' use of Strong at Mennonite Brethren Bible College also represents a workable accommodation of orthodoxy and modernity in the context of a Mennonite ethno-religious "tradition" seeking theological identity through a gradual rediscovery of its own "history." A generation after Strong, Toews used his theology, not so much to provide a mediating position between orthodoxy and modernity, as to provide an expansionary framework for moving students from a narrow sectarian theology to a broader conception of the nature and task of theology within a conservative, orthodox, and Evangelical-Anabaptist framework. Strong served as an important, if not decisive tool, for enlarging the theological horizons of Mennonite Brethren students whose exposure to the broader Christian tradition was minimal, if not negligible.

Toews' primary use of the conservative orthodox side of Strong had a limiting influence on Mennonite Brethren theology. Toews' use of him brought not only an orthodoxy (rationalism) into MB theologizing, but also introduced an unfamiliar method of theologizing into MB theological education.

The rationalism and ahistoricism of Strong's theology was somewhat of an enigma for Mennonite Brethren theologizing. Strong's theologizing remained foreign to a tradition grounded more firmly in its own history. Though Strong was interested in the questions of the late nineteenth and early twentieth century, his theological framework did not easily permit the incorporation of other theological narratives, particularly one insisting on a historical understanding of biblical revelation.

Toews' engagement of the question of modernity and historical consciousness cannot be defined solely, or even primarily, in terms of his use of Strong. Rather, his role, as historian, was to make Mennonite Brethren more conscious of their own Anabaptist theological history and identity.[47] As the primary instructor in the book of Acts, Toews more than Strong, made a notable shift from tradition to history, from orthodoxy to modernity. Toews the theologian was increasingly tempered by Toews the historian in making the break with tradition. To be sure, Toews had the advantage of living later in the more historicized ethos of the mid-twentieth century. Yet the basic difference between the two men lay in the fact that Toews more easily accepted God's truth being revealed through the particularities of history.

Toews, through his use of Strong, symbolized microcosmically in the Mennonite Brethren context what Strong symbolized macrocosmically in the broader North American religious context, namely, the clear intent to push beyond the constrictive boundaries of fundamentalist orthodoxy (whether Evangelical or Mennonite) and provide some sort of a synthesis between tradition and the modern context. On the Mennonite side, Toews, via history, accomplished this through his promotion of the Anabaptist vision appropriate for the Mennonite Brethren.

What Wacker writes of Strong is equally true of Toews. Neither Strong nor Toews were men "who towered above their age"; nor men "who disdained to be touched by it"; and certainly not men "who lived ahead of it." They were "touchingly human figures: too conservative to discard the nurture of their youth, too honest to discount their own religious experiences, yet too intelligent and well-read to ignore the verdict that the modern understanding of history had rendered on the case for orthodoxy."[48]

If Toews was like Strong, he also differed from him in a significant way. Both because of, and in spite of, Toews' use of Strong, he was able to avoid being tragically caught in the modernist-historicist dilemma. He was more historically conscious and more easily able to move from tradition to history. Mennonite Brethren are indebted to Toews for this significant transitional role. On the other hand, the use of Strong posed a major dilemma for Toews and Mennonite Brethren theological education. Toews' own intellectual pilgrimage and scholarly efforts contributed to an increasing discrepancy and enduring theological tension internal to the tradition.

MENNONITE BRETHREN THEOLOGICAL IDENTITY AND THE LEGACY OF STRONG

The purpose of this essay is to illuminate the development of Mennonite Brethren theological identity as it intersected, at one point, with the theology of Strong. The first section described Toews' use of Strong at Mennonite Brethren Bible College, identifying three areas of significance—epistemology, theology, and soteriology. The second section explored the meaning of that intersection from a broader denominational as well as cultural and theological perspectives. Now we turn to considering what Mennonite Brethren did not receive from Strong, and what continue to be enduring issues in Mennonite Brethren theology.

The Problem of Historical Consciousness

Toews did not use Strong to explore the larger epistemological issues related to the interface of orthodox rationalism and historical consciousness.[49] Mennonite Brethren theology had little, if any, conception of the modern form of this problem. Still, Toews' use of Strong at MBBC, centrally raised the epistemological question. It became increasingly evident that Toews' use of Strong was not merely a short-term asset in providing a theological orientation for Mennonite Brethren in the absence of one. Rather it symbolized a fundamental problem with which the MB tradition continues to struggle: the problem of historical consciousness and what form it should take in theological education.

In the last chapter of his study, Wacker attempts to put into perspective some ways in which thoughtful Protestants responded to this historic confrontation between the two conceptual worlds of orthodoxy and modernity. He suggested four "persistent patterns": 1) consistent ahistoricism, 2) accommodating ahistoricism, 3) accommodating historicism, and 4) consistent historicism.[50] Wacker contends that Strong moved from the second form of historical consciousness to the third, and then returned to the second toward the end of his career. It is reasonable to contend that Toews, more consistently than Strong, moved from the first to the second, and perhaps to the third toward the end of his career. The tension at Mennonite Brethren Bible College during Toews' early tenure was, at times, between the first and second forms of historical consciousness. Toews' reluctance to even deal with Strong's doctrine of Scripture is illustrative of that tension.

Yet, inspite of these tensions at the college, or in the constituency, very few academically trained Mennonite Brethren individuals in Canada promoted what might be considered a rigid orthodoxy or a historical fundamentalist theology. According to Dueck, those influences came primarily at the popular level and contributed significantly to "the ambivalent attitudes toward the intellectual aspects of the faith and toward education which are prevalent in fundamentalism." Consequently, "Mennonite Brethren really don't know who their closest theological kin in America are and will continue to struggle until a more common basis for theological education is established."[51] Toews' use of the progressive Strong during the formative decades of Mennonite Brethren Bible College partly addressed the problem. It also illuminated the problem since Strong's systematic theology was largely ahistorical.

The Nature and Role of Theology

The use of Strong's *Systematics* at a Mennonite Bible college presented a highly significant issue: namely, what is the nature and role of theology with respect to the Bible and history? Toews followed classical understandings in his instruction of systematics which raised some fundamental questions for Mennonite Brethren theology.

First, the tradition itself was historically suspect of systematic theologies, especially those that gravitated to a philosophical mode of discourse. Second, even granted a certain legitimacy of the use of Strong, the next generation of Mennonite Brethren scholars (not to mention some of Toews' contemporaries), judged the use of Strong to be of secondary importance, if not anachronistic. This judgment may not be entirely justified; but it does raise the question of what mode MB (and Mennonite) theologizing should take, and to what degree Strong contributed toward, or detracted from, the task of theological identity-formation.

Strong's systematics fits clearly into one of the major historical types concerning the nature and role of theology. The major models of Christian theology can be classified as knowledge, as science, as practice, as hermeneutics, as confession. Strong's systematics falls into the classical model of theology conceptualized as science. Of all the models, ironically, this one is the most distant from the Anabaptist, and therefore, the Mennonite Brethren tradition—even if one factors into Mennonite Brethren identity a significant Pietist influence. This model does not provide for the deepest instincts in the faith-narrative of the Mennonite tradition. It certainly reveals the tension in a tradition whose theology has been largely implicit, but increasingly made explicit through its strong embrace of the twentieth-century biblical theology movement.

To be sure, the model that Strong embodied has the advantage of reminding Mennonite Brethren, together with all Christians, that good theology does not neglect doctrine; and that right theology does not pull back from rigorous intellectual pursuit. However, it did not sufficiently reinforce the fact that theology must be inextricably linked to knowledge as wisdom, to praxis and experience, to interaction and confession. While Strong may have been useful at a particular juncture (in the absence of theological resources, and in the popular context of an anti-intellectualism) to assist Mennonite Brethren in theological education, his theology did not articulate and embody the deepest theological instincts and needs of the tradition. Strong may have helped Mennonite Brethren begin to understand the nature and necessity of the more full-orbed task of theology in the past generation, but his model of theology cannot be the standard by which they shape their understanding of the nature and necessity of theology. In this respect, Strong illustrated an enduring problem for the MB (and Mennonite) theological tradition: namely, the nature and role of systematic theology. The answer to that question remains in its formative stage.

The Place of Theological Ethics

The ambiguity regarding the nature and role of theology in the Mennonite Brethren tradition has consequences for the place of theological ethics. For a tradition in which the premiere theological emphasis has been on personal faith and discipleship, the use of Strong's theology symbolized this problem. It represented a theological framework that excluded the entire field of theological ethics.

It is true that Strong recognized the great ethical facts of Christian theology—freedom, responsibility, sin, and guilt—and that Toews affirmed the Baptistic slant that Strong provided. However, his use of Strong's formal, rationalistic, and objectivist theology (Reformed-Baptistic influence) reinforced the informal, experiential, and subjectivistic side (German Pietistic influence) of the Mennonite Brethren tradition since neither permit a naturally strong incorporation of ethics into their theology. To the degree that Mennonite Brethren appropriated that ethical accent, they are indebted more to their Anabaptist origins than to Strong's influences upon them. Thus the dark side of the MB's distinctive, theological trait and Strong's systematic theology created a major lacuna in Mennonite Brethren theological education. Such an omission contributed to reducing Mennonite Brethren understanding of the gospel and the task of theology.[52]

A *de facto* endorsement (through the use of Strong) of a "great divide" between doctrine and ethics not only robbed the tradition of a badly needed integrative approach to theology, but, in the end, it also reduced significantly the role of theology in the actual life of the church. Separating theology and ethics continues to be an issue for the MB (and Mennonite) tradition. The use of Strong's systematics a generation ago is not only illustrative of this enduring problem, but also reinforced an inherent tendency in the larger Mennonite tradition.

Strong is useful for helping us understand Mennonite Brethren theology in light of what Wacker calls the "upheaval that wrenched the foundations of late nineteenth-century Protestant thought."[53] Wacker argues that Strong was caught in a major, and tragic dilemma precipitated by the confrontation of two worlds. He symbolized both the difficulty and the challenge for Christian theology in a time of crisis, when there was a geological shift of paradigms, the effects of which we still experience today.

For over two decades, Strong's theology represented a challenge for theological students at MBBC. One and even two generations after Strong, they studied in a theological environment and cultural milieu where his theology could still expand the theological horizons of a conservative (and sometimes sectarian) mindset. However, the use of his *Systematics* increasingly symbolized and illustrated theological problems endemic to the MB (and Mennonite) tradition. The present generation will no longer be able to use Strong (or theologies like his) as J.A. Toews' generation did at MBBC. However, the life and thought of this Baptist theologian can encourage us to think and act so that an identifiably Christian witness will continue to exist in an emerging, postmodern culture where the clash of major world views presents all of the opportunities and obstacles they did for Strong a century ago.

JAMES WM. McCLENDON, JR.

The Mennonite and Baptist Vision[1]

However diverse they may otherwise be, readers of a book such as the present one share some concerns. Perhaps these can be grouped under three headings. One concern is *historical*: where have the communities with whom we pray and break bread together originated? What is their true source? Such inquiry is not merely a quest for information, but a drive toward self-understanding; we *embody* our spiritual ancestors; we know who we are when we identify them. Not everyone cares about the past, but those who have worked through these pages share an interest in their own and others' history.

A second shared concern is *communitarian*, though it may at first glance divide more than it unites. How wide is the circle of our fellowship? Human beings are part of the wide human circle; some would draw a nominally smaller circle around the "religious," but is this not again all of us? Certainly a smaller circle defines those who identify themselves as Christian, and smaller still, our own group of Christians. Here, too, the matter of self-knowledge and self-definition arises. How wide, how tight, is the circle we name "our own"? If I am a Baptist, do I limit that to the General Conference Baptists or to churches connected (some tenuously connected, these days) with the Southern Baptist Convention, or if not, where do I draw the line? And if I am a Mennonite, does that term limit me to the General Conference Mennonites, or to the Mennonite Brethren, or to these Mennonite Brethren? To what margins does it extend? Are my convictions merely my own, or are they in some degree set for me by my "family" of co-believers? The problem may seem answered by asking if my religious body is one that names itself a (national or international) "Church," and more difficult if mine is a mere fellowship or association or (as some have argued about Southern Baptists) only a cooperative arrangement for financing missions. Yet in actuality the same sorts of convergence and dissension arise in either

211

polity. This is a practical question, but it is also a theological one: If theology is a communitarian task, where are the limits of the data base? To listen to no voice but one's own is solipsistic; to receive every voice alike is chaotic and contradictory; where between those two is the line of demarcation? What is the appropriate community of reference for theological work?

A third quality readers of this book are likely to share is concern about the *future*. Does a divided Christianity make sense in a world in which Christians are a struggling minority? Does Jesus' prayer "that they may all be one" (John 17:21) point the way into the future? Is ecumenism a Christian duty? What will a true ecumenism entail for the Christian body of which "my own" brothers and sisters and I are a part? These three interrelated sets of questions, about the past, the present, the future, are of common interest to present readers. This interest is not diminished, but underlined, by the fact that some will say I do not even have the questions straight. When we do get them straight, we will have answers we need.

My present contribution is to propose that Mennonites (however defined) and Baptists (however defined) have an extraordinary amount in common, that they belong together in the closest of the circles described above, and that this commonality bears upon the *past*, the *present*, and the *future*. This proposal does not mean to sweep differences under the rug. For hard-nosed historians, Mennonites have their origin as part of the sixteenth-century movement called (following the language of the oppressors) Anabaptists. Baptists originated in the seventeenth century in a movement historians call Puritan (again, not a complimentary term). For present-day sociologists, Baptists are an almost amorphous group, bridging every imaginable category of wealth and poverty, education and ignorance, fundamentalism and liberality. Mennonites are more homogeneous because they are strongly identified by ethnicity as well as by religious conviction. As for future hopes, one can argue that there is too much diversity among both Baptists and Mennonites to justify any common grouping. So I have my work cut out for me. Nevertheless, consider one initial point of convergence: neither group believes that "only we are the saved." In that agreement, neither Mennonites nor Baptists are to be classified among "sectarian" believers.[2]

I hope to show that we are neither Protestant or Catholic or Orthodox, but belong to another great Christian type, to which historians have assigned many names, but which I will call simply "baptist" (note the small b). My task is to show that baptist Christianity is a theologically coherent type of Christian faith, drawing together Mennonite and Baptist (and still other) understandings of past and present and future as well.

Those who reject the view that one group of Christians constitutes the true church, others being consigned to heresy and to hell, have another option: outward forms simply do not matter—religion is an inward affair, so that what we say and practice are matters of indifference.[3] Most Christians subscribe to this theory at least in part. Some things do not matter. These are the "adiaphora," the undecided doctrines, the variable customs, the local adaptations of the Christian way. Fourth-century Bishop Ambrose makes this point in his sage advice to a traveler: "When in Rome, do as the Romans." Yet it remains true that the Christian way is a body of practice, not merely an inward feeling. Common practices finally require common institutions as well. Only the spiritualists seek to avoid this conclusion, and their impact has been at least as divisive as any other.

Beside the ways of sectarian "orthodoxy" and individualistic spiritualism, a third option exists: the way of historical development.[4] This understanding of Christian unity acknowledges the importance of many varieties of Christian conduct, yet it holds that none is infallible or flawless. Each stream of Christian life can express part of the truth of Christ, though none has expressed it all. All the tongues make Pentecost. Yet the several streams cannot be combined by rejecting the special features of each, for each has its historic destiny to fulfill, each its own true course that must be followed if it would signify the Kingdom of God.

On this understanding, what is wanted in a true ecumenism is neither simpleminded endorsement of other churches nor simpleminded anathemas for those we dislike—or do not understand. The true ecumenists will not abandon their own tongues, their own truths, nor will they naively adopt others' ways. Instead, the task of each great Christian stream is to examine itself from within, discovering its own true witness to Christ. Only when this witness is brought fully into view can it be appropriated by the others.[5]

Viewed historically, what sort of Christians are baptists? Opinions differ. One theory, the *deviation* theory, holds that baptists are only a variety of some more basic Christian type: English and American Baptists are only Puritans, the Swiss Brethren are a variant upon the Zwinglian reform, Dutch Mennonites only a variation upon Erasmian biblicism, etc.[6] A second theory, the *successionist*, holds that Baptists, Mennonites, Anabaptists, and many others before them are genetically linked in a long causal chain rivaling Rome's. Durnbaugh, though not its advocate, gives this view fair treatment.[7]

There is a third theory, which I will call the *theory of types*, advocated by Albert Henry Newman, Roland Bainton, George Williams, John Howard Yoder, Donald Durnbaugh, and still others.[8] It sees in the baptist movement, not a successionist history, and not a mere deviation, but a recurrent type. Mennonites and modern Baptists are examples of this recurrence, originating in the sixteenth and seventeenth centuries respectively, while the Church of the Brethren is an eighteenth, and the Disciples, a nineteenth-century instance. There are other examples from other centuries—perhaps the Hussite Chelcicky movement in the fifteenth and the Pentecostal movement in the twentieth century. On this view, what is vital is not that these movements influenced one another (though no doubt they sometimes did), but that under certain circumstances they took up in turn, in their own ways, a particular understanding of the gospel and of the Christian life. This baptist type is distinctive—it has its own role and destiny in the Kingdom of Christ. For historical reasons I find persuasive, I follow this third view, without denying that there is some truth in the other views.

This brings us back to names. Some have called this movement the "Radical Reformation" (Williams) or the "Left Wing of the Reformation" (Bainton), but those names are purely historical, as is the name long favored by American Mennonite scholars, "Anabaptist," while this last one is pejorative as well.[9] Newbigin has proposed the name "Pentecostal," others have spoken of the "Free Church" (Littell) or "Believers' Church" (Durnbaugh).[10] However, "Free Church" means all things to all people, while, "Believers' Church" seems uncomfortably self-congratulatory. So as I have said I prefer "baptist" with a small *b* (the equivalent of *Täufer*) to match "catholic" with a small *c* and "protestant," with a small *p*. Yet if others choose another term than mine, I will not quarrel.

* * * * *

My central task is not to provide a name, but to call attention to the wider *movement* of which modern Mennonites and Baptists are only a part. The movement itself is the thing. The theological task is to find the true, inner light of this movement, so that its pure color may (with others) make its contribution to the white light of God's revelation in Christ. Many suggestions have been made as to this distinctive light. From a longer list, consider these candidates for "the baptist vision." First there is the *biblicist* proposal. Offered by many,[11] it is in essence this: the baptists of whatever century are the people of the Book. For example, the Swiss Brethren: Blaurock, Grebel, Mantz, Reublin, and Brötli were inspired by the biblical teaching of a priest named Zwingli. But when Zwingli counseled caution, these met in a private home to consider the Bible further. Then, "Dread began to come over them, yea, they were pressed in their hearts. . . . After the prayer, George Cajacob arose and asked Conrad Grebel to baptize him, for the sake of God, with the true Christian baptism upon his faith and knowledge. And when he knelt down with that faith and desire, Conrad baptized him. . . . After that was done the others similarly desired George to baptize them, which he also did."[12] Here, none could deny, was baptist practice. The proposal is that its core vision is biblicism. There is something right about this proposal, yet "biblicism" is not a winsome word. Biblicism smacks more of a narrow fundamentalism than of the wide-ranging baptist vision, and it fails to distinguish the baptist way of approach to Scripture, its reading strategy. (For every Christian community has some place for Scripture.) We must look further into this.

But first, consider two alternative proposals. One sees a close connection between the baptist movement and *liberty*. Here the name "Free Church" becomes relevant. The Anabaptists were feared and hated in sixteenth-century Europe, not because in one or two cases they constituted a state church and defended their Münster or Oldeklooster with arms, but because, in most places, they rejected that link between civil and church government that had been at least a 1,200 year European tradition. This liberty, which we now seem to take for granted in the West, was dearly bought by suffering martyrs in the baptist movement. Hence, Edgar Young Mullins, followed a little later by Ernst Troeltsch, understood liberty as the very essence of the baptist vision.[13] Mullins expressed this in his phrase "soul competency"—the capacity of the individual soul in all matters under God. He expanded this motto into a series of "axioms"—theological, political, ecclesiastical, and so on—that together expressed a viewpoint that was indeed baptist, but in the form of a rugged individualism perhaps better suited to early twentieth-century liberalism (as exemplified by "Rough Rider" Theodore Roosevelt) than to the Kingdom of Christ. The liberty theme might yet be adopted and socialized by today's Liberation Theology, but this is work remaining to be done, rather than an accomplishment I can report here.

The *communitarian* note (a third proposal) has been sounded by historical scholars working in the field of Anabaptist studies: Franklin H. Littell, Harold S. Bender, and John Howard Yoder in particular.[14] These have seen the organizing vision as "a view of the church" (Littell), an "Anabaptist vision" of discipleship (Bender), a recovery of "the politics of Jesus" (Yoder). Discipleship does not mean *solitary* imitation of Jesus—that is a contradiction in terms. Jesus formed an alternative community, a different kind of community, and discipleship now means sharing in a community bound like his to the way of the cross.

A little reflection will show that the second proposal and the third, liberty and community, are each defective without the other. Community without liberty is oppressive; liberty without community is chaos. Where, then, is that vision that can bind these two into one? Let us return to the beginning. The authority of the Bible must be at least a clue: baptist confessions through the centuries have pointed to it. So, how do baptists interpret the Bible? Not, I have already suggested, by an exact biblicist literalism; that is more characteristic of the Reformed movement than of baptists.[15] Such literalism caused great trouble when Reformed Puritans used it to apply Old Testament law to England and America. It creates a problem of another sort when a John Calvin finds (and imitates) one church order in the New Testament, while in a later century an Eduard Schweizer finds another order there.[16]

Let me suggest, then, that the reading strategy of the baptist vision is a narrative one. This recognizes that the story now is continuous with the story then—but to say this is not enough. By such a rule all heresies can be validated! Rather, *the story then is the story now; we are the disciples of the Gospel story; its Lord is our Lord; the Kingdom it proclaims is the Kingdom coming now.*[17]

According to Acts 2, this is the reading strategy that was employed already on the day of Pentecost. Psalm 16, Psalm 110, and Joel 2 are quoted in Acts 2 as testimonies to the crucified and risen Christ; the Hebrew Bible describes the ecstasy of the Pentecostal community! Intelligent Bible readers, in that day as well as this, must have known that if this was meant literally, it was a mistake. The Psalms were celebrations of the faith in which they had been composed long before. Joel's vision of prophecy by sons and daughters, slave and free, young and old (2:28-31) was itself an application to his own day of the earlier teaching of Moses in Numbers 11 ("Would that all God's people were prophets, that all had the Spirit"). What Joel had done in 400 B.C., Acts does again in the first century. To say "this" (what happens now) "is that" (what happened then) is not to deny the calendar or the facts of history, facts of which first-century Jewish folk had a sophisticated awareness, thanks to their own great historians. Rather the meaning, the sense, of present events is transformed by placing them in a biblical frame.

The frame gives a sense of the picture within it. Hold up a picture frame before a living human being. Let it be a Florentine frame of the *cinque cento*—the high Renaissance. Now we may be in position to say, "this is that": This living beauty is realized in a new way because of the old frame. Today's subject, this living man or woman, is seen within the frame as the Renaissance artist might have seen him or her.

Now change the image. Let it be not a still portrait but a moving picture of the church today. Let the frame be not Florentine but biblical. Let it be not a mere border but a story in its own right, and you have the prophetic vision—I say the baptist vision—a way of seeing both Scripture and present community anew as one is seen through the lines of the other. That is the vision, understood here as a distinctive reading strategy for the people of God.

* * * * *

This reading strategy occurs and recurs in the chapters of the Bible itself. According to Amos, God says to the little nation whose capital was Samaria, "I brought *you* from the land of Egypt" (2:10). "Us? Why, that happened five hundred years ago. What has it to do with us now?" Again, consider the Deuteronomist telling other parents how to be a parent. When your Jewish child says, "Papa, why do we have to keep all these rules?" tell him "We were Pharaoh's slaves in Egypt, and the Lord brought us out" (Deuteronomy 6:20f.). *We* were Pharaoh's slaves—as if it had happened to this very family, to us! This is the reading strategy those in relationship to a living, historical God employ. Nor does the New Testament lack this *prophetic* vision—else what does it mean when Jesus asks the disciples, "Who do people say that I am?" and they answer, "John the Baptist, or Elijah, or Jeremiah"? This is not reincarnationism. It is the prophetic vision, "this is that." The problem the disciples faced was *how to get that vision right.*

Is the prophetic vision also the baptist vision? If it is, it should illuminate the baptist movement through its long and varied history, and it should interpret and bind together those other possible foci of the baptist vision, liberty and community, as well. To test this interdependence, consider four true stories. The first comes from the pages of Thieleman van Braght's *Martyrs Mirror.* In 1535 the Holy Roman Emperor Charles V issued an edict requiring that those who practiced anabaptism be brought "to the most extreme punishment." There was, happily, some discrimination: Leaders must be burned to death, but mere members, if repentant, could be executed with a sword, and the women buried (alive, of course) in a pit. The next year, the alert bailiff at Zierichsee, in the Netherlands, arrested Peter Gerrits, Peter Joris, Peter Leydecker, and Johanna Mels. When these four were interrogated under the edict, they answered from the Bible, but the Burgomaster said, "We care not for your Word of God, but hold to the mandate of the emperor," warning the four that they faced death. Then they answered, "Lord Burgomaster, by this you prove yourself to be a protector of the kingdom of Babel and of Bel for which you will indeed reap some reward here on earth, but hereafter, with antichrist and the crowned beast, eternal damnation in the lake of fire."

I would like to tell you that after they provided so insightful a diagnosis, the Burgomaster set these four young baptists free. Alas, it was not so; I spare you the detail of their torture and death. "Thus," concludes *Martyrs Mirror*, "they offered up their sacrifices."[18] I would simply note that when their crisis came, the three Peters and Johanna held steadfast by their perception that "this is that." Their present peril could be understood only by reading the dramatic stories of the Old and New Testaments. They were Daniels in distress, their tormentors were the evil King Astyages and his god, Bel. Thus disciples suffering in solidarity are supported by the baptist vision.

My next story is more cheerful, though not less moving. Eighteenth-century English Baptists had nearly withered away under the reasoning of a systematic theologian named John Gill (1697-1771). Their hyper-Calvinism had led them to reject all efforts to save the lost, since such efforts contradicted the primacy of God's electing decree. Then a genius Northamptonshire shoemaker and preacher named William Carey dared to challenge that iron logic, and Carey became the means by which a missionary society was organized that sent him to India—the inauguration (1792-1793) of modern missionary methods. Those facts are well known.[19] What is less well known is that despite Carey's brilliance and eloquence, the society would hardly have been organized, or Carey sent, had not a neighboring pastor, Andrew Fuller of Kettering, supported Carey's proposal and backed it with his own solid argument. Now Fuller, like Moses, was not eloquent. Yet Herbert Skeats, in his classic nineteenth-century *History of the English Free Churches*, writes that in arguing for mission "Fuller established his almost unrivalled power as a theological controversialist. Possessed of an intellect of extraordinary grasp and ability, which, by its sheer momentum, bore down with an irresistible force upon his opponents, and acute in detecting the smallest sophistries, he was a man whose sympathy and active aid were worth the assistance of troops of ordinary adherents."[20] Fuller was opposed by ultra-Calvinists, Arminians, and Sandemanians, all of whom said he was utterly wrong; nonetheless, he swept the field before him. The Society was subscribed, and Carey went to India.

What was the non-eloquent Fuller's secret? If we consult his classic sermon, "The Gospel Worthy of All Acceptation," we find the now-familiar pattern. Fuller addresses the "this" of his earnest but mistaken listeners, mired in a rigid theology that taught preachers not to call sinners to repentance and faith (for that, they said, was "preaching the law"). To such a "this" he applies the corrective "that" of the practice of apostolic preaching as found in the New Testament. "We have," he declared, "such a compromising way of dealing with the unconverted as to have well nigh lost the spirit of the primitive preachers; and hence it is that sinners of every description can sit so quietly as they do, year after year, in our places of worship. It was not so with the hearers of Peter and Paul."[21] As I have told you, Fuller and Carey, pinning their argument (and staking their lives) upon that baptist vision of apostolic ministry, carried the day, and it is a reasonable inference that many latter day baptists are here today only because they did.

Yet these narratives, chosen from a wealth of others, are not exceptional. I shall briefly remind you of just two more. One is the story of New England's Roger Williams (1603?-1683). Williams was surrounded all his life by Puritans who sought to use the Old Testament as a handbook for civil and church government—and used it as warrant to persecute those whose religion differed from their own. Williams answered, in a series of classic writings, that Old Testament theocracy was a *type*, completely fulfilled in Christ the King. Since that was so, he reasoned, we have in the Old Testament no warrant for further fulfillment, far less imitation, of a manner of life opposite to Christ. Thus there can be no warrant in Old Testament kings and battles, or witch-burnings and persecutions, for any of these things in seventeenth-century New England.[22] Thereby Roger Williams provided a control upon typology that can guide the baptist vision in every generation: Only in faithfulness to Christ and his way can we claim identity with his disciples. Our liberty is the gift of God. Therefore, it is presumptuous for governments, preempting God's place, to cancel those gifts. Thus Williams believed we dare not, on the grounds of God's sovereignty, set up any part of our society in the place of God to rule over the human spirit. His doctrine of religious liberty was not a theory of human rights, it was merely a doctrine of the inability of men and their government to occupy the throne of Deity.

It may surprise some that I have defined the baptist vision

without special reference to its name-giver (believer's) baptism. Yet that has only been to save this paradigmatic case for last: Baptism is a *living* instance of this vision at work. For baptism, rightly practiced, is the prophetic sign of the convergence of two life stories: our Lord's and our own. In it, once again, "this is that": The "this" of my wayward journey is overtaken by the "that" of Jesus' ongoing narrative. In believer's baptism his story becomes my own as I become his; his hope, my hope; the life of the Kingdom is declared in this sign to be also my life; its Lord, my Lord.[23] Baptism is a commissioning ceremony.[24] It is the believer's "ordination" as a minister or servant of the Lord. That service is not to be different in kind from the commission Jesus lived out in his own life of ministry. Thus "this is that" means here the taking of Jesus' way to be my own way. The believer's baptism corresponds to, mystically *is*, Jesus' own baptism at the river Jordan. The acceptance of his grace as equipment for Kingdom tasks corresponds to Jesus' endowment by the Spirit of God on his baptismal day long ago.

Thus, baptism paradigmatically shows how the vision embraces both the *liberty* that some have correctly seen it must presuppose and the *community* that others have correctly understood it must entail. For in authentic baptism, the freedom of God, God's liberty to be God for us, is graciously expressed precisely in the evocation of a free human response. The youth or adult who responsibly comes to this rite evinces a freedom for God that could provide the model of all human freedom, political, economic, artistic, intellectual. In his or her free yes to God, life begins anew. Yet that same sign initiates as well a life in community, a solidarity in the disciples' task that cannot be fulfilled in a lonely individual commitment to godliness, but requires the give and take of life together expressed in baptism's partner-sign, the eucharistic meal. Here is baptism fulfilled in shared service and shared worship alike.

* * * * *

Our quest has been for an understanding of the baptist idea, its organizing theme or vision. The best expression of that idea will be one that incorporates all other, partial expressions, yet displays the uniqueness of this distinctive baptist variety of Christian faith. The stories just retold point to the power of the baptist vision to do this. When understood as "this is that," when understood, that is, as a scriptural reading strategy, this vision incorporates both liberty and community. The story of Roger Williams shows the theme of liberty dependent upon the baptist vision in which Christ only is Lord, God alone is sovereign. The story of Andrew Fuller's persuasiveness reveals a false and in-turned sense of community—the easy contentment of the elect—being overturned by that same apostolic vision. It thus issued in a revolutionary, missionary sense of community that reached out to the human need of the lost and sin-stricken in distant lands to include them as well in a redeemed community. The stories of the martyr-witnesses, on the other hand, do not seem to single out either liberty or community as such. In them, the martyrs' note of costly witness dominates both the other elements, suggesting to the thoughtful reader that no liberty of choice, and no discipleship, is adequately Christlike if it lacks the yieldedness (*Gelassenheit*) of accepting unresistingly the world's enmity and cruelty. Yet that yieldedness will not be rightly read save as the mirror of the Christ who takes up his cross to bear it and calls followers to take theirs, too. Their suffering is misguided or misconstrued if it be not Christ's own. In martyrdom supremely *this is that.*

Two lessons come into view from this lookout place we have now gained. The first is theological: those who have seen the center of baptist thought as biblical have not been wrong. The focus is Scripture before it is anything else. Yet something more emerges. Not every reading of Scripture is a baptist reading; not every appeal to the Old or New Testament is a baptist appeal. We own a distinctive reading strategy, exemplified in Scripture, that has the capacity to give a particular shape to the life of the people of God. Thus theology finds its task in the employment of this very strategy as a guiding hermeneutic for the discovery, understanding, and—God willing—creative transformation of the convictions of a people who are themselves so guided, so shaped. This understanding of the theological task may comfort "conservatives" who rejoice in the centrality of the Bible. It may also comfort "liberals" who delight in change in all earthly things. It should comfort neither to the extent that the baptist theological task calls into question the easy assumptions both parties make.

The other lesson returns us to the pentecostal scene of Acts 2, mentioned above. What sort of Christian self-understanding today can do justice to Pentecost's twin themes of variety and unity—the *variety* of tongues, peoples, responses to the Spirit, together with the *unity* of gospel and grace and God in resurrection light? I claimed that the movement some call Anabaptist, or the Free Church, and here called baptist, is neither a mere deviation from some more central type of Christian life, some True Church, nor is it, itself, that True Church—all others having simply missed the way. It is not sectarian, but it is different. That difference may have obscured for some the other Pentecostal concern: "They were all with one accord in one place" (Acts 2:1b). The baptist vision fails if it does not also point the way to Christian unity.

On the surface, God's baptist people must often seem a motley bunch of followers of the Risen One. How can others see us as one while we do not even see ourselves in clear gospel light? How can we be of one accord with other Christians, if we are not even of one accord with one another? Yet it is exactly this vision that has provided the profound unity we experience. While other Christian types have much to teach us, much to share, we have this vision to share with one another and with them—to show that "this is that," that the church, now, *is* the primitive church, that the Kingdom coming *is* the Kingdom at hand.

When asked about their Christian identity, some may be satisfied simply to refer to the current ecclesiastical organization. But theologically, is that adequate? Some Mennonites have learned to answer "Anabaptist," using the old term of reproach to stake a claim upon the past. Some (very sophisticated) Baptists may even say "Puritan," another such claim upon the past. Yet such labels go no distance at all to acknowledge the gulf that separates today's Mennonites from the sixteenth century, or today's Baptists from the seventeenth. (To say nothing of the differences that divided old Anabaptists from one another!) What if both Mennonites and Baptists learned to answer the identity question by saying "baptist" (or any other name that meant the same), i.e., present sharers of the distinctive vision that sees that *this* (what we do and are now) is to be understood only in light of *that* (what Scripture shows us of Christ Jesus), and that *then* (what God intends for us) is *now*. That would be a theological self-designation, not a historical one, but in a different way it does look to the past and finds in it our present oneness.

A parallel point can be made about our self-understanding as related to the (present and) future. If asked about the Ecumenical Movement, the Councils of Churches, and the like, some Mennonites will likely respond favorably, some not. The same is true of Baptists. If, however, either is asked about the claim that Jesus' prayer "that they all may be one" has upon us now, Mennonites and Baptists may answer alike: Though the prayer is unrealized, it expresses a *present* demand. The baptist vision, "then is now," recognizes that we must live today in light of God's intended future. This requires that we now become the people (peoples?) God intends us to be, so that others can finally see us as we truly are. My argument is that by this vision Baptists and Mennonites are even now one because we do share just such a vision of past and present and future. The rest of the ecumenical task may take more time.

Endnotes

INTRODUCTION

1. On the early history of Anabaptism in England see Irvin B. Horst, *The Radical Brethren: Anabaptism and the English Reformation to 1558* (The Hague: Nieuwkoop, B.De Graaf, 1972). On the history of English Puritanism in the Netherlands see Keith Sprunger, *Dutch Puritanism: A History of English and Scottish Churches of the Netherlands in the Sixteenth and Seventeenth Centuries* (Leiden: E.J. Brill, 1982).

2. James R. Coggins, *John Smyth's Congregation: English Separatism, Mennonite Influence and the Elect Nation* (Scottdale, Pa.: Herald Press, 1991), 44-45.

3. "Who are the Members of the Mennonite Brethren Church," *Mennonitische Blätter* 1 May 1896, 33-35; reprinted in *Zionsbote* 20 May 1896, 3; John F. Harms, "Our Answer," *Zionsbote* 20 May 1896, 3-4.

4. Frank C. Peters, "The Early Mennonite Brethren Church: Baptist or Anabaptist?," *Mennonite Life* 14 (October 1959):176-178.

5. For a description of the multiple religious currents in the Russian Mennonite world see David G. Rempel, "The Mennonite Colonies in New Russia: A Study of their Settlement and Economic Development from 1789-1914," (Ph.D. diss., Stanford University, 1933); John B. Toews, *Czars, Soviets and Mennonites* (Newton, Kan.: Faith and Life Press, 1962) and *Perilous Journey: The Mennonite Brethren in Russia, 1860-1910* (Winnipeg, Man.: Kindred Press, 1988); James Urry, *None But Saints: The Transformation of Mennonite Life in Russia, 1789-1889* (Winnipeg, Man.: Hyperion Press, 1988) and "The Social Background to the Emergence of the Mennonite Brethren in Nineteenth Century Russia," *Journal of Mennonite Studies* 6 (1988): 8-35; Harvey L. Dyck, "Russian Mennonitism and the Challenge of Russian Nationalism, 1889," *Mennonite Quarterly Review* 56 (1982):307-341; and Paul Toews, "Differing Historical Imaginations and the Changing Identity of the Mennonite Brethren," in *Anabaptism Revisited: Essays on Anabaptist/Mennonite Studies in Honor of C.J. Dyck*, ed. Walter Klaassen (Scottdale, Pa.: Herald Press, 1992):155-172.

I

SIXTEENTH-CENTURY ANABAPTISM AND THE PURITAN CONNECTION: REFLECTIONS UPON BAPTIST ORIGINS

1. The critical German text is found in Balthasar Hubmaier, Schriften, eds. Gunnar Westin and Torsten Bergsten (Gütersloh: G. Mohn, 1962), pp. 72-74.

2. John Christian Wenger, ed. and trans., *Conrad Grebel's Programmatic Letters of 1524: With Facsimiles of the Original German Script of Grebel's Letters* (Scottdale, Pa.: Herald Press, 1970), pp. 18-19.

3. George Huntston Williams and Angel M. Mergal, eds. *Spiritual and Anabaptist Writers: Documents Illustrative of the Radical Reformation*, The Library of Christian Classics, vol 25 (Philadelphia: Westminster Press, 1957), p. 76.

4. Wenger, *Grebel's Programmatic Letters*, p. 32.

5. Hubmaier, *Schriften*, pp. 95-100. See also John Howard Yoder, "The Turning Point in the Zwinglian Reformation," *Mennonite Quarterly Review* 32 (April 1958):128-140.

6. Ibid., p. 100.

7. William L. Lumpkin, *Baptist Confessions of Faith* (Valley Forge: Judson Press, 1959), p. 22.

8. J. C. Wenger, ed., *The Complete Writings of Menno Simons: c.1496-1561*, trans. Leonard Verduin (Scottdale, Pa.: Herald Press, 1956), p. 731.

9. W. T. Whitley, ed., *The Works of John Smyth, Fellow of Christ's College, 1594-1598*, 2 vols. (Cambridge: University Press, 1915), 1:158-159.

10. Ibid., p. 166.

11. Ibid.

12. Ibid., lxii.

13. See Irvin B. Horst, *Anabaptism and the English Reformation to 1558* (Nieuwkoop: De Graf, 1966).

14. James Robert Coggins, "John Smyth's Congregation: English Separatism, Dutch Mennonites and the Elect Nation," (Ph.D. dissertation, University of Waterloo, 1986), pp. 41-44.

15. William Bradford, *Of Plymouth Plantation*, ed. Harvey Wish (New York: Capricorn Books, 1962), p. 28.

16. Keith L. Sprunger, *Dutch Puritanism* (Leiden: E. J. Brill, 1982), p. 81.

17. Whitley, *The Works of John Smyth*, 1:250.

18. Ibid., p. 273.

19. Champlin Burrage, *The Early English Dissenters in the Light of Recent Research (1550-1641)* 2 vols. (Cambridge: University Press, 1912; reprint ed., New York: Russell & Russell, 1967), 1:236.

20. Ibid., p. 237.

21. Whitley, *The Works of John Smyth*, 2:572.

22. Ibid., p. 564.

23. Ibid., p. 681.

24. Lumpkin, *Baptist Confessions of Faith*, p. 114.

25. Ibid., p. 140.

26. Ernest A. Payne, *Thomas Helwys and the First Baptist Church in England* (London: Baptist Union of Great Britain and Ireland, 1966), p. 4.

27. The Hampton Court Conference in 1603 gained few concessions from King James. The one notable achievement was the king's authorization of a new translation of the English Bible. This was the year John Smyth gave up attempting to regain his position as City Lecturer in Lincoln.

28. Whitley, *The Works of John Smyth*, 1:lxii.

29. Although at one time, Richard Clifton led this congregation, it seems that by 1607 the leadership was in the hands of John Robinson.

30. Burrage, *The Early English Dissenters*, 1:232.

31. Whitley, *The Works of John Smyth*, 2:565.

32. Burrage, *The Early English Dissenters*, 1:239.

33. Whitley, *The Works of John Smyth*, 2:571.

34. Ibid., p. 572.

35. Ibid.

36. Ibid., p. 573.

37. Timothy George, "Between Pacifism and Coercion: The English Baptist Doctrine of Religious Toleration," *The Mennonite Quarterly Review* 58 (January 1984):30-49.

38. Walter H. Burgess, *John Smith the Se-Baptist, Thomas Helwys and the First Baptist Church in England; With Fresh Light Upon the Pilgrim Fathers' Church* (London: James Clarke & Co., 1911), p. 179.

39. Ibid., p. 181.

40. Ibid., p. 186.

41. John Robinson reacted vigorously to Helwys' charge that it was unchristian to seek a refuge in the Netherlands. "And for drawing over the people, I know none of the guides, but were as much drawn over by them, as drawing them. The truth is, it was Mr. Helwisse, who above all, either guides or others, furthered this passage into strange countries: and if any brought oars, he brought sails, as I could show in many particulars, and as all that were acquainted with the manner of our coming over, can witness with me. Neither is it likely, if he, and the people with him at Amsterdam, could have gone on comfortably, as they desired, that the unlawfulness heady and indiscreet courses, and otherwise disabled himself, that natural confidence, which abounded in him, took occasion, under an appearance of spiritual courage, to press him upon those desperate courses, which he, of late, hath run" (Robinson, *The Works of John Robinson; Pastor of the Pilgrim Fathers*, 3 vols. [London: John Snow, 1851], 3:159).

42. Burrage, *The Early English Dissenters*, 2:181.

43. Article six (Translation from Latin): That Jesus Christ, in the fullness of time, was manifest in the flesh, made of woman, conceived and born of her; the Holy Spirit enveloping her, fruit of her womb, seed of Abraham, of Isaac, of Jacob and of David, according to the flesh. Thus a true man, he was circumcised, baptized, he prayed, he was tempted, he experienced fear, unaware of the day of judgment, he suffered hunger, he was thirsty, he was tired, he ate, he drank, he took rest for his eyes, he grew in height and in knowledge. He was crucified, he died and was buried, he arose, he ascended into heaven, with all the power in heaven and on earth given over to him, manifest as the only king, priest and prophet of his church. In one person a true God and true man (Ibid., p. 182).

44. Ibid.

45. Ibid., p. 179.

46. Article nine (Translation from Latin): That the church is the union of the faithful people, baptized in the name of the Father, Son and Spirit at the time when they confess their faith and their sins; having the power of Christ, of foretelling the word, baptism, of administering the Lords' Supper, of choosing and rejecting its ministers, and of receiving and casting out its members according to the canons of Christ (Ibid., p. 183).

47. Ibid., p. 184.

48. (Translated from Latin) And thus through the mercy of God, according to his word, we have learned to know Christ. Nevertheless realizing that we ourselves are

simple and ignorant, and always prepared with all reverence and humility to be instructed by God through means of this type which our Lord has called forth in truth for our greater edification; and blessing God for excellent intermediaries of this type, which have been furnished in abundance by you for us, humbly calling upon our Lord Jesus Christ that through his Spirit he may direct you and us into complete truth. Let there be grace to you and peace from God our Father and from our Lord Jesus Christ (Ibid.).

49. Ibid.

50. Ibid., pp. 184-187.

51. Ibid., p. 186.

52. Ibid., pp. 186-187.

53. Burgess, *John Smith the Se-Baptist*, p. 212.

54. Burrage, *The Early English Dissenters*, 2:185.

55. Ibid., pp. 185-186.

56. Ibid., p. 186.

57. Ibid., p. 187.

58. Lumpkin, *Baptist Confessions of Faith*, p. 120.

59. Burgess, *John Smith the Se-Baptist*, p. 218.

60. Thomas Helwys, *The Mistery of Iniquity* (Notingham: Gray's Inn and Broxtowe Hall, 1612; reprint ed., London: The Kingsgate Press, 1935), xxiv.

61. Ibid., p. 69.

62. Burrage, *The Early English Dissenters*, 2:215. This petition bears all the earmarks of Helwys. Here he is arguing for equality under the law. He cites that the only crime with which he and his fellow petitioners are charged is a matter of conscience.

63. Ibid., p. 216.

64. A. C. Underwood, *A History of the English Baptists* (London: The Baptist Union of Great Britain and Ireland, 1947), pp. 50-51.

65. Sprunger, *Dutch Puritanism*, pp. 84-90.

II
BAPTIST INTERPRETATIONS OF ANABAPTIST HISTORY

1. Henry Eilas Dosker, "Early Dutch Anabaptists," in Papers of the *American Society of Church History*, ed. Samuel Mackeley Jackson (New York: Red Diamond Press, 1910), pp. 189-198. Dosker would later publish a full-length monograph on the subject: *The Dutch Anabaptists* (Philadelphia: Judson Press, 1921). This work contained the Stone Lectures he delivered at Princeton Theological Seminary in 1918-1919. The tone of this study is very different from that early lecture.

2. Dosker, "Early Dutch Anabaptists," p. 189.

3. Ibid.

4. Keller responded to his critics in *Grundfragen der Reformationsgeschichte. Eine Auseinanderstzung mit litterarischen gegnern* (Berlin: R. Gaertner, 1897).

5. As late as 1868, the Waldenses were described as follows: "For sixteen hundred years, at least, the Waldenses have guarded the pure and primitive Christianity of the Apostles. . . . No one knows when or how the faith was first delivered to these mountaineers. . . . Irenaeus, Bishop of Lyons, in the second century found them a church. . . . These gallant hill-men have kept the tradition of the Gospel committed to them as pure and inviolate as the snow upon their Alps. . . . They have maintained an Evangelical form of Christianity from the very first, rejecting image worship, infallibility, and the dogma of purgatory; taking the Scripture as the rule of life, and admitting no sacraments but Baptism and the Lord's Supper. . . . No bloodier cruelty disgraces the records of the Papacy than the persecutions endured by the ancestors of the twenty thousand Waldenses now surviving. . . . Never did men suffer more for their belief" (*London Daily Telegraph*, 30 April 1868, p. 1, quoted in Pius Melia, *The Origin, Persecutions and Doctrines of the Waldenses* [London: J. Toovey, 1870], vii).

Alexis Muston wrote, "The Vaudois (Waldenses) of the Alps, are, in our view, primitive christians, or inheritors of the primitive church, who have been preserved in these valleys from the alterations successively introduced by the church of Rome into the evangelical worship. It is not they who separated from catholicism, but catholicism which separated from them, in modifying the primitive worship. Hence the impossibility of assigning a precise date to the origin" (Muston, *The Israel of the Alps: A History of the Persecutions of the Waldenses*, trans. Wm. Hazlitt [London: Ingram, Cooke and Co., 1853], p. 1). To a certain extent, Keller and the Baptists fell prey to this kind of older scholarship.

6. E. H. Broadbent, *The Pilgrim Church* (London: Pickering & Inglis, 1955), viii.

7. Ibid., vi.

8. See his *The Dutch Anabaptists* of 1921.

9. Broadbent, *Pilgrim Church*, xi.

10. Jack Hoad, *The Baptist: An Historical and Theological Study of the Baptist Identity* (London: Grace Publications Trust, 1986), p. 19.

11. Ibid.

12. Ibid.

13. Ibid.

14. Ibid., p. 5.

15. Ibid., pp. 5-6.

16. Ibid., p. 1.

17. Brown's essay was first published in the *Baptist Memorial* in 1846 and was later published in book form by the American Baptist Publication Society of Philadelphia in 1853.

18. Ibid., p. 15.

19. Ibid., p. 16.

20. Ibid., p. 21.

21. Ibid., p. 26.

22. The first in this line of succession may well have been Thomas Crosby, *The History of the English Baptists from the Reformation to the Beginning of the Reign of King George I*, 2 vols. (London: By the Author, 1738-1740). See Robert G. Torbert, *A History of the Baptists*, 5th ed. (Valley Forge: Judson Press, 1963), p. 18.

23. Cramp, *Baptist History*, p. 54.

24. Ibid., p. 117.

25. Ibid., pp. 151-152.

26. Ibid., p. 158.

27. Ibid., pp. 212-230.

28. It seems unlikely that Cramp's first edition could have been published before 1860, since the second edition appeared in 1865 and the English and German editions in 1870 and 1871 respectively.

29. Edward Bean Underhill, *Tracts on Liberty of Conscience and Persecution 1614-1661* (London: J. Haddon, 1846; reprint ed., New York: Burt Franklin, 1966), lxxiii.

30. Ibid., lxxiv.

31. Ibid., lxxxi.

32. Ibid., lxxx.

33. Ibid., lxxiii.

34. Ibid., cxxiv.

35. John Foxe's *Acts and Monuments*, Jean Crespin's *Histoire des martyrs persécutez et mis à mort pour la vérité de l'Évangile*, and Van Braght's *Martyr's Mirror* all begin with the heretics of the Middle Ages who came into their own in the age of the Reformation, perhaps inspired by the older histories of the Waldenses. See Jeannine E. Olson, "Jean Crespin, Humanist Printer among the Reformation Martyrologists," in *The Harvest of Humanism in Central Europe*, ed. Manfred P. Fleischer (St. Louis: Concordia Publishing House, 1992), pp. 317-340.

36. Wm. Byron Forbush, ed., *Fox's Book of Martyrs* (Philadelphia: John C. Winston, 1926), p. 1.

37. Ibid., p. 43.

38. Thieleman J. Van Braght, *The Bloody Theater or Martyrs Mirror*, trans. Joseph F. Sohm, 5th ed. (Scottdate, Pa.: Mennonite Publishing House, 1950), p. 16.

39. Ibid., p. 26.

40. Ibid., pp. 363-366.

41. John Lawrence Mosheim, *An Ecclesiastical History*, 6 vols., trans. Archibald Maclain (Charlestown, Mass.: Samuel Etheridge, 1810), 4:427-428.

42. See Frank E. Manuel, *Isaac Newton, Historian* (Cambridge: Harvard University Press, 1963), p. 152.

43. *The Works of Richard Hurd, D.D., Lord Bishop of Worcester* (London: Cadell & Davies, 1811), vol. V: 297-332. John Henry Newman wrote, "The School of Hurd and Newton hold, as the only true view of history, that Christianity slept for centuries upon centuries, except among those whom historians call heretics" (J. H. Newman, *An Essay on the Development of Christian Doctrine* [New York: Longmanns, Green, 1949], p. 84).

44. August Rauschenbusch and Walter Rauschenbusch, *Leben und Wirken von August Rauschenbusch*, ed. Walter Rauschenbusch (Cleveland: P. Ritter, 1901), pp. 241-242.

45. Ibid., p. 242.

46. Brown, *Menno*, pp. 5-6.

47. Ibid., p. 50.

48. Albert Henry Newman wrote, "Writings of Anabaptist leaders, especially those of Hubmaier, Denck, Hätzer, Hofmann, Riedemann, Philips, Menno, Bünderlin, and Czechowitz (most of this literature is excessively rare. The best American collection of *Anabaptistica* is probably that collected by Dr. Howard Osgood and deposited in the library of the Rochester Theological Seminary)" (A. H. Newman, *A Manual of Church History*, 2 vols. [rev. and enl. ed., Philadelphia: American Baptist Publication Society, 1933], 2:148).

49. Henry S. Burrage, *A History of the Anabaptists in Switzerland* (Philadelphia: American Baptist Publication Society, 1882; reprint ed., New York: Burt Franklin, 1973), xiv.

50. Henry C. Vedder, *Balthasar Hubmaier, The Leader of the Anabaptists* (New York: G. P. Putnam's Sons, 1905; reprint ed., New York: AMS, 1971), iv.

51. See *National Union Catalogue*, s.v. "Burrage." His son, Champlin Burrage, followed in his father's footsteps, visited Ludwig Keller in Münster and wrote a 2 vol. study on *The English Dissenters in the Light of Recent Research 1550-1641* (New York: Cambridge University Press, 1912).

52. Burrage, *Anabaptists*, ix.

53. Ibid., x.

54. Ibid., pp. 40-108.

55. Ibid., p. 76.

56. Ibid.

57. Ibid.

58. Ibid., pp. 89-90.

59. Ibid., p. 110.

60. Ibid., pp. 154-156.

61. Ibid., p. 117.

62. Ibid., p. 221.

63. Ibid., p. 222.

64. 7 June 1880, Burrage to Keller, Ludwig Keller Correspondence, Mennonite Library and Archives, North Newton, Kansas. I am very grateful to Dale Schrag, Librarian, and John D. Thiesen, Archivist, for their most gracious hospitality in granting ready access to this most important collection of letters for Anabaptist historiography.

65. 6 July 1882, Burrage to Keller, Keller Papers.

66. Keller Papers.

67. 5 April 1883, Burrage to Keller, Keller Papers; *Baptist Quarterly Review*, no. 25 (1885), pp. 28-47.

68. 14 April 1885, Underhill to Keller, Keller Papers. How or where Underhill and Keller met is nowhere indicated. But Underhill was only the first of a number of notable English Baptist scholars who entered into correspondence with Keller (Burrage was the first American Baptist scholar to do so).

69. Ibid.

70. 12 March 1884, Schwab to Keller, Keller Papers.

71. Ibid.

72. W. Rauschenbusch, *August Rauschenbusch*, p. 173.

73. Ibid., p. 221.

74. Ibid., p. 242.

75. 29 May 1885, A. Rauschenbusch to Keller, Keller Papers.

76. Paul M. Minus writes that during the years 1868-1869, August Rauschenbusch was in Germany researching Anabaptist history "in pursuit of German antecedents of the Baptist movement" (Minus, *Walter Rauschenbusch: American Reformer* [New York: Macmillan, 1988], p. 10). August Rauschenbusch retired from Rochester Baptist Seminary to return to Germany in 1889 where he died in 1899. He spent his last years teaching at the Baptist seminary in Hamburg. On 22 November 1897, Heinrich Braun from South Russia, an uncle of my mother and student at the time at the Hamburg Baptist seminary, wrote to Keller, saying: "It is my ambition (I am a Mennonite from Southern Russia), to learn as much about the origins of our history as possible during my stay here in Germany. Since you have written so much about the age of Reformation, I would very much like to acquire your books. But since I am not in a position to purchase them, I would like to ask you, most learned Sir, if you would be so kind as to send me the following of your works: 1) The Reformation and the older Reformparties; 2) The Waldensians and the German Bible Translations; 3) Johann von Staupitz and the Beginnings of the Reformation; 4) The Counter-Reformation in Westphalia and the Lower Rhine, 2 vols" (Translated from German, Keller Papers). Keller noted that he had sent him the following three works: *Die Anfänge der Reformation und die Ketzerschulen*; *Die altevangelischen Gemeinden*; and *Die Böhmischen Brüder*. It may well have been August Rauschenbusch, then at the Hamburg Baptist seminary, who stimulated Braun's thinking about Anabaptist history and turned him to the works of Keller. Heinrich Braun was later part owner of the Raduga Press in the Molotschna Colony and a friend and ally of P. M. Friesen. Could Keller have come to Friesen through Braun? The title, and the thesis on Anabaptist origins developed in Friesen's book, clearly bear the imprint of Keller's theories: *Die Alt-Evangelische Mennonitische Brüderschaft in Russland*.

77. *Baptist Quarterly Review*, no. 21 (1884), p. 49.

78. Ibid., p. 58.

79. Ibid., p. 59.

80. Ibid., p. 60.

81. Ibid., p. 61.

82. Ibid., p. 66.

83. Ibid., p. 67.

84. Ibid.

85. *Baptist Quarterly Review*, no. 27 (1885), p. 300.

86. Ibid., p. 322.

87. This is in contrast to Dosker's assessment of Theodor Kolde's attack cited in the opening quotation.

88. 15 September 1886, Newman to Keller, Keller Papers.

89. Published by the American Baptist Publication Society (Philadelphia, 1897).

Newman was professor of Church History at McMaster University, then in Toronto, before returning to the United States.

90. Ibid., p. 3.

91. Ibid., p. 4.

92. Ibid.

93. Ibid., pp. 21-22.

94. Ibid., p. 24.

95. Ibid., p. 30.

96. Ibid., p. 40.

97. Ibid., p. 43.

98. Ibid., pp. 77-87. On Zimmermann, see my *Reformation and Utopia: The Marxist Interpretation of the Reformation and its Antecedents* (Wiesbaden: F. Steiner, 1974).

99. A. H. Newman, *Anti-Pedobaptism*, pp. 84-85.

100. Ibid., p. 166. In another place, Newman speaks of "the most objectionable features of Denck's system" (Ibid., p. 245).

101. Ibid., p. 187.

102. Ibid., p. 292.

103. Ibid., p. 293.

104. Ibid., p. 296.

105. Ibid., p. 342.

106. Ibid., p. 339.

107. Ibid., pp. 392-393.

108. Ibid., p. 394.

109. See "Introduction" to George H. Williams and Angel M. Mergal, eds., *Spiritual and Anabaptist Writers*, The Library of Christian Classics, vol. 25 (Philadelphia: Westminster Press, 1957), pp. 19-38.

110. A.H. Newman, *A Manual of Church History*, 2:157.

111. Ibid., p. 162.

112. Ibid., p. 160.

113. Ibid., p. 169.

114. Ibid., p. 174.

115. Ibid., p. 183.

116. On the Baptist Union, see Ernest A. Payne, T*he Baptist Union: A Short History* (London: Carey Kingsgate Press, 1958).

117. Richard Heath, *Anabaptism, From its Rise at Zwickau to its Fall at Münster 1521-1536* (London: Alexander and Shepheard, 1895).

118. Minus, *Walter Rauschenbusch*, p. 71.

119. See A. Friesen, *Reformation and Utopia*, pp. 177-180. Heath is cited by Belfort Bax, *Rise and Fall of the Anabaptists* (New York: Macmillan, 1903; reprint ed., New York: Burt Franklin, 1966), p. 381.

233

120. Heath, *Anabaptism*, viii & ix.

121. Ibid.

122. Ibid., p. 8.

123. Ibid., p. 10.

124. Ibid., p. 13.

125. Ibid.

126. Ibid., p. 18.

127. See especially my "Menno and Münster: The Man and the Movement," in *Menno Simons, A Reappraisal*, ed. Gerald R. Brunk (Harrisonburg, Va: Eastern Mennonite College, 1992), pp. 131-162, especially p. 140.

128. 21 March 1891, Heath to Keller, Keller Papers.

129. Ibid.

130. Minus, *Walter Rauschenbusch*, note 22, p. 222.

131. Ibid., p. 82.

132. Ibid.

133. Ibid. In another part of his book, Minus observed: "Martin Luther's work, however consequential for subsequent Christian history, did not constitute the most important development of the Reformation era, because he and the other major Protestant reformers remained attached to much of traditional religion. In Rauschenbusch's eyes, the truly heroic figures of the Reformation were the Anabaptists, because more than other Protestants they recognized the church's failures and courageously sought a restoration of primitive Christianity" (Ibid., p. 153).

134. Walter Rauschenbusch, "The Freedom of Spiritual Religion," sermon preached at the Northern Baptist Convention in Chicago, 8 May 1910, quoted in Don E. Smucker, "Walter Rauschenbusch and Anabaptist Historiography," in *The Recovery of the Anabaptist Vision*, ed. Guy F. Hershberger (Scottdale, Pa.: Herald Press, 1957), p. 296.

135. Ibid., pp. 296-297.

136. Ibid., p. 297.

137. (London, 1904).

138. Ibid., x.

139. Ibid.

140. Ibid., p. 20.

141. Ibid., p. 22.

142. Vedder, *Hubmaier* (New York: G. P. Putnam's Sons, 1905).

143. Ibid., p. 9. Vedder was not uncritical of Keller, however, adding: "And if at times his conclusions have outrun his facts, and depend for their soundness rather on his historical insight than on any definite proofs he has been able to bring forward, this cannot be said to vitiate the greater part of his work" (Ibid.).

144. Ibid., p. 20.

145. Ibid., pp. 171-172.

146. Ibid., p. 23.

147. Subtitled: *A Study in Intellectual Origins, Studies in Anabaptist and Mennonite History*, no. 16 (Scottdale, Pa.: Herald Press, 1974).

148. J. K. Zeman, *The Anabaptists and the Czech Brethren in Moravia 1526-1628* (The Hague: Mouton, 1969).

149. Ibid., p. 28.

150. Ibid., p. 271.

151. Jan J. Kiwiet, *Pilgrim Marbeck* (Kassel: J. G. Oncken Verlag, 1957); Ekkehard Krajewski, *Leben und Sterben des Zürcher Täuferführers Felix Mantz* (Kassel: J. G. Oncken Verlag, 1957); and Torsten Bergsten, *Balthasar Hubmaier, Seine Stellung zu Reformation und Täufertun, 1521-1528* (Kassel: J. G. Oncken Verlag, 1961), trans. by W. R. Estep, Jr., as *Balthasar Hubmaier: Anabaptist Theologian and Martyr* (Valley Forge: Judson Press, 1967). Estep himself has contributed a popular account of the Anabaptists entitled: *The Anabaptist Story*, and an edition of early Anabaptist documents.

152. See my "Humanism and Anabaptism: A Study in Paradigmatic Similarities," in *Harvest of Humanism*, ed. M. P. Fleischer, pp. 232-261.

153. I have begun to work through the Keller correspondence and intend to complete such a study in the near future.

III
BAPTISTS AND MENNONITES IN POLAND AND PRUSSIA

1. See, for example, Peter M. Friesen, *The Mennonite Brotherhood in Russia (1789-1910)*, trans. J. B. Toews et al. (Fresno, Calif.: Board of Christian Literature, General Conference of Mennonite Brethren Churches, 1978), especially pp. 461-467, 476-477.

2. For a sketch of his life see Eduard Kupsch, *Geschichte der Baptisten in Polen, 1852-1932* (Zdunska-Wola: By the Author, 1932), pp. 17-31.

3. Ibid., pp. 25-26.

4. A contemporary description of these events has been recorded in *Missionsblatt der Gemeine getaufter Christen* 17 (1859):27.

5. Kupsch, p. 31.

6. Ibid., pp. 46-58.

7. Hans-Christian Diedrich, *Siedler, Sektierer und Stundisten: Die Entstehung des russichen Freikirchentums* (Berlin: Evangelische Verlagsanstalt, 1985), p. 155.

8. *Missionsblatt* 20 (1862):126-128.

9. Kupsch, *Baptisten in Polen*, p. 62.

10. Robert L. Kluttig, *Geschichte der deutschen Baptisten in Polen* (Winnipeg, Man.: Christian Press, 1973), p. 53.

11. *Missionsblatt* 24 (1866):138.

12. Joseph Lehmann, *Geschichte der deutschen Baptisten: von 1848 bis 1870, II. Teil* (Kassel: J. G. Oncken Verlag, 1922).

13. Ibid., pp. 125-126.

14. Günter Balders, *Theurer Bruder Oncken* (Kassel: J. G. Oncken Verlag, 1978), p. 136.

15. Kupsch, *Baptisten in Polen*, p. 112.
16. Ibid., pp. 116-117.
17. *Festschrift zur Feier des 50-jährigen Jubil ums des Predigerseminars der deutschen Baptisten zu Hamburg-Horn* (Hamburg: n.p., 1930), pp. 69ff.
18. Friesen, *Brotherhood*, p. 340.
19. *Missionsblatt* 24 (1866):127.
20. *Missionsblatt* 34 (1876):12.
21. Ibid., pp. 12-13.
22. Michael Klimenko, *Anfänge des Baptismus in Süd-Russland (Ukraine) nach offizielen Dokumenten* (Erlangen: Friedrich-Alexander-Universität, 1957), p. 76.
23. E. Cramer, *Jeder Baptist ein Missionar!* (Kassel: Christliche Trakatgesellschaft, n.d.), p. 16.
24. Ibid.
25. Joseph Lehmann, *Geschichte der deutschen Baptisten*, I. Teil (Kassell: Verlagshaus der deutschen Baptisten, 1900), pp. 89-90.
26. Ibid., pp. 171-172.
27. Rudolf Donat, *Das Wachsende Werk* (Kassel: J. G. Oncken Verlag, 1960), p. 81-83. Attempts to expand into Danzig proved difficult. Not until 1875 were Baptists successful in founding their own church.
28. Cramer, *Jeder Baptist ein Missionar!*, p. 17.
29. Ibid.
30. "Die Baptisten," *Mittheilungen aus dem religiösen Leben* (1848):8.
31. "Gottes Feld vor unsrer Tür," *Die Gemeinde* 17 (January 1962):1.
32. Hans Luckey, *Johann Gerhard Oncken* (Kassel: J. G. Oncken Verlag, 1958), pp. 134-136.
33. *Protokoll-Buch des Executiv-Comitees der Missions-Schule, 1884-1889* (Hamburg: Oncken Archive, n.d.), p. 39.
34. Erich L. Ratzlaff, *Im Weichselbogen* (Winnipeg, Man.: Christian Press, 1971), pp. 55-57, 98-109.
35. Ibid., p. 106.
36. Author's conversation with Erich Ratzlaff.

IV
BAPTISTS AND MENNONITE BRETHREN IN RUSSIA: (1790-1930)

1. James Urry, "John Melville and the Mennonites: A British Evangelist in South Russia, 1837- c.1875," *Mennonite Quarterly Review* 54 (October 1980):305-322.
2. R. C. Scott, *Quakers in Russia (London: Michael Joseph Ltd.,* 1964), p. 113ff.
3. Cornelius Krahn, "A Pietist Revival Comes to South Russia," *Mennonite Life* 33 (March 1978):4-11. Also A. Kroeker, *Pfarrer Edward Wüst* (Hillsboro, Kans.: Central Publishing Co., 1903) and J. Prinz, *Die Kolonien der Brüdergemeinde* (Moscow: G. Lissner & A. Geshel, 1898).

4. The tensions are rather well-illustrated in the recollections of Cornelius Hildebrand, "Aus der Kronsweider Erweckungszeit," *Der Botschafter*, 21, 25, 29 January; 1, 5, 8, 12, 15, 19, 22, 26 February; 1, 5 May 1913. Also see the Jacob Epp Diary, 5 February 1860, 15 April 1862, 12 May 1862, 30 April 1865 and 24 May 1865, Mennonite Heritage Centre, Winnipeg, Manitoba.

5. See H. Luckey, *Johann Gerhard Oncken und die Anfänge des deutschen Baptismus* (Kassel: J. G. Oncken Verlag, 1958).

6. Jacob P. Bekker, *Origin of the Mennonite Brethren Church* (Hillsboro, Kan.: Mennonite Brethren Historical Society of the Midwest, 1973), p. 179.

7. Ibid., pp. 180-181.

8. For documentation and comments on the baptism question see Peter M. Friesen, *Der Alt-Evangelische Mennonitische Brüderschaft in Russland (1789-1910) im Rahmen der mennonitischen Gesamtgeschichte* (Halbstadt: Verlags Gesellschaft "Raduga", 1911), pp. 240-247; 380-386.

9. Albert W. Wardin, "Baptist Influences on Mennonite Brethren with an Emphasis on the Practice of Immersion," *Direction* 8 (October 1979):33-38.

10. Heinrich Epp, *Notizen aus dem Leben verstorbenen Ältesten Abraham Unger* (Halbstadt: H. J. Braun, 1907), p. 29.

11. Abraham Friesen is the first Russian Mennonite name listed in the student registrar of the Baptist Seminary in Hamburg. See *Festschrift zur Feier des 50 jährigen Jubiläums des Predigerseminars der deutschen Baptisten zu Hamburg-Horn* (Hamburg: n.p., 1930), p. 70. For another interesting case study see Albert W. Wardin, "Jacob J. Wiens: Mission Champion in Freedom and Repression," *Journal of Church and State* 28 (Autumn 1986):495-514.

12. This was apparently a question of different administrative structures, not different Mennonite Brethren identities. See P. Penner, "Baptist in All But Name: Molotschna Mennonite Brethren in India," *Mennonite Life* 46 (March 1991):17-23.

13. David G. Rempel "The Mennonite Commonwealth in Russia: A Sketch of its Founding and Endurance, 1784-1919," *Mennonite Quarterly Review* 47 (October 1973).269, 283-286.

14. For a detailed analysis of this process see Alexander Karev, *The Russian Evangelical Baptist Movement*, trans. Frederick P. Leman (Evansville, Ind.: typescript photocopy, n.d.) pp. 15-19, 23ff. Alexander Karev was of Molokan background. He joined the evangelical-Baptist movement when he became convinced that the Scriptures clearly taught the necessity of baptism, which the Molokans, though biblicists, rejected. He was active in the Evangelical Christian Baptists after it was founded in the 1920s and even during its shadowy existence in the 1930s. He joined the All-Union Council of Evangelical Christian Baptists after it was founded in the 1940s and became its general secretary, travelling widely in the postwar period. See also Heinrich Löwen, *In Vergessenheit geratene Beziehungen* (Bielefeld: Logos-Verlag, 1989), pp. 61-65.

15. Hans Christian Diedrich, "Ursprünge und Anfänge des russischen Freikirchentums" (dissertation, Humbold-Universität Berlin, 1979), p. 246. Also Johann Pritzkau, *Geschichte der deutschen Baptisten in Süd-Russland* (Odessa: Wenske and Lübeck, 1914), p. 12.

16. Pritzkau notes that the Alt-Danzig group officially became Baptist with Johann Oncken's visit in 1869 (Ibid., pp. 36-38). Some Mennonite Brethren were also present at a Baptist organizational conference in Alt-Danzig in 1874 (Ibid., p. 76). During the

237

1870s Gerhard Wieler's brother, Johann, was involved with the Baptists in and about Odessa (Diedrich, "Russischen Friekirchentums", pp. 253ff).

17. This in no way implies that the Mennonite Brethren were a key formative force on the rise of Protestant Evangelicalism in Russia. International, national, and regional forces were involved in this complex scenario. Some of the major studies on its origins include W. Gutsche, *Westliche Quellen des russischen Stundismus* (Kassel: J. G. Oncken Verlag, 1956); John Nesdoly, "Evangelical Sectarianism in Russia: A study of the Stundists, Baptists, Pashkovites and Evangelical Christians, 1865-1917" (Ph.d. dissertation, Queens University, 1971); Michael Klimenko, *Die Anfänge des Baptismus in Südrussland nach offiziellen Dokumenten* (Erlangen: Friedrich-Alexander-Universität, 1957); and H. Brandenburg, *The Meek and the Mighty: The Emergence of the Evangelical Movement in Russia* (London: Oxford University Press, 1976).

18. Karev, *Russian Evangelical Baptist Movement*, pp. 110-114.

19. On Johann Wieler, see the very interesting document in Lawrence Klippenstein, "Johann Wieler (1839-1889) Among Russian Evangelicals: A New source of Mennonites and Evangelicalism in Imperial Russia," *Journal of Mennonite Studies* 5 (1987):44-60.

20. For Kargel's personal account of his involvement with the evangelical movement in Russia, see J. G. Kargel, *Zwischen den Enden der Erde. Unter Brüdern in Ketten* (Wernigerode am Harz: Licht im Osten, 1928).

21. Adolf Reimer, "Bilder aus der Arbeit unter den Russen," *Friedensstimme*, 17 March 1907, pp. 128-129 and Adolf Reimer, "Von der Reise," *Friedensstimme*, 31 October 1909, p. 4.

22. Peter Riediger, "Mission der Mennoniten in Russland unter den Russen," B. B. Janz Papers, Centre for Mennonite Brethren Studies, Winnipeg, Manitoba.

23. Ibid., pp. 8-9.

24. Ibid., p. 26.

25. Ibid., p. 8.

26. Gerhard P. Schroeder, *Miracles of Grace and Judgment* (Lodi, Calif.: By the Author, 1974), pp. 178-179, 221-228.

27. "Offener Brief des Ältesten H. Dirks," *Der Botschafter*, 19 November 1910, pp. 3-4.

28. H. J. Braun, "Mennoniten oder Baptisten?," *Friedensstimme*, 5 May 1910, pp. 3-5.

29. As a result of the Blankenburg *Allianz* influence among the South Russian Mennonites, both Mennonite Brethren and Old Church members joined to organize several Mennonite *Allianz* fellowship groups, yet took their continued membership in the larger Mennonite world for granted. Similarly, the legalistically inclined Peter's Church or definable schismatics, like the Mennonite Seventh Day Adventists, often lived in the same village and still "felt" more Mennonite than anything else. Consciously or unconsciously all foreign contacts occurred within the context of an operational "border patrol". *Allianz* preachers and teachers visiting the Mennonites in Russia at best contributed new ideas and insights to an existing peoplehood. For example, the Old Church Mennonite, Peter Schellenberg, affirmed an *Allianz* style conversion, attended the *Allianz* Bible School in Berlin and accompanied E. A. Broadbent, an English Plymouth Brethren historian and minister, during his travels in Siberia and Turkestan (*Friedensstimme*, 25 February 1912, pp. 2-3). There was no perceived threat in inviting evangelists from Switzerland or England (*Friedensstimme*, 18 July

1909, p. 3; 19 September 1909, pp. 3-4). When Mennonite leaders discussed the need for their own theological school, they simply assumed it was inherently important and never articulated any concern about the danger of Mennonite students studying abroad. Meanwhile young people aspiring to ministry continued to study at the *Allianz* Bible School in Berlin (later Wiedenest), St. Chrischona in Switzerland, or the missions school in Barmen. Whatever traditions and teachings they absorbed while abroad somehow became "Mennonite" when they returned. While some theological dislocation and modification was inevitable, it rarely catapulted the individual beyond the peoplehood which gave him or her birth.

30. See A. J. Klassen, "Early Mennonite Brethren Ecumenical Relations," *The Journal of Church and Society* 4 (Spring 1968):46-56.

V
MENNONITE BRETHREN AND BAPTISTS IN RUSSIA: AFFINITIES AND DISSIMILARITIES

1. For the history of German Baptists in Germany before the First World War, see Joseph Lehmann, *Geschichte der deutschen Baptisten*, 2 vols. (Hamburg and Kassel: J. G. Oncken, 1896-1900); Rudolf Donat, *Wie Das Werk begann* (Kassel: J. G. Oncken, 1958); and Rudolf Donat, *Das wachsende Werk* (Kassel: J. G. Oncken, 1960). The second volumes of Lehmann and Donat include material on the spread of the German Baptists in the Russian Empire. For a recent treatment of the German Baptists in Russia/Soviet Union, see *The Modern Encyclopedia of Religions in Russia*, 1991 ed., s.v. "Baptists (German) in Russia and USSR," by Albert W. Wardin, Jr. which includes a bibliographic essay on sources.

2. Donat, *Das wachsende Werk*, pp. 94-96; and Kulius Köbner, "The Baptist Missionary Society," *Evangelical Christendom* 5 (1851):495-496.

3. J. H. Rushbrooke, *The Baptist Movement in the Continent of Europe* (London: Carey Press and Kingsgate Press, 1915), pp. 19-31; William L. Wagner, *New Move Forward in Europe* (Pasadena, Calif.: William Carey Library, 1978), pp. 8-9, 12-16; and Köbner, "Baptist Missionary Society," pp. 495-496.

4. On C. Plonus' ministry in St. Petersburg, see Otto Ekelmann, *Gnadenwunder: Geschichte der Ersten Ostpreussischen Baptistgemeinde in Memel und ihrer Missionsfelder in Ostpreussen und Russland* (Memel: By the Author, 1928), pp. 86-87; and A. R. Schiewe, "Brief," *Sendbote*, 28 May 1884, pp. 170-171. Probably Schiewe's date of 1855 rather than Ekelmann's date of 1856 for Plonus's arrival is correct. For German Baptist beginnings in Poland, see Eduard Kupsch, *Geschichte der Baptisten in Polen 1852-1932* (Zdunska-Wola: By the Author, 1932), pp. 23-82.

5. *Missionsblatt der Gemeine getaufter Christen* 22 (June 1865):92-94; 22 (October 1865):157; 26 (September 1869):143-144; J. Prizkau, *Geschichte der Baptisten in Süd-Russland* (Odessa: Wenske and Lübeck, 1914), pp. 2-9, 15-20, 124-130; and K. Veltistov, "Nemetskii baptizm v Rossii," *Missionerskoe obozrenie* 7 (March 1902):467-469.

6. *Unions-Statistik der Baptisten-Gemeinden in Russland*, 1901 (Riga: A. v. Grothuss, 1902), p. 8.

7. The most valuable source for primary material on the beginnings of the Mennonite Brethren is P. M. Friesen, *Die Alt-Evangelische Mennonitische Brüderschaft in Russland (1789-1910) im Rahmen der mennonitischen Gesamtgeschichte* (Halbstadt: Verlags Gesellschaft "Raduga", 1911) [For an English translation, see Friesen, *The*

Mennonite Brotherhood in Russia (1789-1910), trans. J. B. Toews et al. (Fresno, Calif.: Board of Christian Literature, General Conference of Mennonite Brethren Churches, 1978). Citations of pages from Friesen will first be from the German original followed in parenthesis by pages from the English translation.] Another helpful primary source is Jacob P. Bekker, *Origin of the Mennonite Brethren Church* (Hillsboro, Kans.: The Mennonite Brethren Historical Society of the Midwest, 1973), which is an English translation of the author's manuscript written around 1890. A modern treatment of the Mennonite Brethren is the very helpful volume by John A. Toews, *A History of the Mennonite Brethren* Church (Fresno, Calif.: Board of Christian Literature, General Conference of Mennonite Brethren Churches, 1975).

8. Friesen, *Brüderschaft*, pp. 240-247, 380-386 (284-291, 459-467); Toews, *History of the MB Church*, pp. 55-57, 83, 100-101. The volume by Heinrich Löwen, *In Vergessenheit geratene Beziehungen* (Bielefeld: Logos, 1989) is a carefully documented work on the relations between Mennonite Brethren and Baptists in the Russian Empire. It is the first work by a Mennonite Brethren scholar to attempt to provide a full accounting of Baptist influences on the Mennonite Brethren in Russia.

9. For a discussion of the introduction of the concept of immersion in the Molotschna, see the article by Albert W. Wardin, Jr., "Baptist Influences on Mennonite Brethren with an Emphasis on the Practice of Immersion," *Direction* 8 (October 1979):33-38; Bekker, *Origin of the MB Church*, pp. 70ff; Heinrich Epp, *Notizen aus dem Leben und Wirken des verstorbenen Altesten Abraham Unger, dem Gründer der "Einlager-Mennoniten Brüdergemeinde"* (Halbstadt: By the Author, 1907), pp. 6-9; *Baptist Missionary Magazine* 50 (January 1870):17; and Friesen, *Brüderschaft*, pp. 245-246 (289-290).

10. Friesen, *Brüderschaft*, pp. 244-245 (288-289); Bekker, *Origin of the MB Church*, p. 181; and Kupsch, *Baptisten in Polen*, p. 64.

11. Friesen, *Brüderschaft*, pp. 246-247 (290-291).

12. *Quarterly Reporter of the German Baptist Mission*, January 1862, pp. 14-15; January 1867, p. 215; Friesen, *Brüderschaft*, pp. 291-292, 380-386, 431 (340, 459-467, 515); Epp, *Abraham Unger*, pp. 20-23, 25-26, 28; *Sendbote*, 8 June 1904, p. 357; *Missionsblatt* 23 (August 1866):125; 26 (December 1869):180-181; Toews, *History of the MB Church*, pp. 53-54, 72; and Hans Kasdorf, "Reflections on the Church Concept of the Mennonite Brethren," *Direction* 4 (July 1975):340.

13. Friesen, *Brüderschaft*, pp. 381, 385-386, 430-431 (460-461, 466-467, 514-515); *Missionsblatt* 30 (May 1873):84-87; 30 (August 1873):139-141; and 31 (December 1874):221-223.

14. *Quarterly Reporter*, April 1862, p. 27; April 1869, pp. 357-359; July 1869, p. 375; July 1870, pp. 836-838; Lawrence Klippenstein, ed. and trans., "Johann Wieler (1839-1889) Among Russian Evangelicals: A New Source of Mennonites and Evangelicalism in Imperial Russia," *Journal of Mennonite Studies* 5 (1987):44-60; Bekker, *Origin of the MB Church*, pp. 147-148; Epp, *Abraham Unger*, pp. 23-24; Michael Klimenko, *Anfänge des Baptismus in Südrussland (Ukraine) nach offiziellen Dokumenten* (Erlangen: Friedrich-Alexander-Universität, 1957), pp. 61-62; and S. D. Bondar, *Sekta mennonitov v Rossii* (Petrograd: n.p., 1916), pp. 156-166; and Löwen, *Beziehungen*, pp. 62-66.

15. *Missionsblatt* 18 (March 1861):36-37; 19 (July 1862):107; 20 (August 1863):126-127; *Quarterly Reporter*, January 1865, pp. 73-79; and Epp, *Abraham Unger*, p. 14.

16. *Quarterly Reporter*, October 1873, pp. 58-60; and *Missionsblatt* 26 (October 1869):153-160.

17. Kupsch, *Baptisten in Polen*, pp. 64-65; Friesen, *Brüderschaft*, pp. 244-245, 383-385, 397-398 (288-289, 463-466, 478-479); and Epp, Abraham Unger, pp. 24-25.

18. Friesen, *Brüderschaft*, pp. 395-396, 398-401 (476-477, 479-481); and Epp, Abraham Unger, pp. 26-28.

19. Friesen, *Brüderschaft*, pp. 383-384, 395-396 (463-464, 476-477); Epp, Abraham Unger, pp. 24-25; *Missionsblatt* 23 (August 1866):125; and Kupsch, *Baptisten in Polen*, pp. 64-65.

20. For early Mennonite Brethren mission outreach among Germans, see Bekker, *Origin of the MB Church*, pp. 35-39, 182; *Missionsblatt* 19 (July 1862):107; 22 (October 1865):156-157; 26 (October 1869):159; Bondar, *Mennonitov v Rossii*, pp. 140, 161; Löwen, *Beziehungen*, pp. 51-53; and Friesen, *Brüderschaft*, pp. 427-430 (511-514). See Friesen, *Brüderschaft*, p. 429 (512-513) concerning problems of non-Mennonites becoming Mennonites.

21. Bekker, *Origin of the MB Church*, p. 181; Friesen, *Brüderschaft*, p. 430 (514); Toews, *History of the MB Church*, p. 98; *Wahrheitszeuge*, 25 April 1908, p. 136; A. H. Unruh, *Die Geschichte der Mennoniten-Brüdergemeinde 1860-1954* (Hillsboro, Kan.: The General Conference of the Mennonite Brethren Church of North America, 1955), pp. 257-280; and John B. Toews, *Perilous Journey: The Mennonite Brethren in Russia 1860-1910* (Winnipeg, Man.: Kindred Press, 1988), pp. 60-63. For an account of a member of the Mennonite Brethren who became identified with the Russian evangelicals, see Albert W. Wardin, Jr., "Jacob J. Wiens: Mission Champion in Freedom and Repression," *Journal of Church and State* 28 (Autumn 1986):495-514.

22. For various mission and benevolent funds of the German Baptists in Russia see *Der Hausfreund*, 21 March 1907, p. 95; and the *Minutes of the Union of Baptist Churches in Russia, 1909* (Riga: J. A. Frey, 1909).

23. *Sendbote*, 1 June 1904, p. 346; 8 June 1904, p. 357; and *Friedensstimme*, 5 May 1910, pp. 3-5.

24. Toews, *History of the MB Church*, pp. 99-103.

25. *Sendbote*, 9 May 1883, p. 146; 8 June 1904, p. 357; Toews, *History of the MB Church*, p. 99; and Friesen, *Brüderschaft*, pp. 447, 560-568 (532-533, 674-687).

26. *Der Hausfreund*, 28 July 1910, p. 238; and *Baptist Missionary Magazine* 88 (January 1908):24-25.

27. J. Heinrichs, "Abstract of Report of Rev. J. Henrich's [sic] Visit to Russia in May and June, 1909," p. 6, Correspondence 1900-1910, American Baptist Foreign Mission Society, Archives, Valley Forge, Penn.

VI
RUSSIAN MENNONITES AND BAPTISTS (1930-1990)

1. See the new official history of the Evangelical Christian Baptists: S. N. Savinsky, P. D. Savchenko and J. P. Dyck, eds., *Istoriia evangel'skikh khristian-baptistov v SSSR* (Moskva: Izdanie vsesoiuznogo soveta ev. khristian-baptistov, 1989), pp. 310-316. (An official, documentary history, hereafter *Istoriia*, AUCECB).

2. On these events see John B. Toews, *Czars, Soviets and Mennonites* (Newton, Kan.: Faith & Life Press, 1982), pp. 82-94.

3. Still the best published discussion of the Evangelical Christian-Baptist relationship is Wilhelm Kahle, *Evangelische Christen in Russland und der Sowjetunion* (Wup-

pertal: J. G. Oncken Verlag, 1978).

4. Al Reimer, "Peasant Aristocracy: The Mennonite Gutsbesitzertum in Russia," *Journal of Mennonite Studies* 8 (1990):76-88, 81-82 in particular.

5. Prominent scholars such as Stephen Cohen, Robert Tucker and Pavel Campeaneau have examined the nature and roots of Stalinism at length. For an overview of current Soviet reflection on the Stalinist burden see: Alec Nove, *"Glasnost" in Action: Cultural Renaissance in Russia* (Boston: Unwin Hyman, 1989); and Alexander Tsipko, *Is Stalinism Really Dead?* (San Francisco: Harper, 1990).

6. For more details than space allows here, *Mennonite Encyclopedia*, 1990 ed., s.v. "Spetskomandatura," by Walter Sawatsky; and Walter Sawatsky, "From Russian to Soviet Mennonites 1941-1988," in *Mennonites in Russia 1788-1988: Essays in Honour of Gerhard Lohrenz*, ed. John Friesen (Winnipeg, Man.: CMBC Publications, 1989), pp. 301-304.

7. The three standard works are: Nicholas Bethell, *The Last Secret: The Delivery to Stalin of Over Two Million Russians by Britain and the United States* (New York: Basic Books, 1974); Nikolai Tolstoy, *Victims of Yalta* (London: Hodder and Stoughten, 1977); and Mark R. Elliot, *Pawns of Yalta: Soviet Refugees and America's Role in Their Repatriation* (Urbana:-University of Illinois Press, 1982).

8. For a detailed discussion, see Walter Sawatsky, *Soviet Evangelicals Since World War II* (Scottdale, Pa.: Herald Press, 1981), pp. 78-90.

9. Reported in V. K. Krest'ianiv, *Mennonity* (Moscow: Izdatel'stro politicheskoi literatury, 1967), p. 14.

10. For more details, see Sawatsky, *Soviet Evangelicals Since World War II*, pp. 157-254. The official history, for the first time quotes several of the offending clauses in the constitution, and cites then President Logvinenko in an interview with *Moscow News* (3 April 1988) admitting that the documents "restricted the canonic and spiritual life of the church" (*Istoriia*, AUCECB, p. 241). The authors also claim that the majority of the churches refused to respond or expressed disagreement with the action.

11. For a recent overall survey, see Walter Sawatsky, "Protestants in the USSR," in *Religious Policy in the Soviet Union*, ed. Sabrina P. Ramet (New York: Cambridge University Press, 1992).

12. Literally meaning "self-publishing," the term *Samizdat* has come to refer to all uncensored writings from single page letters to books, that were copied and circulated illegally. Discovery of *Samizdat* materials in one's possession could lead to three or five year prison terms. The Soviet evangelicals were the first to utilize *Samizdat* systematically (in the twentieth century). A complete collection is available at Keston College, England.

13. In statistical terms, about five thousand of the estimated 50,000 believing Mennonites were active in the CCECB. Initially 16,000, then 18,000 by 1968 and finally 30,000 by 1985 were considered part of the AUCECB, and about 15,000 independent, mainly Kirchliche Mennonites.

14. For details see Albert W. Wardin, Jr. "Jacob J. Wiens: Mission Champion in Freedom and Repression," *Journal of Church and State* 28 (Autumn 1986):495-514.

15. Georgi Vins, *Testament From Prison*, trans. Jane Ellis (Elgin, Ill.: David C. Cook, 1975). Vins was featured in Michael Bourdeaux, *Faith on Trial in Russia* (London: Hodder & Stoughton, 1975). After increasing isolation following his deportation, Vins, in the autumn of 1990, resumed at least a cordial relationship with other Baptists and Mennonites and visited the Soviet Union.

16. Here, as elsewhere, the author is relying on extensive unpublished interview data from Soviet emigrants (1975-1981) Umsiedler, plus private conversations with many leaders in the Soviet Union.

17. For details see *Bratskii Vestnik*, March 1976, pp. 67-74; Sawatsky, *Soviet Evangelicals*, pp. 280-282; and Walter Sawatsky, "What Makes Russian Mennonites Mennonite?" *Mennonite Quarterly Review* 53 (January 1979):5-20.

18. For an English translation with commentary see Walter Sawatsky, "A Call for Union of Baptists and Mennonites Issued by a Russian Baptist Leader," *Mennonite Quarterly Review* 50 (July 1976):230-239.

19. They included Traugott Kviring, Abram Fast, Peter P. Ens, Johannes P. Dyck, plus numerous local pastors.

20. The published report of the congress, found in *Bratskii Vestnik*, February 1990, p. 70, reported his election, almost as an afterthought. Generally that report ranked the greeting of the Mennonite World Conference executive secretary Paul Kraybill below that of the smaller Slavic church unions from America.

21. All Mennonite and Mennonite Brethren congregations receiving registration, to my knowledge, omitted the pacifism clause. Mennonites have also kept apart from the recent movement to reinstate the right of conscientious objection into Soviet legislation.

22. Their view of the Mennonite-Baptist distinction was stated in Heinrich Wölk and Gerhard Wölk, *A Wilderness Journey; Glimpses of the Mennonite Brethren in Russia 1925-1980*, trans. Victor Doerksen, Perspectives on Mennonite Life and Thought, no. 4 (Fresno, Calif.: Center for Mennonite Brethren Studies, 1982), pp. 132-133.

VII
THE RUSSIAN MENNONITE BRETHREN AND AMERICAN BAPTIST TANDEM IN INDIA (1890-1940)

1. John A. Toews, *History of the Mennonite Brethren Church: Pilgrims and Pioneers* (Fresno, Calif.: Board of Christian Literature, General Conference of Mennonite Brethren Churches, 1975), pp. 72-75; see also Clarence Hiebert, "The Development of Mennonite Brethren Churches in North America—Some Reflections, Interpretations and Viewpoints" and J. B. Toews, "Mennonite Brethren Identity and Theological Diversity," in *Pilgrims and Strangers: Essays in Mennonite Brethren History*, ed. Paul Toews (Fresno, Calif.: Center for Mennonite Brethren Studies, 1977), pp. 122-123, 139-141.

The American Mennonite Brethren, two decades in Kansas, Nebraska, and Minnesota, wrestled with the question of maintaining their independence from the Baptists. See *Konferenzberichte der Mennoniten Brüdergemeinde von Nord Amerika 1883-1919* (Hillsboro, Kans.: Mennonite Brethren Publishing House, 1920), pp. 186-190.

2. See Peter Penner, "Baptist in All But Name: Molotschna Mennonite Brethren in India," *Mennonite Life*, March 1991, pp. 17-23.

The reference is to the missionary correspondence of the Russian Mennonite Brethren in the American Baptist Archive Center (ABAC), Valley Forge, Pa. They seem to have remained untapped until now, at least since Gerhard W. Peters researched them at the New York Head Office of the American Baptist Foreign Missionary Society (ABFMS) in the mid-1940s for his *The Growth of Foreign Missions in the Mennonite Brethren Church* (Hillsboro, Kans.: Board of Foreign Missions, General

Conference of Mennonite Brethren Churches, 1952) pp. 53-69. At that time, he reached the same conclusions as does this chapter about the Russian and American Mennonite Brethren relations.

3. Peter M. Friesen, *The Mennonite Brotherhood in Russia (1789-1910)*, trans. J. B. Toews et al. (Fresno, Calif.: Board of Christian Literature, General Conference of Mennonite Brethren Churches, 1978), pp. 682, 1032 (footnote 18); cf. with *Konferenzberichte der Mennoniten Brüdergemeinde 1883-1919*, p. 208.

4. C. Unruh, "Rev. Abraham Friesen: A Tribute," *Mennonitische Rundschau*, 11 October 1922, p. 12; P. M. Friesen, *Brotherhood*, p. 675; cf. Peters, *The Growth of Foreign Missions*, p. 57.

The American Baptist Missionary Union (ABMU) in India was a branch of the ABFMS, headquartered in Boston for 94 years. During this time, the headquarters, called "The Rooms", was located in Tremont Temple Baptist Church, just off the Common in Boston. In 1920 the ABFMS relocated to Fifth Avenue, New York.

5. P.M. Friesen, *Brotherhood*, pp. 682-683, 873; and A.J. Friesen to Boston, many references between 10 May 1890 and 28 June 1901, A.J. Friesen Collection, ABAC. Unless otherwise noted the subsequent archival collections cited are from the ABAC Papers. Both Maria and Abram Friesen died in Russia, she on 19 April 1918 and he on 5 November 1920. See Unruh, "Rev. Abraham Friesen: A Tribute."

6. Friesen to Samuel W. Duncan, 28 February; 18 June; 23 July 1895, Friesen Collection.

7. Friesen, from Ootacumund, to Thomas S. Barbour, 15 April 1903, Friesen Collection.

8. "Plan of Cooperation Between the M.B. of Russia and the Executive Committee of the Missionary Union" (1904), ABAC, quoted in Peters, *The Growth of Foreign Missions*, pp. 59-60.

9. Friesen to Barbour, 16 August 1905; 28 August 1907, Friesen Collection.

10. Abraham H. Unruh, *Die Geschichte der Mennoniten-Brüdergemeinde, 1860-1954* (Hillsboro, Kans. and Winnipeg, Man.: General Conference of Mennonite Brethren Churches, 1955), pp. 328-330. Unruh does not provide a date for this constitution. For references to Braun see J. A. Toews, *History of the Mennonite Brethren Church*, pp. 103, 104, 113, 381; P. M. Friesen, *Brotherhood*, pp. 727-730, 835-838; and *Mennonite Encyclopedia*, 1955 ed., s.v. "Braun, Heinrich Jakob." by Cornelius Krahn.

11. Friesen to H. Mabie, 20 February 1900; 28 June 1901; Friesen to Barbour, 22 October 1902, Friesen Collection; Hübert to Barbour, 23 August 1904, A.J. Hübert Collection; cf. *Konferenzberichte der Brüdergemeinde von Nord Amerika 1883-1919*, pp. 206ff, 241.

12. Hübert was reprimanded by George B. Huntingdon for spending too much on the bungalow, 29 June 1906, Hübert Collection.

13. C. Unruh to Joseph C. Robbins, 3 October 1923, C. Unruh Collection; A. J. Hübert to Robbins, 30 December 1931; 17 November 1936, Hübert Collection. Katharina Hübert died there in 1948, as did Abram some years later.

14. P. M. Friesen, *Brotherhood*, pp. 681-687. On their first furlough the Unruhs left the four eldest: Henry, Marie, Martha, and Arthur, in Russia, where they were taught by Katharina Reimer, mentioned earlier. This information was supplied by Marie (Unruh) Crocker [Kroeker], Canim Lake, B.C., 20 December 1988.

15. Franz and Marie Wiens, "Über Br. H. Unruhs Krankheit, Leiden, Sterben und Begräbnis; III.," *Das Erntefeld*, no. 22 (1912), pp. 280-283; Franz Wiens, "Unseres

heimgegangenen Bruders letzte Worte an uns," *Das Erntefeld*, no. 23 (1912), pp. 298-301; and John H. and Maria Voth, "Aus Indiens Fluren," *Zionsbote*, 25 December 1912, pp. 2-3.

16. Henry C. Unruh [son of C. H. Unruh], a family "Memoir" [89 pages, c. 1980], p. 29 [copy presented to author]; C. H. Unruh to Baldwin, 12 August 1914, from Altona, Germany; and Fred P. Haggard, ABFMS, to W. J. Bryan, Secretary of State, Washington, 27 November 1914, Unruh Collection.

17. She died in 1915 after bearing five children; M. A. Solomon, *Joy for Mourning: Life and Ministry of Daniel F. Bergthold: Missionary to India*, (Andhra Pradesh: B. Aseervadam, 1980), pp. 8-12.

18. She died in Vineland, Ontario, in 1939, ABAC; Anna Peters, "Er, gestern, heute, und in Ewigkeit derselbe," *Das Erntefeld*, no. 10 (1909), pp. 9-12; no. 1 (1910), pp. 11-12; Anna Peters, "Äußere Mission," *Das Erntefeld*, no. 15 (1912), pp. 194-195; and no. 19 (1912), pp. 242-244.

19. She married a man named Hamm and died in 1963. Aganetha Neufeld, "Ein Bericht von der Reise in die 'blauen Berge'," *Das Erntefeld*, no. 9 (1914), pp. 141-142; and *Missionary Album, 1889-1963* (Hillsboro, Kan.: Board of Missions of the Conference of the Mennonite Brethren Church, 1963), p. 115.

20. Johann G. Wiens, from Tschongraw, to Huntingdon, 4 August 1910; 24 October 1913, J.G. Wiens Collection; See John H. Lohrenz, *The Mennonite Brethren Church* (Hillsboro, Kan.: The Board of Foreign Missions of the Conference of the Mennonite Brethren Church, 1950), p. 55, where he implies that Wiens actually went to Ramapatnam; J. G. Wiens (1922) to the Reference Committee, ABMU, India, in C. Unruh Collection; and J. A. Toews, *History of the Mennonite Brethren Church*, pp. 113-114.

21. Friesen to Barbour, 7 July 1909; 11 September 1911; and K. Unruh, "Indien," *Das Erntefeld*, no. 4 (1911), pp. 42-46.

22. Friesen to the Secretary of the ABFMS, 26 November 1912, Friesen Collection.

23. See Friesen, "Auf Reisen [Touring]," *Das Erntefeld*, no. 9 (1914), p. 144; and Franz and Maria Wiens, "Von den Missionsstationen Nalgonda und Jangaon, Indien," *Das Erntefeld*, no. 11 (1913), pp. 145-147.

24. Huntingdon to Wiens, 26 December 1913, Franz Wiens Collection.

25. Franz and Maria Wiens, "Äußere Mission," *Das Erntefeld*, no. 8 (1909), pp. 4-5. The Wiens family with three sons, Jacob, Henry and Frank, first tried a venture in orange growing, and then moved to Reedley.

There, on 31 July 1922, Franz Wiens lost his life in tragic circumstances. Coming to the Kings River bridge after dark, he misunderstood orders to stop from a civilian posse and tried to run their blockade against an escaped murder suspect. One of the shots fired killed him at the wheel of his car. Missionary John A. Penner, on furlough at the time, was with him, but escaped injury.

Jacob F. Wiens, "Our Heritage from our Parents and Forefathers," a family memoir (1979) [copy presented to author]; Marie Warkentin Wiens, "Unser Leben fähret schnell dahin, als flögen wir davon," *Zionsbote*, 15 November 1922, pp. 9-11; and John A. Penner to J. C. Robbins, 4, 18 August 1922, John A. Penner Collection.

26. *Das Erntefeld*, no. 19 (1913), p. 244; no. 22 (1913), pp. 277-279; no. 13 (1914), pp. 204-207; the Penners had three sons: Nicholas, John, and Waldo (for many years a missionary in India with the Canadian Baptists), and three daughters: Erna, Hulda, and Margaret.

27. Baldwin to his ABFMS (late 1914), A. J. Hübert Collection; Friesen to Arthur G. Baldwin, 1 January 1915; and Baldwin to Friesen, 2 February; 2 March 1915, Friesen Collection.

28. Friesen to Baldwin, 1 January 1915, Friesen Collection.

29. K. Unruh, "Indien," *Das Erntefeld*, no. 4 (1911), pp. 42-46; Baldwin wrote Hübert very clearly that they wanted to retain the three stations, 20 November 1914.

30. J. H. Pankratz, "In Nalgonda und Suriapett gewesen," *Das Erntefeld*, no. 5 (1904), pp. 42-44; no. 6 (1904), pp. 45-46; John H. Lohrenz, *The Mennonite Brethren Church*, pp. 53-56, 230-238; J. H. Voth, "Deverakonda," in *Ein Jahr unter den Telegus: Jahresbericht 1928-1929* (Hyderabad: A.M.B. Mission, n.d.), pp. 5-8; and J. H. and Maria Voth, "Aus Indiens fluren," *Zionsbote*, 25 December 1912, pp. 2-3.

The single women accepted for service between 1898 and 1910 were: Anna Suderman (the third Mrs. Bergthold), Elizabeth Neufeld (later Wall), Katharina Schellenberg (MD), and Katharina Lohrenz.

31. By 1915 the American Mennonite Brethren were faced with demands for support from China and Africa. See *Konferenzberichte der Mennoniten Brüdergemeinde*, 1883-1919, pp. 452ff.

32. H. W. Lohrenz and J. C. Robbins to each other, 18, 22 December 1936, J. A. Penner Collection, ABAC.

33. Robbins to C. Unruh, 19 February 1932, C. Unruh Collection.

34. C. Unruh to Barbour, 18 September 1907; cf. Friesen who questioned his first salary cheque, 10 May 1890. Known as the Coimbatore Conference, the awakening of 1906 had a widespread impact. J. Wiens, "Eine Erfüllung von Joel 3,1 in Coimbatore, Indien," *Das Erntefeld*, no. 8 (1906), pp. 101-111; A. Friesen, "Pfingstensegen in Indien," *Das Erntefeld*, no. 9 (1906), pp. 121-128; A. Friesen, "Erweckung in Nalgonda," *Das Erntefeld*, no. 10 (1906), pp. 137-141; and Peter Penner, "The Holy Spirit and Church Renewal: Coimbatore, India 1906," *Direction* 20 (Fall 1991):135-142.

35. Unruh to Boston, [2 February 1909]; 19 October 1909, C. Unruh Collection.

36. Robbins to Unruh, 18 July 1919; 23 July 1920; 7 June 1921, C. Unruh Collection.

37. John A. Penner to Robbins, 14 June 1920; 25 June 1921; 21 April 1922; 7 August 1923, Penner Collection.

38. Cornelius Unruh, 14 December 1912; 12 July 1913; 26 April 1922; 20 June 1924. When Heinrich died in 1912, Anna took Cornelius John [today John C.] and Elizabeth to Russia to be reunited with the eldest four. They survived the War and Revolution.

39. C. Unruh to Robbins, 3 October 1923, C. Unruh Collection; A. J. Hübert, 30 December 1930; J. P. Klahsen, 28 July 1953, Hübert Collection.

40. *Mennonitische Rundschau*, 8 April 1925, pp. 8-9.

41. Ibid. Unruh had warmest commendation for Pankratz' work, 26 May 1923; Pankratz actually backed away from his criticism when he discovered that some field preachers were more to blame than C. Unruh (J. H. Pankratz to C. Unruh,, 13 July 1925, Mennonite Brethren Missions/Services, India Mission Records, CMBS, Fresno, Calif.).

42. Unruh to Robbins, 10 April 1929; and Unruh report (1936), C. Unruh Collection.

43. Henry C. Unruh, "Memoir", pp. 46ff; C. Unruh to Robbins, 2 June; 7 April; 8 October; 16 December 1930; 15 April; 29 May 1933, C. Unruh Collection; Cornelius and Henry went on to graduate schools and distinguished themselves in their respective firms.

44. Unruh to Wiens, treasurer of the AMBM, 16 December 1930; to Robbins, 1929 Report; 20 July 1931; 7 January 1935; 1 June 1935; 9 August 1938, C. Unruh Collection. See note 32.

45. Unruh to Robbins, 14 September 1934; and Robbins to Unruh, 30 March 1937, C. Unruh Collection.

46. Unruh to Robbins, 31 May 1939; JRW, a secretary of the ABFMS, to Martha Unruh, Kitchener, 30 December 1941, C. Unruh Collection; interview with Robert Eric Frykenberg, the son of K. E. Frykenberg, 30 July 1990, Madison, Wisconsin. The Frykenbergs, of Swedish Baptist background, particularly liked the C. Unruhs, as well as the John and Viola Wiebe and J. N. C. and Anna Hiebert families of the AMBM.

47. Hulda Penner to the author, 12 June 1990; and Isaac Tiessen copy of interview with J. P. Klahsen, age 91 (1990).

48. H. S. Hines, [John Everett] *Clough: Kingdom Builder in South India* (Philadelphia: Judson Press, 1929).

VIII
MENNONITE BRETHREN-BAPTIST RELATIONS

1. "Kirchliche Mennonite" is a designation associated primarily with the main body of Mennonites in Russia. Sometimes they were also referred to as "Grosse Gemeinde" in contrast to a small group that seceded from them 1812-1814 known as the "Kleine Gemeinde." The Kirchliche Mennonites who immigrated to America in 1874 and following did not retain this name. Most of them affiliated with a reform/renewalist-oriented body of Mennonites that came to be known as the General Conference Mennonite Church. At first they were known by various designations like: "Oberholtzers" (reform leader), the "New Mennonites" (in contrast to the Old Mennonites) or dubbed "Gay Mennonites" (symbolizing their shift from somber-colored, prescribed pattern clothes). Their official name indicated their intention to be a large umbrella-type conference welcoming all Mennonites who espouse basically-held Mennonite teachings and practices.

2. In Russia at that time, Baptists were designated as a "sect." Reinhold Johannes Kerstan, "Historical Factors in the Formation of the Ethnically Oriented North American Baptist General Conference" (Ph.D. dissertation, Northwestern University, 1971), 175.

3. See Frank H. Woyke, *Heritage and Ministry of the North American Baptist Conference* (Oakbrook Terrace, Ill.: North American Baptist Conference, 1979), 178, 247. Woyke notes that German Baptists were especially interested in the Mennonite Brethren group, a branch of Mennonites sometimes thought of as the "Baptist Mennonites." (p. 178).

4. Peter M. Friesen, *The Mennonite Brotherhood in Russia (1789-1910) [Alt-Evangelische Mennonitische Brüderschaft in Rüssland, (1789-1910) im Rahmen der Gesamtgeschichte]*, trans. and ed. J. B. Toews et al. (Fresno: Board of Christian Literature, General Conference of Mennonite Brethren Churches, 1978), 477; John A. Toews, *A History of the Mennonite Brethren Church: Pilgrims and Pioneers* (Fresno: Board of Christian Literature, General Conference of Mennonite Brethren Churches,

1975), 73-74.

5. Kerstan, "Historical factors in the Formation of the Ethnically Oriented North American Baptist General Conference," 165; Woyke, *Heritage and Ministry of the North American Baptist Conference*, 25.

6. Richard Sallet, *Russian-German Settlements in the United States*, trans. LaVern J. Rippley and Armand Bauer (Fargo, N.D.: North Dakota Institute for Regional Studies, 1974), 6.

7. "The Germans from Russia (Volga Region and Black Sea Protestants) who had been baptized by immersion by either Mennonite Brethren or 'German' Baptist ministers or evangelists may have migrated to Kansas, Nebraska and South Dakota as nominal 'Mennonites' in order for them to get exit papers more easily in Russia. The Mennonite Brethren designation may also have given them a framework in which to get more favorable terms from the Santa Fe or Burlington Railroads from which they were purchasing land." Raymond F. Wiebe, letter to author, 8 November 1992.

8. It is evident that emigrations of this kind trigger serious and haunting questions. Processing alternative ways of looking at what has been and what could be offer opportunities for broader understandings. Modified worldviews may result.

9. C. Henry Smith, *The Story of the Mennonites* (Berne, Ind.: Mennonite Book Concern, 1941), 665-666.

10. Raymond F. Wiebe, *Hillsboro, The City on the Prairie* (Hillsboro, Kan.: Multi-Business Press, 1985), 87-106.

11. Ebenfeld Mennonite Brethren Church Record Book, 1874-[1884], Hillsboro, Kansas, edited by Solomon L. Loewen, Center for Mennonite Brethren Studies, Hillsboro, Kan.

12. John F. Harms, *Geschichte der Mennoniten Brüdergemeinde* (Hillsboro, Kan.: Mennonite Brethren Publishing House, 1925), 75.

13. Peter M. Friesen, *Alt-Evangelische Mennonitische Brüderschaft in Rüssland (1789-1910): im Rahmen der mennonitischen Gesamtgeschichte*, Teil II: Die Mennoniten in Nord Amerika (Halbstadt, Taurien: Verlagsgesellschaft "Raduga," 1911).

14. Ben C. Ollenberger, "Ebenfeld: History, Interpretation and Mennonite Brethren Identity," photocopy, n.d.

15. Friesen, *Alt-Evangelische Mennonitische Brüderschaft*, Teil II, 8.

16. Friesen, *Alt-Evangelische Mennonitische Brüderschaft*, Teil II, 9; Toews, *A History of the Mennonite Brethren Church*, 134.

17. Friesen, *Alt-Evangelische Mennonitische Brüderschaft*, 9-10.

18. *Verhandlungen der vierten Jahres-Versammlung der Suedwestlichen Konferenz der deutschen Baptisten-Gemeinden von Nordamerika, 1884*, 33.

19. Wiebe, *Hillsboro, The City on the Prairie*, 88-90. A review of the annual reports of the Südwestliche Konferenzen der deutschen Baptisten-Gemeinden von Nordamerika, 1880-1930. These are on file in the archives of the North American Baptist Seminary, Souix Falls, South Dakota.

20. Ollenburger, "Ebenfeld: History, Interpretation and Mennonite Brethren Identity," 30-31.

21. Feelings of ethnocentric superiority are common, particularly where there is relatively little social interaction with those of other ethnic traditions. When one ethnic group has dominant power, pressure is often exerted formally or informally for

others to conform. At times this is so strongly programmed alongside of theological enculturation that culture and theology cannot readily be differentiated by insiders to that culture. It is at this level that outsiders experience frustration in being pressured to conform.

22. Seventh-day Adventism had already become attractive to some who were Mennonites in Russia. See Friesen, *The Mennonite Brotherhood in Russia*, 506, 540, 565.

23. *General Catalogue-German Department, 1818-1928*, The Colgate-Rochester Divinity School, 258-273.

24. A typical catalogue of general information and course offerings and the Institute for German Baptists noted that there were two basic educational programs. A summary of the German-American Academy listed the following curriculum:

FIRST YEAR (25 class hours per week)
 1. German (rhetoric, poetry, literature)
 2. English (grammar, rhetoric, reading of classics)
 3. Latin (Cicero and Virgil and grammar)
 4. Greek (Xenophon and Homer and grammar)
 5. History (middle-ages and the new age)
 6. Science (geology, astronomy)
 7. Philosophy (logic, ethics, philosophy)
SECOND YEAR (25 class hours per week)
 1. Advanced courses of the first five courses of the first year.
 2. Add Geometry, Zoology, Physics
THIRD YEAR (26 class hours per week)
 1. Advanced courses in German, English, Latin and History.
 2. Added courses in Algebra, Anatomy, Geography
 3. Additional available course in Business Accounting.

The Theological Seminary included advanced Academy courses and additional courses:

FIRST YEAR (19 class hours per week)
 1. Biblical Theology (Old and New Testament and Greek Exegesis)
 2. Systematic Theology (Christology and Soteriology)
 3. Historical Theology (Reformation, Denominationalism, Baptists)
 4. Pastoral Theology (Preaching, Leadership, Pastoral Care)
 5. Written Research to be submitted.
SECOND AND THIRD YEAR (18 class hours per week)
 1. Advanced courses in all of the five first year courses.
 2. Special studies were available in Greek, Hebrew and Music.

25. J.A. Pankratz, "Missionsfest in Marion, Kans." *Der Sendbote* 7 (Juni, 1899); The German Baptist weekly publication, *Der Sendbote*, carried "newsy" articles about specific communities through appointed correspondents who submitted such reports. Through these publications and the yearly Conference Proceedings (*Verhandlungen der Jahres Versammlungen*) one can trace the activities of those ex-Mennonite Brethren who had become Baptist leaders. Raymond Wiebe regards these years as a time that included a "period of local level competitions between the professional (paid) German Baptist ministers and evangelists and the unpaid and less polished MB local elders, ministers and evangelists. . . a time when each group accused the other of 'sheep stealing' and spreading rumors about each other's motives. Raymond Wiebe Letter to author 8 November, 1992).

26. Eduard Schewe, *Dem Herrn Vertrauen: Blueten und Fruechte eines Lebens fuer*

Gemeinde, Mission und Diakonie, ed. Guenter Bolders (Wuppertal und Kassel: Oncken, 1979) 178-179. Other kinds of mission festivals were conducted in other ways. Mountain Lake, Minnesota regularly held an all-day, July 4, missions rally. At Henderson, Nebraska there were also yearly missions festivals.

27. A number of reports in *Der Sendbote* describe the aggressive work of Regier among Russian German-speaking immigrants.

28. Frank C. Peters, "The Early Mennonite Brethren Church: Baptist or Anabaptist?," *Mennonite Life* 25 (October 1959):178.

29. *Konferenzbeschluesse, 22-24 Oct., 1896, Ebenfeld, Marion County, Kansas*, 186-189.

30. Hans Kasdorf, "A Century of Mennonite Brethren Mission Thinking, 1885-1984" (Ph.D. thesis, University of South Africa, 1987), 354-367, 409-416; Woyke, *Heritage and Ministry*, 181-182.

31. Kasdorf, "A Century of Mennonite Brethren Mission Thinking," 412-413.

32. For the story of the Mennonite Brethren years at McPherson College and the beginnings of Tabor College see Clarence Hiebert, "Early Influences in the Shaping of H.W. Lohrenz," paper presented to the symposium "H.W. Lohrenz and the Mennonite Brethren Tradition: Shaping a Tradition (1900-1945)," 15-16 April 1983, Fresno, Cal., Historical Commission Records, Center for Mennonite Brethren Studies, Fresno, Cal.

33. Numbers are gathered from a perusal of student records and catalogs at Tabor College.

34. The data were gathered from an examination of the Mennonite Brethren Biblical Seminary catalogues.

35. See Kerstan, "Historical Factors in the Formation of the Ethnically Oriented North American Baptist General Conference," 222.

IX
BAPTISTS AND MENNONITE BRETHREN IN CANADA

1. Jarold K. Zeman, ed., *Baptists in Canada: Search for Identity Amidst Diversity* (Burlington, Ont.: G. R. Welch, 1980).

2. John A. Toews, *A History of the Mennonite Brethren Church: Pilgrims and Pioneers*, ed. A. J. Klassen (Fresno, Calif.: Board of Christian Literature, General Conference of Mennonite Brethren Churches, 1975).

3. Frank H. Epp, *Mennonites in Canada, 1786-1920: The History of a Separate People* (Toronto: Macmillan of Canada, 1974); and Frank H. Epp, *Mennonites in Canada, 1920-1940: A People's Struggle for Survival* (Scottdale, Pa.: Herald Press, 1982).

4. Peter Penner, *No Longer at Arms Length: Mennonite Brethren Church Planting in Canada* (Winnipeg, Man.: Kindred Press, 1987).

5. Harry A. Renfree, *Heritage and Horizon: The Baptist Story in Canada* (Mississauga, Ont.: Canadian Baptist Federation, 1988).

6. Philip G. A. Griffin-Allwood, George A. Rawlyk, and Jarold K. Zeman, eds., *Baptists in Canada, 1760-1990: A Bibliography of Selected Printed Resources in English*, Baptist Heritage in Atlantic Canada, vol. 10 (Hantsport, N.S.: Lancelot Press, 1989); Zeman, *Baptists in Canada*; G. A. Rawlyk, ed., *Canadian Baptists and Christ-*

ian Higher Education (Kingston, Ont. and Montreal: McGill-Queen's University Press, 1988); Leslie K. Tarr, *This Dominion, His Dominion* (Willowdale, Ont.: Fellowship of Evangelical Baptist Churches in Canada, 1968); and Colin Campbell McLaurin, *Pioneering in Western Canada: A Story of the Baptists* (Calgary, Alta.: C. C. McLaurin, 1939).

7. See detailed account in Toews, *History of the Mennonite Brethren Church*, pp. 152ff.

8. Constant H. Jacquet and Alice M. Jones, eds., *Yearbook of American and Canadian Churches 1991* (Nashville: Abingdon Press, 1991), pp. 137-138.

9. Ibid., p. 143.

10. See especially G. A. Rawlyk, "A. L. McCrimmon, H. P. Whidden, T. T. Shields, Christian Education, and McMaster University," in *Canadian Baptists and Christian Higher Education*, pp. 31-62.

11. Jacquet and Jones, *1991 Yearbook*, p. 150.

12. Constant H. Jacquet, ed., *Yearbook of American and Canadian Churches 1989* (Nashville: Abingdon Press, 1989), pp. 127-128.

13. The only known Mennonite Brethren leader who has completed a program at McMaster Divinity School appears to be Isaac Block, a long-time faculty member at the Mennonite Brethren Bible College.

14. Shillington graduated several months after joining the Mennonite Brethren Church.

15. Rudy H. Wiebe, Letter to the Author, 28 February 1990.

16. A survey questionnaire was sent to all pastoral staff in Canada. There were ninety-seven responses out of a total of approximately 250 questionnaires sent out. The questionnaire focused on such issues as relationships with Baptist churches at the local level, transfers of members to and from Baptist churches, theological education of pastors, and perceived differences between Baptists and Mennonite Brethren. Responses in many cases were quite impressionistic and would be difficult to verify scientifically.

17. Ed Boldt, 2 March 1990, Letter.

18. H. H. Janzen's biography was published in a series of installments in the *Mennonitische Rundschau* beginning 6 October 1976 and ending 23 November 1977. The first twelve installments were written as an autobiography by H. H. Janzen himself whereas subsequent installments were written by his wife, Katherina Janzen.

19. Ed Boldt, Letter to the Author, 2 March 1990.

20. Ibid.

21. Tarr, *This Dominion, His Dominion*, pp. 115ff.

22. Walter E. Ellis, "Baptists and Radical Politics in Western Canada, 1920-1950" in *Baptists in Canada, 1760-1990*, p.169.

23. My own recollections pertaining to Coaldale bear this out.

24. Ellis, "Baptists and Radical Politics in Western Canada," p. 170.

25. Erich L. Ratzlaff, *Ein Leben für den Herrn: Biographie und Predigten von David Borisovich Wiens* (Winnipeg, Man.: Historical Committee of Canadian Conference of Mennonite Brethren Churches, 1982), p. 16.

26. Penner, *No Longer at Arms Length*, pp. 38, 59, 60.

27. Ibid., p. 27. Note that much of the subsequent material pertaining to mission churches relies on Penner's study.

28. Ibid., pp. 128ff.

29. Ibid., pp. 32, 57.

30. See Maria Rogalski, *McDermot Avenue Baptist Church 100th Anniversary, 1889-1989: 100 Years and Growing* (Winnipeg, Man.: McDermot Avenue Baptist Church, 1989).

31. Anna Thiessen, *The City Mission in Winnipeg*, trans. Ida Toews (Winnipeg, Man.: Centre for Mennonite Brethren Studies, 1991), p. 2.

32. See J. Arthur Koop, "Winnipeg Mennonite Brethren and the McDermot Avenue (German) Baptist Church in Winnipeg, 1907-1939," paper prepared for Mennonite Studies II in March 1992. Centre for Mennonite Brethren Studies, Winnipeg, Manitoba.

33. Ibid., pp. 4-9. Copies of transfer documents are included as appendices.

34. Judith Ibbs, Letter to the Author, 5 March 1990.

35. John G. Baerg was quoted as saying, "God is infusing new blood into us. We are not an ethnic group" (Harold Jantz, "CBI Dominates B.C. Convention," *Mennonite Brethren Herald*, 24 June 1977, p. 13).

36. Interview with Nick Dyck is the source of much of this information.

37. Penner, *No Longer at Arms Length*, p. 76.

38. Ibid., pp. 82-83.

39. Ibid., p. 137.

40. Renfree, *Heritage and Horizon*, p. 273.

41. Jacquet and Jones, *1991 Yearbook*, p. 138.

42. Penner, *No Longer at Arms Length*, p. 114.

43. Again, comparative information for other denominations, particularly the Conference of Mennonites and the Alliance Church, would help to determine the significance of the statistics gathered.

44. The survey results clearly indicate this.

45. Ed Boldt writes, "There seems to have been a 'natural affinity' between Baptists and Mennonite Brethren, perhaps since Baptists formed a significant proportion of the larger group of churches we now recognize as 'Evangelical,' along with the Alliance, Missionary, and several other denominations" (2 March 1990, Letter). He also cites Anne Wiebe who states that from the very beginning Mennonite Brethren did not really feel a part of their (Old) Mennonite hosts, kind and generous as most of them were.

X
AUGUSTUS H. STRONG: BAPTIST THEOLOGIAN FOR THE MENNONITE BRETHREN

1. Biographical data on Strong is available in the following theological dictionaries: *The Westminster Dictionary of Church History* (WDCH); *The New International*

Dictionary of the Christian Church (NIDCC); *Evangelical Dictionary of Theology* (EDT); *New Dictionary of Theology* (NDT).

2. Carl F. H. Henry states that "Strong considered his 1907 theology, which appeared in one and three volume editions running 1166 pages, including 107 index pages, as a revision and enlargement of his 1886 work, of which seven previous editions had appeared, each embodying 'successive corrections and supposed improvements'" (Henry, *Personal Idealism and Strong's Theology* [Wheaton: Van Kampen Press, 1951], p. 143).

3. *New Dictionary of Theology*, 1988 ed., s.v. "Strong, Augustus Hopkins (1836-1921)," by T. J. Nettles.

4. *Evangelical Dictionary of Theology*, 1984 ed., s.v. "Strong, Augustus Hopkins (1836-1921)," by W. R. Estep, Jr.

5. Ibid.

6. *New Dictionary of Theology*, 1988 ed., s.v. "Strong, Augustus Hopkins (1836-1921)," by T. J. Nettles.

7. Ibid.

8. A representative list of those studying at Rochester Theological Seminary between 1890 and 1930, for seminary and missionary training, includes the following: P. C. Hiebert, Franz J. Wiens, J. H. Pankratz, Peter H. Wedel, Johann Berg, John H. Voth, Henry F. Toews, Frank A. Janzen, Bernhard J. Friesen, John J. Franz and David Dyck. In conjunction with Central Baptist Theological Seminary the *Tabor College Bulletin* January 1950, noted that twelve Tabor students had or were currently studying at Central. Most, if not all, of these would be Mennonite Brethren students, since Tabor had few non-Mennonites prior to 1950. The roster included: A. J. Harms, Clarence Fast, Waldo Hiebert, Marvin Hein (post-1950), Franklin Jost, Robert Vogt (post-1950), Joseph Schmidt, Orrin Berg (post-1950), Chester Fast (post-1950), Lando Hiebert, John H. Lohrenz, Cornelius Plett, Henry F. Toews. There were Mennonite Brethren students also at other Baptist seminaries during the pre- and post-WWII period: Northern Baptist (John S. Dick, John J. Franz, H. W. Lohrenz, Henry C. Thiessen, John Caldwell Thiessen); Western Baptist (J. B. Toews); Los Angeles Baptist (Henry D. Wiebe, Elias Wiebe), Berkeley Baptist (Henry Schenkofsy); Southern Baptist (D. Edmond Hiebert); Southwestern Baptist (Larry Martens, George Konrad, J. B. Toews, B. J. Braun).

9. August H. Strong's *Systematic Theology* (Philadelphia: Judson Press, 1907) was used as a primary text by several instructors at Mennonite Brethren Bible College from 1945-1967 (see endnotes 11, 12, 14). At Tabor College Strong's text served as a main resource for the "Essentials of Christianity" course, taught by J. B. Toews. This was the senior Bible course required for graduation. Toews taught it one semester every year from 1954-1962. Strong also served as a reading resource and provided a frame of reference for Toews' lectures in his course "Introduction to Theology" which he taught at Mennonite Brethren Biblical Seminary from 1962 to the late 1970s. Toews was also president of the seminary from 1965-1972. This data was obtained through conversation with J. B. Toews.

10. The information relating to faculty, students, and courses at Mennonite Brethren Bible College has been obtained, with permission, from the Mennonite Brethren Bible College records, Centre for Mennonite Brethren Studies, Winnipeg, Man.

11. J. B. Toews, as president, was the first to use Strong in his systematic theology, which he taught seven times in the years 1945-1948. Between 1948 and 1951 G. D. Huebert taught systematic theology six times using Strong; C. Wall from 1950-

1951, four times. In the winter of 1951 John A. Toews for the first time taught the systematics course. Until 1967 he used Strong continuously in every systematics class. While attending graduate school he was assisted in one section in the spring semester, 1960-1961 by F. C. Peters, and relieved in one section in fall semester in 1963-1964 by H. H. Voth.

12. The total number of students taught at Mennonite Brethren Bible College, in forty-nine sections of the systematic theology series, with Strong as the primary text, was 1144. J. B. Toews taught 167 students in seven sections during 1945-1948; G. D. Huebert 113 in six sections during 1948-1951; Cornelius Wall seventy-five in four sections during 1950-1951; J. A. Toews taught 757 students in thirty-one sections over a period of seventeen years, 1951-1967; and H. H. Voth thirty-two in one section when he was substituting for J. A. Toews in the fall semester of 1963-1964. The student count is based on total head count. The actual number of students (that is, student names) would be less since most would have taken both sections of the systematic theology series. The actual number of names enrolled in the various sections over the years has not been tallied.

13. For a profile of Toews' career, see David Ewert, "John A. Toews: in Memoriam," in *People of the Way: Selected Essays and Addresses by John A. Toews*, eds. Abe J. Dueck, Herbert Giesbrecht, and Allen R. Guenther (Winnipeg, Man.: Historical Committee Board of Higher Education, Canadian Conference of Mennonite Brethren Churches, 1981), pp. 1-23.

14. From 1947-1967 Toews taught twenty-six different courses a total of 145 times. The majority of them were church history courses, his field of academic expertise. He taught a major course in each area during most of his teaching career at Mennonite Brethren Bible College. Respectively, those courses were: "Acts," "Mennonite History," "Systematic Theology," and "Homiletics." He taught the first three more, by far, than any other courses, and "Systematic Theology" the most frequent of all. The course "Christian Doctrine" was also regularly taught at MBBC in the first two decades.

15. For this study I have not provided a text-critical analysis of the sort that carefully determines the various "layers" of Toews' notes on Strong and attempts to periodize them. I have only made such observations (a) where those kinds of distinctions are sufficiently obvious and (b) where they are pertinent for our discussion.

16. A detailed summary of Toews' lecture notes on Strong's *Systematics*, which functioned as a primary data-base for this study, can be found at the Centre for Mennonite Brethren Studies, Winnipeg, Manitoba and at the Center for Mennonite Brethren Studies, Fresno, California.

17. James Garrett, "Representative Modern Baptist Understanding of Biblical Inspiration," *Review and Expositor* 71 (Spring 1974):183.

18. Assuming the integral relation of religious and scientific world-views, Strong asserts that the possibility of theology is found in a God who has relations with the universe, in the capacity of the human mind for knowing God and certain of his relations, and in the provision of a revelation linking God and humanity (Henry, *Strong's Theology*, p. 149). For Strong, external revelation in nature and history precedes and conditions internal revelation. God is disclosed in nature but supremely in Scripture. All biblical truth supplements rather than contradicts or corrects natural theology, which prepares the way for biblical theology (Ibid., pp. 149-150). Our idea of God thus comes from rational intuition.

19. Garrett, "Biblical Inspiration," p. 184.

20. Ibid., p. 185.

21. Henry, *Strong's Theology*, p. 154. Until Grant Wacker's recent study, *Augustus H. Strong and the Dilemma of Historical Consciousness* (Macon, Ga.: Mercer University Press, 1985), Henry's work was the most thorough study of Strong's theology. According to Crerar Douglas, Henry launched a "formidable barrage against the liberalism of the Boston personalists and the later Strong" (Douglas, "The Hermeneutics of Augustus Hopkins Strong," *Foundations* 21 [January 1978]:72). The central issue for Henry was a hermeneutical one. Had Henry taken into account the fact that Strong's hermeneutics could only be adequately understood against the backdrop of his study of literature and poetry, he might not have been such a strident critic of the later Strong (Ibid., pp. 71-76).

22. Henry, *Strong's Theology*, p. 154.

23. Ibid., p. 151.

24. Ibid., p. 155.

25. Ibid., p. 156.

26. Grant Wacker states that "in retrospect it is clear that the story of Strong's growing consciousness of history was part of a larger story of cultural change and conflict in American Protestantism" (Wacker, *Strong and the Dilemma*, p. 110). Wacker continues noting that "the most persistent cause of conflict was a growing divergence over the nature of biblical authority. More often than not, the central question was whether the Bible is a direct—and therefore inerrant—communication from God, or whether it is the principal record of humanity's faltering quest for God" (Ibid., p. 112).

27. Henry, *Strong's Theology*, p. 161.

28. Ibid., p. 162.

29. Wacker contends that four major views have emerged in attempting to typecast Strong: an early fundamentalist, a (Reformed) conservative, a mediator between liberalism and orthodoxy, and a closet liberal (Wacker, *Strong and the Dilemma*, pp. 7-8). It would appear that Toews engaged Strong mainly as a (Reformed) Baptist theologian who periodically accommodated himself too much to modernistic ideas. See also Paul M. Minus' recent biography, *Walter Rauschenbusch: American Reformer* (New York: Macmillan, 1988), for a portrayal of Strong in regard to the critical role Rauschenbusch played on Strong's faculty at Rochester Theological Seminary.

30. See Henry, *Strong's Theology*, pp. 172-184 for a more detailed analysis of Strong's soteriology.

31. A more nuanced assessment of the cumulative impact the use of Strong's systematic theology had on the theological orientation and formation of the Mennonite Brethren church and its leadership, goes beyond the scope of this study. That requires a more in-depth analysis of the socio-historical dimensions surrounding the interface of culture and religion.

32. Abe J. Dueck, "The Changing Role of Biblical/Theological Education in the Mennonite Brethren Church," in *The Bible and the Church: Essays in Honour of Dr. David Ewert*, eds. A. J. Dueck, H. J. Giesbrecht, and V. G. Shillington (Winnipeg, Man.: Kindred Press, 1988), p. 134.

33. Ibid.

34. Ibid., pp. 134-135.

35. Ibid., pp. 137-39. According to Dueck, both Anabaptism and Evangelicalism

"emerged at about the same time and came to relative maturity in the 1950s" (Ibid., p. 140).

36. Dueck points out that the first generation of Mennonite Brethren teachers in the post-WWII period received their education and taught in what George Marsden called the fourth stage of evangelicalism. The first stage was the more expansive phase, from the mid-nineteenth century to 1918 (Strong belonged to this period). The second stage was the dramatic phase dating from about 1919 to 1926 when the antimodernist crusade peaked and fundamentalism became an identifiable movement. The third stage, from about 1926 to 1940 was one of withdrawal and regrouping, characterized by sectarianism and dispensationalism. The fourth period commenced about 1940 and consisted of the generation following the post-war period where the original fundamentalist movement divided into two distinct movements: evangelicalism and separatist fundamentalism. George Marsden, "From Fundamentalism to Evangelicalism: A Historical Analysis," in *The Evangelicals: What They Believe, Who They Are, Where They are Changing*, eds. David F. Wells and John D. Woodbridge (Nashville: Abingdon Press, 1975), pp. 128ff, quoted in Dueck, "Changing Role of Biblical/Theological Education," p. 138. Thus, to use Marsden's categories, here was a fourth stage Mennonite Brethren historical theologian using a first stage Baptist systematic theologian. There is something congruent about the expansiveness regarding the first and fourth stages of evangelicalism, and their interfacing in an unusual way at Mennonite Brethren Bible College in mid-twentieth century.

37. Epistemologically, orthodox rationalism refers to the "common sense supposition that all sane people perceive and think about the external world in pretty much the same way" (Wacker, *Strong and the Dilemma*, p. 10). Historical consciousness refers to the acute "consciousness of the historical origin of culture" (Ibid.).

38. Ibid., p. 12. Wacker contends that the "link between religious knowledge and historical process constantly deepened as he grew older" (Ibid., p. 13). Therefore, because he "gradually came to see that creeds, like all human artifacts, are products of history . . . the doctrinal superstructure of Strong's thought was left precariously suspended in midair as the cornerstone—his conception of the origin of religious knowledge, and more exactly, his growing awareness of the role of historical conditioning in the formation of such knowledge—shifted ground" (Ibid.).

39. Ibid., p. 14. Wacker outlines the epistemic revolution of the late nineteenth century with the growing recognition of the power of history to condition human understanding. For him "the real roots of modern historical consciousness started to take form in the eighteenth century" when men and women "began to think in serious, systematic, and nontheological terms about the nature of the historical process" (Ibid., p. 33). By the early twentieth century this view had become the main ideology.

40. Ibid., p. 42.

41. Ibid., p. 46. For Strong these developments and changes occurred through his metaphysical study of consciousness, the powerful new impulse around the 1890s "to conceive reality as one and to see the divine as immanent within the human historical process" (Ibid., p. 59) and "that Christ is the connective tissue that makes these epistemic transactions possible" (Ibid., p. 65). According to Wacker, Strong's work increasingly conceded the following to modern thought: the basic building blocks of religious knowledge are embedded in the structure of consciousness; a pronounced affinity for a evolutionary interpretation of civilization; the lure of the modernist impulse—to look to history and contemporary culture for amplification of the meaning of revelation. By the 1890s, at his prime, Strong had grown keenly sensitive to the principle of the continuity of the historical process. Four currents characterized his thinking: an inclination to blur the distinction between special and general revelation;

the molten, developmental nature of the matrix in which revelation is conveyed; an embrace of the spiritual progress evident in modern culture; an abiding conviction that the onward, upward rush of history carries within itself an old-fashioned gospel whose truth never changes (Ibid., pp. 75-80).

42. As one might expect the response to Strong in American Protestantism was mixed. Strong's systematic theology propelled him into the big leagues at the height of his career. However, no one considered him too daring on historical questions, some found him not daring enough, others found him hopelessly old-fashioned or even confused (Ibid., p. 89). There were those who saw him clinging to the relics of scholasticism while trying to embrace the realism of modern science and philosophy (Ibid., p. 90); a butterfly struggling to emerge from the cocoon of orthodox scholasticism; a dangerous influence among Baptists. Most of the conservative reviews (of the 1907 edition) were largely insensitive to the problems raised by historicism (Ibid., p. 94). Thus he was both too radical and too conservative.

43. Ibid., p. 122. For Wacker "this elusiveness is the tip-off that the real reason that Strong is difficult to assess is not because his creedal formulations were inconsistent but because his epistemic assumptions were. The stress is not in his massive doctrinal system, but beneath the system, in the shadowy underworld of suppositions about the origin and nature of religious knowledge itself" (Ibid., p. 9).

44. Ibid., p. 125.

45. Wacker attempts to chart four ways in which thoughtful Protestants responded to the pressures created by the larger confrontation between the two conceptual worlds of orthodox and modern epistemologies (Ibid., pp. 139-166), and locate Strong in terms of them. *Consistent ahistoricism* represented an "uncompromising resistance to the deepening historical consciousness of the age" (Ibid., p. 139). Representatives of this position were Princeton (Hodge), Westminster (Machen), Niagara Bible Conference (Stewart). *Accommodating ahistoricism* were more open to embracing the historical method. Representatives of this group were Northern Baptists, Holiness tradition, Reformed circles, A. J. Gordon, A. B. Simpson. *Accommodating historicism* still held in some form to the enduring truths of salvation, but softening the angularities of orthodoxy. Its representatives were Bushnell, Fosdick, Briggs, Clarke. *Consistent historicism* embraced historicism barehanded and without compromise. It was represented by McGiffert and University of Chicago (Smith, Case). It rebuked mystics such as Rudolf Otto and dialecticians such as Karl Barth who assumed the virtual bankruptcy of history as a source for the modern person's doctrinal assurances (Ibid., p. 157). It did not differ with the working assumptions of the leading scholars in the humanities and the social and natural sciences. Wacker contends that Strong moved from the first to the third and came to rest finally in the second, accommodating ahistoricism (Ibid., 162).

46. Ibid., p. 15.

47. John A. Toews wrote the most definitive work on Mennonite Brethren history to date: *A History of the Mennonite Brethren Church* (Fresno, Calif.: Board of Christian Literature, General Conference of Mennonite Brethren Churches, 1975). One of its major contributions was placing Mennonite Brethren roots squarely in the Anabaptist (not simply Baptist-Pietist) tradition.

48. Wacker, *Strong and the Dilemma*, p. 172.

49. Although Toews did not explicitly use Strong for the purpose of focusing the orthodoxy-modernist agenda, he did reflect his own theological biases regarding orthodox-modernist issues as we have seen. Toews used Strong in order to present a theological framework in the absence of an explicit theology and adequate resources

in the Mennonite tradition, at times using him to expose students to a more expansive orthodoxy, at other times to reinforce certain aspects of the conservative-fundamentalist agenda.

50. Wacker, *Strong and the Dilemma*, pp. 139ff. See note 44 for a further explanation of these four "persistent patterns."

51. Dueck, "Changing Role of Biblical/Theological Education," p. 142.

52. A. James Reimer in "The Nature and Possibility of Mennonite Theology," *Conrad Grebel Review* 1 (Winter 1983):33-35 has persuasively argued that contemporary Anabaptist-Mennonite theology carries an unduly strong bias toward the historical-ethical side of theology.

53. Wacker, *Strong and the Dilemma*, p. 172.

XI
THE BAPTIST AND MENNONITE VISION

1. This article is adapted from my graduation address at the Baptist Theological Seminary, Rüschlikon, Switzerland, in 1985. I express gratitude to the Seminary for its hospitality on that occasion. Thanks also to my wife, Dr. Nancey Murphy, and to Dr. Wayne Pipkin, then of Rüschlikon, now of Associated Mennonite Biblical Seminaries, Elkhart, Indiana, for helpful advice. Another version of this paper has been accepted by Dr. Pipkin for publication among the Rüschlikon Baptist Papers; he has very kindly granted permission for its appearance in this form here.

2. Ernst Troeltsch, *The Social Teaching of the Christian Churches*, trans. Olive Wyon (New York: Harper & Row, 1931; London: George Allen & Unwin, 1931; reprint ed., Chicago: The University of Chicago Press, 1981), provided a more sophisticated typology of church, sect, and mystical religious types in the late Middle Ages. I use Troeltsch's term, but here in a popular sense rather than his own.

3. I owe this distinction to an important paper by John Howard Yoder on ecumenical conversations between Anabaptists, Catholics, Reformed, and Lutherans. John Howard Yoder, "A Clarification of Views of the Church," Elkhart, Ind., n.p. 1969.

4. The modern concept of development did not appear until the nineteenth century, when it was most fully explored by John Henry Newman, who in his *Essay on the Development of Christian Doctrine* (London: J. Toovey, 1845; reprint ed., New York: Sheed and Ward, 1960) sought to distinguish true from unauthentic development as a means of defending the true (i.e., Roman Catholic) church. The standard account of Newman's achievement is by Owen Chadwick, *From Bossuet to Newman: the Idea of Doctrinal Development* (Cambridge: Cambridge University Press, 1957). With the rise of the twentieth-century ecumenical movement, however, it began to appear that there might be more than one sort of authentic Christian development, each having its own notae or distinguishing marks of authenticity. Ruth Rouse and Stephen Charles Neil, eds., *A History of the Ecumenical Movement, 1517-1948*, 2nd ed. (London: SPCK, 1967; Philadelphia: Westminster Press, 1967). This twentieth-century notion of development has not been competently explored from a perspective that would take into account the baptist vision—a task for someone willing to work. See for a start, James Edward Lesslie Newbigin, *The Household of God* (New York: Friendship Press, 1960); and James Wm. McClendon Jr., *Ethics: Systematic Theology Volume I* (Nashville: Abingdon, 1986), ch. 1.

5. See Karl Adam, *Das Wesen des Katholizismus*, 7th ed. (Düsseldorf: L. Schwann, 1934); and Robert McAfee Brown, *The Spirit of Protestantism* (New York: Oxford Uni-

versity Press, 1961) for application of these themes to Protestant and Catholic forms of Christianity, respectively.

6. Winthrop Hudson, "Baptists Were Not Anabaptists," *The Chronicle* 16 (1953):171-179.

7. Gunnar Westin, *The Free Church Through the Ages*, trans. Virgil A. Olson (Nashville: Broadman, 1958); and Donald F. Durnbaugh, *The Believers' Church: The History and Character of Radical Protestantism* (New York: Macmillan, 1968; reprint ed., Scottdale, Pa.: Herald Press, 1985), pp. 8-16.

8. Albert Henry Newman, *A Manual of Church History*, rev. ed. (Philadelphia: American Baptist Publication Society, 1899); Roland H. Bainton, "The Left Wing of the Reformation," *Journal of Religion* 21 (April 1941):124-134; George Huntston Williams, *The Radical Reformation* (Philadelphia: Westminster Press, 1962); John Howard Yoder, *The Ecumenical Movement and the Faithful Church* (Scottdale, Pa.: Mennonite Publishing House, 1958); Durnbaugh, *The Believers' Church*; and my own essay, "What is a 'baptist' Theology?" *American Baptist Quarterly* 1 (1982):16-39.

9. "Anabaptist" is pejorative, since the term, meaning "baptizers again" simply assumes what baptists with good reason deny—that infant "baptism" is real baptism, and thus that subsequent believer's baptism is superfluous and repetitive, a mistake repeated as recently as World Council of Churches, *Baptism, Eucharist, and Ministry* No. 111 (Geneva: World Council of Churches, 1982), pp. 4-6.

10. Newbigin, *The Household of God*; Franklin Hamlin Littell, *The Free Church* (Boston: Starr King Press, 1957); and Durnbaugh, *The Believers' Church*.

11. Donovan E. Smucker, "The Theological Triumph of the Early Anabaptist-Mennonites: The Re-Discovery of Biblical Theology in Paradox," *Mennonite Quarterly Review* 19 (January 1945):5-26.

12. George Huntston Williams and Angel M. Mergal, eds., *Spiritual and Anabaptist Writers: Documents Illustrative of the Radical Reformation*, Library of Christian Classics, vol. 25 (Philadelphia: Westminster Press, 1957), pp. 39-46.

13. Edgar Young Mullins, *The Axioms of Religion: A New Interpretation of the Baptist Faith* (Philadelphia and New York: American Baptist Publication Society, 1908; Philadelphia: Griffith & Rowland Press, 1908); Ernst Troeltsch, *Protestantism and Progress: A Historical Study of the Relation of Protestantism to the Modern World*, trans. W. Montgomery (New York: G. P. Putnam's Sons, 1912; reprinted., Boston: Beacon Press, 1958); and Troeltsch, *The Social Teaching of the Christian Churches*.

14. Franklin Hamlin Littell, *The Anabaptist View of the Church: An Introduction to Sectarian Protestantism* (Hartford: American Society of Church History, 1952); Harold S. Bender, "The Anabaptist Vision," in *The Recovery of the Anabaptist Vision*, ed. Guy F. Hershberger (Scottdale, Pa.: Herald Press, 1957); and John Howard Yoder, "A People in the World: Theological Interpretation," in *The Concept of the Believers' Church*, ed. James Leo Garrett, Jr. (Scottdale, Pa.: Herald Press, 1969).

15. Yoder, "A Clarification of Views of the Church."

16. John Calvin, *Institutes of the Christian Religion*, ed. John T. McNeill, trans. Ford Lewis Battles, The Library of Christian Classics, vols. 20 and 21 (Philadelphia: Westminster Press, 1960); and Eduard Schweizer, *Church Order in the New Testament*, trans. Frank Clarke (London: SCM Press, 1961).

17. McClendon, "What is a 'baptist' Theology?"; and McClendon, *Ethics: Systematic Theology*.

18. Thieleman J. van Braght, *The Bloody Theater or Martyrs Mirror of the Defense-*

less Christians, trans. Joseph F. Sohm (Scottdale, Pa.: Mennonite Publishing House, 1951), pp. 442-444. The story of Astyages, Daniel, and Bel is found in the Septuagint version of the Book of Daniel, included in the Bible most sixteenth-century baptists read.

19. Robert G. Torbet, *A History of the Baptists* (Philadelphia: Judson Press, 1978), pp. 103ff.

20. Herbert G. Skeats, *A History of the Free Churches of England from A.D. 1688 - A.D. 1851*, 2nd ed. (London: A. Miall, 1869), p. 510; see also A. C. Underwood, *A History of the English Baptists* (London: The Baptist Union of Great Britain and Ireland, 1947), pp. 161ff.

21. Fuller, quoted in Sydnor Lorenzo Stealy, ed., *A Baptist Treasury* (New York: Crowell, 1958), p. 93.

22. Perry Miller, *Roger Williams: His Contribution to the American Tradition* (Indianapolis: Bobbs-Merrill, 1953), p. 85. Miller's interpretation of Williams was a recovery (with the work of others) of the biblical and Puritan Williams in an age that had transformed him into a modern liberal democrat. See LeRoy Moore, "Roger Williams as an Enduring Symbol for Baptists," *Journal of Church and State* 7 (Spring 1965):181-189. Subsequent discussion, however, has pointed out the misleading aspects of Miller's own account.

23. And what of those who follow him but through historical circumstances are denied this mighty sign, who have the reality but lack the effectual emblem? Here the imagery of Pentecost speaks to us again; the Spirit is poured out on all the disciples, and "this" (our divided, often confused world of faith) is "that" (the Pentecostal scene, where unity and variety are alike the signs of the Spirit of God). How we long, though, for that eschatological fullness when others' gifts may be ours as well, while we share with them believer's baptism, and with the whole world of human need our vision, our fellowship, and our risen Lord.

24. On baptism, see McClendon, *Ethics: Systematic Theology Volume I*, pp. 255-259, and the literature cited there.

List of Contributors

ABE J. DUECK
  Director of the Centre for Mennonite Brethren Studies,
  Winnipeg, Manitoba

WILLIAM R. ESTEP
  Distinguished Professor of Church History, Emeritus,
  Southwestern Baptist Seminary, Fort Worth, Texas

ABRAHAM FRIESEN
  Professor of History,
  University of California, Santa Barbara, California

CLARENCE HIEBERT
  Professor of Religious Studies, Emeritus,
  Tabor College, Hillsboro, Kansas

PETER J. KLASSEN
  Professor of History and Chair of the School of Social Sciences,
  California State University, Fresno, California

HOWARD J. LOEWEN
  Professor of Theology and Academic Dean,
  Mennonite Brethren Biblical Seminary, Fresno, California

JAMES WM. McCLENDON, JR.
  Professor of Theology and Distinguished Scholar-in-Residence,
  Fuller Theological Seminary, Pasadena, California

PETER PENNER
  Professor of History, Emeritus,
  Mount Allison University, Sackville, New Brunswick

WALTER SAWATSKY
  Professor of Church History,
  Associated Mennonite Biblical Seminaries, Elkhart, Indiana

JOHN B. TOEWS
  Professor of Church History,
  Regent College, Vancouver, British Columbia

PAUL TOEWS
  Professor of History, Fresno Pacific College and
  Executive Secretary of the Historical Commission of the
  General Conference of Mennonite Brethren Churches,
  Fresno, California

ALBERT WARDIN
  Professor of History,
  Belmont University, Nashville, Tennessee